DATE.	PLACE.	GUNS.	Buffalo Grouse.	Bush Buck Pheasants.	Roan Partridges.	Hyaena Black Game.	
Sept 5th	Bua River camp						12
" 6th	Chemanto village						27
" 8th	Katangeza's		1				
" 12th	"			1			
" 13th	"				1		
" 14th	Bua River						3
" 15th	Katangeza's		1				
" 16th	"					1	

REMARKS.

Three varieties of geese viz: Spur wing, Egyptian, & Dwarf goose, four varieties of duck, Red Bill, Knob nose, Pochard & yellow Bill not common
A Cow — for meat.
Bull — head moderate, having a late spear at the edge of the marsh
Bull — 25" Horns. Reeds disgracefully at about 250ᵈ
Knob nose, Pochard & Red Bill
Bull — very poor head one of a very large herd. I made a mess of things & lost a good bull, the hyaena was just met day while I was looking for him — a most pleasing shot at 75ˣ at full gallop.

LITTLE BIRDS AND ELEPHANTS

David Macpherson

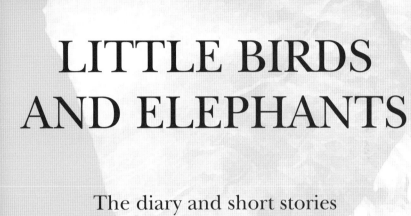

LITTLE BIRDS AND ELEPHANTS

The diary and short stories
of
DAVID MACPHERSON'S
wanderings in
Portuguese East Africa and Nyasaland
1928–1929

Edited by
ISABEL MACPHERSON

2005

Published in 2005 by Denham House for
Isabel Macpherson
Ch. des Chameilles 1
1807 Blonay
Switzerland
email: isabelisabel@mac.com
www.birdsandelephants.com

© 2005 Isabel Macpherson

ISBN 0 904309 04 5

Jacket photograph by:
Richard Anthony Wickenden
e-mail: sales@arundelframing.com

Title page photograph by:
Anthony Heller

Printed in Great Britain by
Halstan & Co. Ltd., Amersham, Buckinghamshire

For Mum
Something you always wanted to do

"You will never be bored child, if you are interested in little birds."

(Dad's wise counsel)

CONTENTS

LIST OF ILLUSTRATIONS AND MAPS

EDITOR'S NOTES
AND ACKNOWLEDGEMENTS

It has long been an ambition in the family to publish 'Dad's Diaries' as they were fondly called. They were kept in the cupboard on the khondi and got out from time to time together with some short stories that he had written. Nobody in the family really knew how to go about this and with young children and busy lives there wasn't the time.

In 1991 after my mother's death I promised to undertake this task. It was quite some years before I put my mind to it. I found a publisher and thought that all that was required was to hand him the typewritten sheets of the diaries and ask him to 'make it all happen'. Mr. Paulin, the publisher, quite rapidly put this all together and handed everything back to be read and checked. "Make sure the bird names are correct and spelt correctly" he said, also "make sure the names of places and rivers are consistent". That's when my problems really started. The diaries had been sent to Grandmamma in Scotland who had had the difficult task of typing them out from the original handwritten copies. Names of birds and places would have been totally foreign to her and her son's handwriting almost impossible to decipher. I put everything back in a box and left it there for a few more years whilst I changed husband, moved house and country. People began asking what had become of the diaries and I started to work at it again, this time with my brain a little more in gear.

My first big problem was with river and place names particularly those in Portuguese East Africa (P.E.A.) north of the Zambezi. I couldn't get hold of a map. There was a map, it hung on the wall on the khondi right through our childhoods. I am ashamed to say I don't think I ever looked at it and I didn't think to save it. I have my niece Julia to thank for finding me a map. The first one came from the British Library, the right date but such small scale. My thanks go to Mr. Joseph Nunn for his research and help. Julia also put me in touch with Dr. Rene Pelissier, an historian and bibliographer of Mozambique, who kindly gave me the name and address of Mr. A. Rita-Ferreira, who had lived and worked in

Mozambique for many years and is now living in Portugal. Thank you Mr. Ferreira for giving me the correct name and co-ordinates of the Lingobri river, the new name of which is the Lingove; he sent me a map and at last I was beginning to get somewhere. He also gave me the correct spelling for the Bivar family and indicated the place he believed their house was situated. My thanks too, go to Mr. Francis Herbert of the Royal Geographical Society who went to so much trouble to find me larger scale maps of this area of P.E.A. I would like to thank Mr. Paul Dutton for putting me in touch with the Map Studio in Durban, and to Vicky Lotter for referring me to the Department of Surveys and Mapping in South Africa and to Nathalie Swan for finding me larger scale maps of P.E.A. now Mozambique.

Eventually I could piece together the rivers and work out the changing place names. I have used the modern names of the important towns and rivers and stayed with village names as my father wrote them.

The Latin names of the birds in the diaries may have changed a little over time, I have left them as far as possible as Dad wrote them. Again the handwriting problem arose with these names. I spent many hours trying to work out what a word might be and sometimes I only had the Latin name to go by. My apologies for any errors in bird names, the mistakes are certainly mine and not my father's.

My thanks to my nephew Cliff Riordan for scanning the photographs and filing them on CD-Rom for me, and to my sister Prinia, for editing and re-editing them for me.

Many thanks go to Brian Burgess of Zomba Plateau for editing the glossary and for helping me with spellings of Portuguese, Chinyanja and Latin words.

A very big thank you Prinia for spending so many hours on the telephone and writing many e-mails contacting people who might want a copy of this book. My thanks too go to all those people who helped with sending out emails and flyers; so many wonderful friends — old and new.

A very special thank you to Dr. John Wilson for writing about the Apalis, telling us about 'the hatching' and for help in so many different ways. Thank you Joe Bernard for allowing me to use your photographs of the parent birds at the nest and congratulations for capturing these very difficult little subjects on film. I was able to confirm the history of the naming of the *Apalis chariessa macphersoni* through Effie Warr, Volunteer, Ornithology Library, Natural History Museum, Tring, Hertfordshire, who kindly sent me the details from Jack Vincent's book *Web of Experience – an autobiography* from which I have quoted in order to set the record straight.

Philip and Jean Jackson together with Michael Chevis of Midhurst in West Sussex gave their time and expertise to bring out the best in the photographs of the White-winged Apalis. A special thank you Jean for your help designing the dust jacket and steering me along the right path.

I would like to thank Frank Johnson of Central Africana for his help, advice and encouragement.

Chip and Dawn Cathcart Kay, thank you for your enthusiasm and help with filling in some of the history and for finding me the two beautiful fold-out maps of Nyasaland.

Profound thanks go to John Pendered for photographing and allowing his paintings of the Bua River by J. C. Harrison to be printed and for the help he gave Prinia and me in 1991 during a very difficult time.

Thank you Cousin Bill for your guidance in matters of history and dates. Grateful thanks too to my nephew Derek in Malaŵi, for being in touch and for filling in some interesting details about Kanongo Estate.

My children, Mark and Kim, thank you for allowing me to use your homes as an 'office' on many occasions and a special thank you David, for your technical expertise, for designing and hosting the web page and for teaching your mother how to use the scanner!

Richard Wickendon has kindly allowed me to use his photograph of a sunset taken in Samburu on a recent trip to Northern Kenya for the dust jacket. He has asked me to make a donation to The Friends of Conservation, 16–18 Denbigh Street, London SW1V 2ER in lieu of payment. Thank you Richard for your generosity.

I thank all those people who have contributed their memories to these diaries, to everyone who helped in their distribution and to anyone whom I have not mentioned, thank you all for your involvement.

My husband Tony has had to put up with me during this time, with copies of maps strewn everywhere, e-mails flooding in and my constantly badgering him for reassurance that this or that read correctly or looked all right and how should I reword this section and for refusing to go out and enjoy the summer because I needed to keep working at the diaries. Thank you Tony, without your help and support in all aspects the publication of these diaries would not have have been possible.

Thank you Mr. Paulin for being so patient and for still being there after retirement to pick this all up after several years' lapse. Lastly, thank you Robin Bannister of Halstan & Co. Ltd. for producing this lovely book — a dream fulfilled.

Isabel Macpherson
Editor

MACPHERSON PEDIGREE

Clan Macpherson Association Badge

Highland Light Infantry Badge

Prinia Macpherson (now Riordan)
b. 28 June, 1936
at Dedza, Malawi, Africa

Ewen Francis William Macpherson
b. 27 November, 1937
at Namitete, Malawi, Africa

Isabel Rose Macpherson (Rapley, now Heller)
b. 25 April, 1943
at Thyolo, Malawi, Africa

David William Kinloch Macpherson
b. 17 May, 1900
at Bankipore, India
d. 8 March, 1982
at Namitete, Malawi, Africa
m. 5 October, 1935
at Dowa, Malawi, Africa

= **Frances McQuire**
b. 20 August, 1906
at East Plumstead, Kent, England
d. 1 February, 1991
at Namitete, Malawi, Africa
m. 5 October, 1935
at Dowa, Malawi, Africa

Douglas Christopher Henry McQuire
b. 27 June, 1861
at Stepney, Middlesex, England
d. 1 August, 1919
at Plumstead, Kent, England
m. 31 August, 1894
at Woolwich, Kent, England

= **Una Ransom**
b. 2 July, 1868
at Woolwich, Kent, England
d. 11 September, 1914
at Epsom, Surrey, England
m. 31 August, 1894
at Woolwich, Kent, England

Peter Frederick McQuire
b.
at
d.
at
m. 29 May, 1858
at Stepney, Middlesex, England

= **Emily Marian Willoughby**
b. 29 December, 1840
at Limehouse, Middlesex, England
d. 13 December, 1920
at Poplar, Middlesex, England
m. 29 May, 1858
at Stepney, Middlesex, England

= **Ruth Baggett**
b. 7 October, 1845
at Greenwich, Kent, England
d. 1 March, 1911
at Woolwich, Kent, England
m. 28 September, 1867
at Plumstead, Kent, England

William Tapley Ransom
b. 17 November, 1845
at Rochester, Kent, England
d. April, 1890
at Woolwich, Kent, England
m. 28 September, 1867
at Plumstead, Kent, England

William Charles Macpherson
b. 11 August, 1855
at Blairgowrie, Perth, Scotland
d. 6 July, 1936
at Blairgowrie, Perth, Scotland
m. 16 October, 1886
at St. Catherine's Church, Blairgowrie, Perth, Scotland

= **Isabella Mary Kinloch**
b. 9 September, 1861
at Poona, India
d. 6 February, 1952
at Edinburgh, Scotland
m. 16 October, 1886
at St. Catherine's Church, Blairgowrie, Perth, Scotland

Allan Macpherson
b. 24 October, 1818
at Blairgowrie, Perth, Scotland
d. 6 November, 1891
at Blairgowrie, Perth, Scotland
m. 30 April, 1853
at Marylebone, Middlesex, England

= **Emma Blake**
b. 29 October, 1833
at Dhobah, Bengal, India
d. 5 November, 1915
at Blairgowrie, Perth, Scotland
m. 30 April, 1853
at Marylebone, Middlesex, England

Col. David James Kinloch
b. 16 October, 1826
at Gourdie, Perth, Scotland
d. 10 November, 1873
at Edinburgh, Scotland
m. 15 November, 1858
at Bombay, India

= **Katherine Mary Young**
b. 1838
at
d. 17 November, 1894
at Gourdie, Perth, Scotland
m. 15 November, 1858
at Bombay, India

17

Newton Castle

INTRODUCTION

David William Kinloch Macpherson

David William Kinloch Macpherson, younger son of William Charles Macpherson and Isabella Mary Kinloch, was born on 17th May, 1900 in Bankipore, India.

He spent his early childhood days in India where his father was a senior and distinguished public servant, having arrived in India in 1877, serving in Bengal and Assam and rising to the post, in October 1903, of Chief Secretary to the Government of Bengal. David, at the age of four was sent to Wester Kinloch House, Scotland to live with his maternal aunts, Annie Cox and Agnes Marjoribanks, both stern disciplinarians, who prepared him for the rigours of school life. He also lived at Blairgowrie House with his grandmother, Emma Macpherson, wife of Allan Macpherson 3rd of Blairgowrie. The estate at Blairgowrie and the family home, Newton Castle, was purchased in 1788 by Colonel Allan Macpherson and has been in the family ever since. David's brother was the 'Cluny' (hereditary Chief of the Macpherson Clan in the Central Highlands of Scotland), and his nephew, Sir William Alan Macpherson, has now inherited the title.

David was educated at Cargilfield Preparatory School in Edinburgh and Clifton College, Bristol. He was something of a classical scholar maintaining an interest in Latin and Greek throughout his life and was a keen ornithologist from his boyhood days. After training at the Royal Military College, Sandhurst, he was commissioned as a Lieutenant in the Highland Light Infantry, served in Africa with the King's African Rifles and was then posted to India. He resigned his commission in 1926 and returned to Africa disembarking at Beira towards the end of 1927. He decided to take the first train out of Beira and 'go to the end of the line' eventually arriving in Limbe, Nyasaland.

Leaning on administration skills learned in the army, his first job was to run Sambankhanga Estate owned by Abe Price and in those days growing tobacco, he also worked for Conforzi Tea and Tobacco at this time.

19

His brother Alan David Macpherson b. 6 Sept., 1887

Studio photographs taken on their 5th birthdays.

David William Kinloch Macpherson b. 17 May, 1900

At Newton about 1914. David with his sister Dr. Sheila

David at Newton – aged about 10 years

21

David at his preparatory school, Cargilfield. David is in the middle row on the left.

He found that there were good farming prospects in the rich agricultural plains in the Bua river catchment, north-west of Namitete, Nyasaland and made up his mind to lease a tract of virgin land on the Namitete river and create a tobacco farm. First he needed to raise the capital.

He had time, and was a formidable rifle shot. Elephant hunting was something he wanted to do, so in 1928 he organized hunting expeditions both in Nyasaland north of the Bua river, and Portuguese East Africa in the Tete area, north and south of the Zambezi river. The diaries cover the very short period of 18 months that he spent hunting and collecting bird specimens in the bush. David endured great hardships, bouts of malaria, trouble with porters, difficulties in getting sufficient supplies to feed everyone in the camp, problems obtaining licences, getting lost in the bush, and last but not least, running out of socks which resulted in painfully blistered feet.

It shows something of the character of the man that he marched unbelievably long distances through inhospitable country while ignoring pain and illness. He succeeded in what he set out to do and spent the days when elephant were hard to find observing and collecting birds and eggs.

Towards the end of 1929, using the money raised from his elephant hunting he purchased the lease on 400 acres of land near Namitete as planned and named his farm Kanongo. Kanongo means *'the place of the porcupine'*, the dambo below the office on the estate being a favourite haunt of these animals. In 1932 the estate was enlarged to its current size.

There was a slump in the tobacco industry during these early years and David still had to look elsewhere to supplement his income.

In 1933 he stood in for the owner Maclean Kay during his absence, running Satemwa Tea Estates in Thyolo (Cholo). It was during this time that he collected many species of birds from the forest on Thyolo Mountain, approaching the mountain from what is known as the Mianga Field 10 road built by Maclean Kay which David was extending into the forest. The original campsite can still be seen today. David donated his collection of birds to the Natural History Museum, Tring, Hertfordshire, England. Included were specimens of a White-winged Apalis hitherto unknown in this area. These specimens were eventually recognized as being a subspecies and were given the name of *Apalis chariessa macphersoni*.

An article on the White-winged Apalis written by Dr. John Wilson appears later in the book.

In 1934 David took up the lease on Kasache Estate on the shores of Lake Nyasa and grew cotton there. The ginnery was owned by the Domira Bay Ginnery Company, the three shareholders being A. F. Barron, R. W. J. Wallace and D. W. K. Macpherson, run by Len Shaw. The ginnery was later sold and David used the land to grow tobacco.

On a visit to Lake Nyasa in 1935 David met Frances McQuire. Frances, the daughter of Douglas Christopher Henry McQuire and Una Ransom came from Kent, 'the garden of England'. She was a qualified midwife and tropical diseases' nurse. A lady of definite views, she took up a nursing post in Blantyre but was dissatisfied with the medical standards and the attitude of the European Hospital Administration. She resigned but decided to take a look at Lake Nyasa before leaving for home. There she met David and after a whirlwind courtship of ten days they were married. On the way to the Mission at Dowa some of the euphoria dissipated when her hat blew out of the open Morris Cowley and she had to 'dance through the thengo' to retrieve it. The ceremony was followed by a long dusty journey to her new home on Kanongo Estate. Her introduction to the simple thatched farmhouse came as a shock. The furniture was sparse — a desk, two chairs and three black tin trunks. The trunks held the 'bird specimens' collected in the bush, one chair was David's and the other was occupied by 'Flo', the Jack Russell bitch. While David sipped his whisky and took pot-shots at the rats as they ran across the rafters, Frances sat down on the tin trunks and wept, threatening to run away.

David aged about 15/16 years at Clifton College.

Frances

Her new husband explained to her that she was 30 miles from anywhere and unable to drive . . . "so, where are you going to run to M'dear?"

In the early days the area around Kanongo Estate was rich in game. Herds of puku were a feature of the dambos, but these sadly have now completely disappeared from Malaŵi. Later on a massive dam was constructed on the farm which has a water surface area of about 12 acres. This beautiful lake has attracted a rich variety of bird life over the years, it is a favourite roosting place for egrets and over a thousand come here in the evening. There have been many interesting ornithological and game records from David Macpherson's observations at the dam and throughout the country during his life in Malaŵi.

David was a keen fisherman and still holds the record for the largest wild rainbow trout in Central Africa; a six and a half pound fish caught on his own tying of a 'silver guinea' fly on the Gaeresi stream in the Eastern District of Zimbabwe on the 14th August, 1970. He was often to be seen casting a dry fly delicately on Chagwa Dam, on Zomba Mountain, in the days when it was stocked with trout.

Frances was not one to give in. She learned to share David's many interests and gave him enormous practical help in the early, difficult farming years. David and Frances made their home on Kanongo Estate, raised their three children, Prinia, Ewen and Isabel, and over the years made an exquisite garden fondly remembered by all who visited them. Frances ran a daily clinic treating anything from wounds, coughs and stomach aches to pneumonia and malaria for all the men, women and children who lived and worked on the estate.

David died on 8th March, 1982; Frances on 1st February, 1991, at home on Kanongo Estate.

See 'Wild Life of the Central Regions', by D. W. K. Macpherson, *The Society of Malaŵi Journal*, vol. XXVI, No. 2, July 1973.

David William Kinloch Macpherson about 1920/1922 somewhere in Scotland with Charlie the spaniel. The car is a Cooper, built with a Coventry-Climax engine and a Moss gearbox.

KANONGO ESTATE IN THE EARLY DAYS

1929

1934

1934

28

1958

1960–1991 — Now sadly demolished.

David and the Chevrolet.

David with Jill.

Ewen and David starting the tractor — the 'box-body' and 'laterite' building in the background.

The back of the house showing the old-fashioned Rhodesian boiler.

Frances in her garden — late 1980s.

34

Primia, Ewen and Isabel.

FOREWORD

PETA McLEAN (*née* Smith)

I am so pleased that Mac's diaries are to be published and that you would like to include some of my recollections in the Foreword. It's fun for me to reminisce about my ties with the Macpherson family.

When we lived in Lilongwe we made numerous trips on that dusty road out to Namitete. We loved visiting the wonderful rambling farmhouse with it's thatched roof and the noisy greeting we received from the little black and tan daschunds and Mac's laboradors. Mac was passionately fond of his superb imported pedigree dogs, Rob and Ruby. We enjoyed wonderful birthday parties when people from the surrounding farms were invited and there used to be get-togethers for adults as well as children. The parties were held in Frances' beautiful garden which was her pride and joy and there was a lot of space to run around and to ride bikes. A highlight for me was riding Prinia's small two-wheeler bike for miles around Mac's tobacco fields. My parents eventually bought that bike from the family and my sisters all learnt to ride on it. That was during the war years when such things were unobtainable in Nyasaland.

My father was referred to as 'Old FC' by most of the men; the women called him 'Smithy'. My mother Nora, and Frances were great friends and when Frances came into Lilongwe to do her weekly shopping our house was her first stop. She would often bring in vegetables from the farm and Isabel would spend the morning with us. The ladies always did a lot of talking — sharing recipes and sewing ideas. It was Frances who taught Nora to smock. They both did a lot of beautiful embroidery.

Duck shoots on the Bua River were an annual event which the menfolk loved. The preparations were quite something, with tents, camp beds, flit guns and food being packed up. Some of the farmers took their gundogs; Mac took Rob. It really was very serious stuff! The shoots were memorable occasions and I can remember FC reminiscing that the mosquitoes were so big up at the Bua River that they bit one right through the canvas on the camp beds! The men certainly bagged a lot of birds and our kitchen staff had the job of cleaning them. The ducks had so little meat on them that we used to eat one each at a meal. We thought they were delicious.

I still shudder when I think of the terrible crocodile attack on my Dad. He was very lucky to escape with his life. My parents moved to Salima in 1952 and started a customs clearing business there. At the time Salima was the end of the rail line and all goods were cleared there before going north by road transport. My parents had their office in Salima, a very hot and dry little town, whilst they had a lovely home on the shores of Lake Nyasa. I remember it as a most beautiful lake with clear water which sparkled in the sunlight and shores of soft yellow sand. We all loved the lake as we were so familiar with it, having spent many family holidays there since I was a baby.

We always knew that there were crocodiles in the lake but it was generally believed that they only inhabited the marsh areas and river mouths.

It became my parents' custom, after driving home from work, to take a swim in the lake to cool off. The evenings became dark quickly in that part of Africa, and so they would take a lamp to the beach with them. They did this for a couple of years until one evening Dad was attacked by a crocodile — attracted by the light, no doubt. My parents and a family friend were standing in waist deep water when a crocodile grabbed at Dad's thighs. He dug his thumb into its eye socket and the croc. let go, only to attack again, this time getting him round the waist. Dad then gripped the crocodile's nose with one hand and with the other dug his thumb into an eye, and the crocodile released him. He yelled for help and Mum and our friend helped him to the beach. It can only have been due to his ability to keep calm and his physical strength that he survived. He suffered horrendous wounds to his stomach and thighs. At the time I was at boarding school but Mum later told me how she ripped up sheets and bound his wounds to stop the bleeding. Then she nursed him whilst a neighbour, Hyde Stansfield, drove them those long 80 miles to the tiny hospital in Lilongwe with no pain killers or antibiotics to help him. When they arrived there was no-one on duty so, as usual, the African watchman had to go and call the doctor.

Mac went to visit FC some days later and on hearing the story of bathing at dusk and the hurricane lamps on the beach said

"Well, you were a bloody fool weren't you!".

FC's wounds healed well. He regained his vitality and energy for life but sadly died from cancer in 1962. Our lovely gentle mother, Nora, continued to live on the Lake shore and with enormous fortitude kept FC's business going for another 12 years on her own.

DAD

We all learned to drive rather young as one does in Africa. We had a Chevrolet saloon when it was my turn, I was lucky, my sister had to learn in the 'box body'. I would have been about 13 and could just about see through the steering wheel when sitting on a cushion, first lessons were taken on the way back from collecting the mail at the Namitete Post Office. Once we had got back to the safety of our private road, Dad would start the lesson with:

"Always remember child, you are aiming a weapon."

By the age of 15, I would drive the last 20 or so miles home from a shopping trip or ulendo. It was during the rains and the road was a sea of mud. We were behind a lorry which was skidding about all over the road and was going very slowly.

"Come along child, we don't want to be here all day. Give it the gun."

Oh. Dear! we didn't argue with Dad, with my heart in my mouth we slid past.

Dad was a keen fly fisherman and used to tie his own flies. We kept chickens and had a very beautiful cockerel. From time to time Dad needed a hackle feather of a certain hue.

"Boy, tenga tambala" (fetch the cockerel)

he would call. Several minutes later, in came the tambala sitting quietly on a large silver tray with his head tucked under his wing. Dad would carefully snip off a few hackle feathers and then send him back to his wives.

Dad knew many things including the best way to sweep a chimney. Normally someone climbed to the top of the chimney, a brick tied to a long piece of rope was lowered and swung from side to side thereby knocking the soot down. A dear friend and neighbour, Dick Everett was complaining one day that his chimney was smoking. "Just fire your shotgun up the chimney, Dick" he advised, "and all the soot will come down into the fireplace." Now this works very well with a straight chimney, but Dick's chimney was not straight and 'down came soot, chimney and all'!

39

The men from neighbouring farms and friends would gather together to shoot duck on the Bua river. Dad had trained his black labrador, Rob, to retrieve and was proud of the dog's abilities. Several of the guns had their own dogs. By this time one or two of Rob's offspring were trained and showing off their skills. It was on about the third day in camp when Braddy came up to Dad and asked if Rob would retrieve a bird he had shot that his own dog had not found. Off went Rob and quite soon returned with a duck.

"No, that's not my bird" said Braddy.

"Hi lorst Rob, hi lorst."

Rob was sent off again and cast about for a few minutes returning with another duck.

"No" said Braddy "this is a yellow-bill mine was a knob-nose."

For the third time Rob was sent off, this time in a different direction.

"Hi lorst Rob, hi lorst"

Rob was not going to let the side down and took a little longer to return. Back he came and gently deposited a duck into Dad's hand. This bird was not quite as fresh as it should have been and Rob's trick was discovered. He had been circling back to camp and retrieving as many duck as his master wished from yesterday's pile.

Peta McLean has told the story of her father's encounter with a crocodile and of Dad's comment, however, I am not quite sure how wise he was when he left his heavily pregnant wife sitting on the beach on Benji Island. We had a tobacco estate down at the lake at Kasache. Just opposite was a small island called Benji. Dad and the manager Len Shaw, went off in Len's boat *The Puffin*, to shoot crocodile and Mum was left on Benji Island with the cook. She sat down on the beach with her knitting and the loaded 'elephant gun' beside her. Mum had never fired the gun, I think she doubted whether she could even pick it up. A little while later there was a noise behind her, she called the cook but he reassured her that it was all right — he had killed a snake. Just then a crocodile came out of the water, looked at Mum and walked around her.

"Well, how do you do?" said Mum.

The crocodile slid quietly back into the lake.

Dad was a keen ornithologist but sadly none of us shared his enthusiasm until very much later on. Perhaps we were taken into the bush too young, scratching our legs on the burnt scrub and worrying about snakes and spiders without appreciating that we were looking at a Golden Oriole.

It was not easy to talk to Dad about birds, he was very pedantic and we had to be correct in describing what we had seen. My dear friend Dotty Henderson and I arrived at the house one day full of excitement.

"We have seen a couple of birds" we said.

"You don't see a couple of birds" Dad said. "It's a pair of birds."

"What colour were their legs? What shape were their bills?

Were they flying or on the ground? Did they hop or walk?"

We changed the subject rapidly. Later when I became interested in birds and was able to discuss things intelligently, I learned that:

"Eagles wear trousers" and

"All kites have forked tails, but not all birds with forked tails are kites"

also

"If it is rare or doesn't occur in this area, you haven't seen it."

It was never easy to find a birthday present for Dad. It is a problem most of us have. I thought I had found the very thing. A little sculpture of a Peregrine falcon, I thought it was rather beautifully painted. Dad looked it over carefully, grunted, as he often did.

"What's it doing with an egg?"

I was a little taken aback, "Why Dad?" I asked.

"It's a cock bird." he answered.

"So what's it doing with an egg?" Dad was not an easy man.

Dad taught us many things about Africa. He was very knowledgeable about the stars. He used to take us out into the night which is as dark as only an African night can be, and point out the constellations and name the stars. It was difficult to concentrate. There would be a crash in the bush. Could it be a leopard? The dogs are with us — leopard's favourite food; a nightjar or bushbaby calling; hyaena in the distance; tom-toms; then the crash again. Where are the dogs? They went back inside a while ago.

"Now child, follow Orion's heels to Sirius, the dog star."

"Yes, Dad."

I loved it and wish I had listened harder and learned more from Dad, one thing I shall never forget though was his:

"Never take liberties with Africa, child".

Tony Bradshaw, Dick Everett, Braddy, Jack Rowell, Mike Hunt and Mac.

Dick Everett and Mac on the Bua.

Rob

Braddy and Mac. "That's not my bird."

Home from the shoot, wet, tired and hungry.

NIGEL HUNTER

An Appreciation

I first met David Macpherson in 1976, when I was invited to visit him at his Zomba Plateau house in order to discuss the *Birds of Malaŵi* with Con Benson and himself. I had been providing records and comments to Con, who was living at the time in Cambridge. However he was visiting David, who was sponsoring the book, and hence the invitation. This meeting gave rise to two outcomes. The first was that I agreed to proof-read the book and see it through the printers, which might sound a chore but was actually a great pleasure. The second was that it began a friendship between Julia, my wife, and myself with David and Frances.

We were at the time living in Zomba on the edge of the rain forest, and the White-winged Apalis, *Apalis chariessa macphersoni*, was a regular visitor to the garden. I mention this because from that Zomba meeting onwards this bird always brings a picture of David to my mind, as he was the first to discover this race of a very beautiful bird a 1,000 miles away from the original Kenya record. This discovery occurred four years after the period covered by the diaries presented in this book, but it is an illustration of the important contribution David made towards developing our understanding of Africa's ornithology.

Shortly after this first meeting, we were transferred to Lilongwe and we then started being regularly invited to tea at the weekend on the Macpherson farm at Namitete. David had a reputation of being quite fierce and not very tolerant of badly behaved children. Luckily our three daughters seemed to understand this and so we were always made very welcome. After tea David and I would then go birdwatching at the farm dam. It was here that we discovered the existence of the Coppery-tailed Coucal, *Centropus cupreicaudus*, in Malaŵi.

Julia and I left Malaŵi in 1980 and we never met David and Frances again, though we kept in regular touch. I am sure David could be difficult, but he appreciated good friendship and we were never stuck for words, but that is true of 'birders' all over the world. So I came to know and enjoy

45

David rather late in his life. He was though one of an old breed. It never ceases to amaze me that these early pioneers created a very good understanding of Africa's ornithology without any of today's technical aids. There may be better known names such as Benson and Moreau, but David was one of these pioneers and these diaries give an insight to what they all contributed and achieved. It was a privilege to know David and I can still recall very vividly watching with him in the evening the cattle egrets come to roost in the Dam reedbeds.

Nigel Hunter
March, 2004

ELIZABETH CAMERON

An Appreciation

While visiting my late husband's mother in Scotland prior to our first posting to Malaŵi in 1966, we were introduced to dear friends of hers, Sheila and Isla, David's sisters. When they heard our destination was Malaŵi, they provided us with David's telephone number.

However, we were first posted to Blantyre, which, in our ignorance, we deemed to be too far away from David for any contact to be made. It was not until a few years later when we were posted to Lilongwe, where my husband Ian, was the Deputy Director of Veterinary Services, that we eventually made contact with David and were immediately invited to Namitete. How we regetted the years we had missed of David and Frances' delightful and stimulating company by not having made use of that phone number earlier!

To Ian's great joy David was able to introduce him to the birds of Malaŵi. David's knowledge and wide experience were fascinating, and many happy hours were spent hearing of his sightings. I well remember mornings spent on the verandah, surrounded by dogs, with David directing our attention to an unusual bird call and promising, if we were to look through his binoculars, that we would see such and such a bird — and he was always right.

Like us, David and Frances were very fond of their dogs, and I shared Frances' love of gardening. Her garden at Namitete was an oasis, always green and serene.

Another common passion was for fishing — we enjoyed many an evening fishing David's dam, and were sometimes fortunate enough to eat our catch for supper that same evening.

David and Frances are always to be remembered for their great hospitality. Christmas luncheons were celebrated in great Scottish style, with of course, Frances' Christmas pudding ablaze with brandy.

The happiest of days to look back on with thankfulness.

Frances fishing on the dam.

49

Apalis chariessa macphersoni

50   This painting was first published as a frontispiece in *Birds of Malawi* by C. W. Benson and F. M. Benson in 1977. It is reproduced here by kind permission of the Benson family. Mrs. F. M. Benson painted the birds directly from the specimens collected by David. The tail of the male bird is shown fanned to draw attention to the markings, in life it is not seen fanned.

APALIS CHARIESSA: THE WHITE-WINGED APALIS

by

Dr. John G. M. Wilson

This remarkably beautiful warbler has a chrome-yellow belly, an orange chest, and a white throat. The male has shiny black upper parts, while the female has a grey cap, wings and tail, and a green back. Their most distinctive feature is the very long, graduated tail. *Apalis chariessa* was originally discovered at Mitole, on the lower Tana River, eastern Kenya by Dr. G. A. Fischer in 1878, who collected two males.

It was not found again until 1933, over 50 years later, when Mr. D. W. K. Macpherson collected a male and a female on Thyolo Mountain in Southern Malaŵi. This was a momentous discovery, since Thyolo Mountain is more than 1,000 miles to the south-south-west of the mouth of the Tana River, and over 900 metres higher.

However, the Thyolo specimens were larger in all dimensions than those from the Tana River, and the chestnut wash on the chest of the Thyolo male was only ill-defined. These characteristics justified the recognition of the Thyolo *Apalis chariessa* as a subspecies, *macphersoni*.

Mr. Jack Vincent, who worked in the British Museum in the 1920's and early 1930's was the first to see this bird whilst on a bird collecting expedition for the museum in 1932. Mr. Vincent writes of this sighting in his autobiography, *Web of Experience*. "In my collecting and bird notes on Cholo — I have never kept a diary as such — I wrote about two things which proved to be of related interest. On the 30th August I said that I called at the Cholo boma, to ask theDistrict Commissioner for permission to shoot in this area, and with him there, met his newly appointed young assistant, Mr. C. W. ('Con') Benson. The following day in the forest I saw two birds which I was sure represented something new. I recorded them in an *Ibis* 1935 paper in the following words: 'I saw a pair of yellow-breasted *Apalis* (a warbler genus) up in the canopy and wounded one which I did not secure. I never saw them again, but have no doubt that they were of the *Apalis* genus, and certainly not applicable to any species mentioned in this paper, having long tails and the male with a black gorget.' I saw these birds very clearly, and was of course disappointed at not being able to list them, and wondered how long it would be before someone was able to confirm their existence. I did not have long to wait, for when working in the British Museum just one year later, skins of a pair of the birds arrived there from Cholo, collected in July 1933. I had the privilege of giving them a name and called them *Apalis macphersoni*. The related interest mentioned is that Con Benson, whom I had just met at Cholo and whom I came to know very well later, stayed about another forty years in Nyasaland, where he became the recognized authority on the birds of that country. In 1977 Mr. Macpherson sponsored Benson's book *The Birds of Malaŵi*. It has a frontispiece painting of the birds I have been talking about, just as I saw them the day they eluded me." (Reproduced here with the kind permission of the Benson family – Ed.)

The White-winged Apalis has subsequently been found to occur in mid-altitude evergreen forest, including riparian forest, on a number of isolated peaks of the Shire Highlands, on the eastern side of the Rift Valley in the southern region of Malaŵi, as follows, from north to south:

Chikala Hill in the Liwonde Hills Forest Reserve.

Zomba Municipality, especially the Mulunguzi gorge. The Apalis is not found above 1,000 metres and hence does not occur on Zomba plateau, which is 1,500 metres high.

The Lissau Saddle on Chiradzulu Mountain Forest Reserve, where the magnificent evergreen forest has been considerably diminished in size and greatly degraded.

Ndirande Mountain Forest Reserve, Blantyre. This evergreen forest now totally destroyed within the last 10 years.

Mpingwe Mountain, Blantyre, the evergreen forest destroyed.

Soche Mountain Forest Reserve, Blantyre, the 200 ha. mid-altitude evergreen rain forest (1,250–1,533 metres) now in the process of being rapidly destroyed.

Bangwe Hill, Blantyre, the evergreen forest destroyed.

Malabvi Forest Reserve, Chiradzulu District (207 ha.).

Thyolo Mountain Forest Reserve, where *Apalis chariessa* occurred below 1,300 metres, and where the unique evergreen forest has been almost totally destroyed in the last five years.

Thyolo tea estates, where lowland rain forest has been preserved in stream depressions at 1,050 metre altitude, with a tall canopy of mainly *Albizia gimmifera* and *Khaya anthotheca* (syn. *K. nyasica*), and where the Apalis survives in relatively high densities of 6–7 pairs per 100 ha.

Khonjeni (500–600 metres) on the south-east scarp of the Shire Plateau.

Michiru Mountain where several observations have been made.

Mulanje Mountain Forest Reserve, in the mid-altitude rain forest from 950–1500 metres (approximately 1800 ha.).

The total Malaŵi population cannot be much above 100 pairs, and thus it is one of the most threatened forest birds in eastern Africa.

It needs stressing that this species is entirely dependent on these small isolated mid-altitude evergreen rainforests for its existence. The destruction of these habitats, as has recently occurred in Malaŵi, results in the disappearance of this wonderful bird forever.

The White-winged Apalis is always in a pair, although in January this year, I observed four together, and they were almost certainly the two parents with two juveniles. They inhabit the very tops of the tallest trees, with a preference for light foliaged, wide-spreading crowns, especially *Albizia spp.* and *Newtonia buchananii* which are at least 30 metres high. It is insectivorous, and gleans from the leaves and twigs in the canopy and at its edges. The song is a strident, rather sharp, very loud, rapid duet of four notes repeated in quick succession (at the rate of 6–7 notes/second) 'tee-lu dee-lu tee-lu dee-lu . . .' (or alternatively rendered as, 'teety-teetup teety-teeup . . .') at least six times, and usually repeated much longer. The male also utters his two notes 'tee-lu . . .', 'tee-lu' leaving a gap for the female part. The call by the female is more subdued and hesitant, or faltering. The call-note between the pair is a single note 'tweety . . .', repeated about six times. The call is normally made from the top of a tall tree.

They are almost the first birds I hear in the early morning, and they continue calling on and off throughout the day. It is mainly by hearing the call that one can detect these small birds, only 15 centimetres long, in the tree canopy over 30 metres up.

Breeding

Only two nests have ever been found. One was found being built on Ndirande Mountain on 11th October, 1944 at 1,300 metres on the edge of riparian evergreen forest. It was composed of 'old man's beard' fibre-lichen, *Usnea barbata*, suspended from a bare branch about 20 metres above the ground, not concealed at all, but very easily overlooked as being any ordinary pendant strand. The nest was open at opposite sides, it was still without eggs when collected on 15th November of that year.

The nest is built by both male and female together, material such as white strands, possibly spider web and dry brown pine needles and white silken seed pappi, probably of an asclepiad. Another nest was found on the edge of a clearing in evergreen forest at 1,500 metres on Mpingwe Mountain on 10th January, 1945 containing three eggs. It was about 8 metres above the ground and, like the Ndirande nest, quite unconcealed. Building activity continued over a period of at least 24 days in the case of the Ndirande nest. Sadly, the evergreen forests where these two nests were originally found have now disappeared.

In my garden in Zomba a pair has attempted to build a nest in a very large pine tree (*Pinus patula*) on and off over the last three years. In the absence of *Usnea* they have attempted to suspend the nest from pine needles, without sucess until this year, March 2004 when, using some strands of *Usnea* that had been collected from Zomba Plateau and strategically placed for their use, they succeeded. By 11th April, 2004, all the chicks had hatched and the parent birds attending the nest have been photographed by Joe Bernard.

The breeding season is October to November, through to January, although nest building has been observed in late March in Zomba, with eggs being laid in March. The eggs are dull-surfaced, narrow and elongate, $16 \cdot 5$–$17 \cdot 1 \times 11 \cdot 3$–$11 \cdot 5$mm. The ground colour is pale green, and they are spotted with yellow-brown and light yellow-brown generally, but not very thickly distributed, with underlying faint slate in one egg forming a definite cap.

The requirement for *Usnea barbata* ('Old man's beard') as a foundation for the nest is most probably a critical limiting factor for the distribution of this very localized resident species. *Usnea* requires a high level of atmospheric moisture, usually in the form of mist, to flourish, and this condition is only found above about 1,000 metres on the south-east facing slopes of mountains in the southern region of Malaŵi, open to the 'Chiperoni' in the dry season, from May to October.

References

F. Dowsett-Lemaire, R. J. Dowsett and M. Dyer, Malaŵi, pp.539–55 in L. D. C. Fishpool and M. I. Evans (eds.), 'Important bird areas in Africa and related Islands', *Pisces and BirdLife Int.*, Cambridge, 2001.

C. W. Benson and F. M. Benson, 'Some Breeding and other Records from Nyasaland', *Ibis*, 89, 1974, pp.279–90.

F. Dowsett-Lemaire, 'Ecology and Biogeographical Aspects of Forest Bird Communities in Malaŵi', *Scopus*, vol. 13, 1989, pp.1–80.

N. J. Collar and S. N. Stuart, 'Threatened Birds of Africa and Related Islands', *The ICBP/IUCN Red Data Book*, Part 1, S:717/718, Cambridge, 1985.

N. G. B. Johnston-Stewart, *The Birds of Thyolo District 3*, Nyala 3(1), 1977, pp.67–96.

Editor's Note: This was not just a matter of David going back to the same site as Jack Vincent and looking again. David was living and working on Cholo Mountain in 1933, found the birds and was able to secure the pair. This bird is very small "162mm of which the tail is 100mm". "It is very rare and spends its time mostly high up in the bigger trees of the streamside. Male and female are often together, and they search the smaller branches, leaves and twigs for their food, climbing about in all attitudes and rarely keeping still." I have quoted above from the letters David wrote to the British Museum describing the birds. They are desperately difficult to see, let alone shoot with a gun or a camera. They were a mystery and the experts were entirely baffled by them, eventually deciding in March 1934 that they were a new species. It was not until May 1934 when Jack Vincent returned from the Congo that he was able to identify them and name the new species *Apalis macphersoni*, "as a compliment to one who has turned my failure into success".

THE WHITE-WINGED APALIS

Photographed in a Zomba garden in April 2004 by Joseph Victor Bernard

These are the first and only photographs of any White-winged Apalis in the wild. These specimens differ in size from those collected in 1933 and therefore may prove to be a previously undiscovered species or race of Apalis. The taxonomy is under review.

Male

57

GLOSSARY

Aasvogel	Vulture in Afrikaans
Ankylostomiasis	Hookworm infection
Askaris	Soldiers
Bango	Reeds
Chimanga	Maize
Chiperoni	Warm, moisture-laden air blown over rising ground which sheds its moisture as drizzle and rain as it rises and cools. *Chiperoni* or *Guti* in Zimbabwe, originates in the Cape of Good Hope as a warm, strong, south-easterly wind and precipitation falling on south-east facing slopes as it rises and travels north, 2,500 miles up the continent to the northern end of Lake Malaŵi in Central Africa.
Dambo	Low-lying marshy ground in rains, generally dry at other times but full of fresh green grass.
Fisi	Mfisi — hyaena
'Fly'	Tsetse fly
Khondi	Verandah
Khuku	Francolin
Laterite	A tropical soil rich in iron oxide. Typically it is porous and clay-like, having been weathered from several different types of rocks.
Lillilooing	Ululating
Machila	Litter — portable bed mounted on two poles carried at each end on the shoulders of porters
Mfumu	Village headman or any Chief
Mlandu	Trouble or Court case
Msita	Heavy bush
Mudzi	Village, dwelling place

Mwenya tree	Muwanga tree — *Pericopsis angolensis* or *Afrormosia angolensis*. A medium to large tree approximately 10 metres tall with fairly smooth, cream-brown or grey-white bark (used to make an infusion to treat headaches and bathe eyes) with small leathery, hairy leaves and pale pink flowers. Common in Mozambique lowlands, virtually indestructable and fireproof (K. Coates-Palgrave). Known only as Afromosia in English.
Mzungu	European
Njobvu	Elephant
Nyama	Meat
Piccanin	Child
Puku	*Kobus vardonii* — a medium-size antelope usually golden-brown in colour and found on grassy plains near rivers, a close relative of the waterbuck.
Thengo	Bush
Ufa	Maize flour
Ulendo	Journey

A DIARY IN
PORTUGUESE EAST AFRICA AND NYASALAND
1928–1929

Nyasaland

August 6th, 1928

I am starting this with the intention of keeping a more or less daily account of any wanderings I may make in Africa and of the circumstances leading up to them. It has been my greatest hope that one day I should be able to push off into the blue for a longer spell than I have ever as yet been able to afford. I have always seemed to have been in a hurry for one reason or another and have only been able to snatch a few odd fortnights, always pressed for time and with the thought that on such and such a date I must indubitably be back at the Boma or on the Estate. Even taking the ammunition convoy from half way to Kilossa, back through Mahenge down to Songea and return, with an extra fortnight's leave thrown in, was a matter of fixed marches mostly on the main road, and a rush from beginning to end; and it is only now when I am no longer in the army and at a loose end, that I think I see my way to be able to afford six months or so seeing a bit of Africa. I will be through with the baccy business here about the 19th of this month and hope to push off soon after the 20th. In these days of low prices it is lunacy to think of starting an estate on my own account; what little capital I could get together, though it might have got me going during a boom, would not be nearly sufficient to carry me over a period of depressed markets. So I have bought a two-seater Morris Cowley, at enormous price, constructed a lean-to lumberman's tent at a cost of some £5 worth of canvas duck, and really mean to push off. I got the design for the tent out of a Boy Scout's book of W's. It is a very crude affair about six feet high by nine feet broad; its main advantage is that it is light, only weighing some 35 lbs. The canvas was machined together with ordinary cotton thread; I don't know if this will prove sufficiently strong; but must risk it as the linen thread wouldn't go into the machine.

61

I have not waterproofed it; I was assured that the canvas was already waterproofed when I bought it, and certainly there is no sign of leakage when a watering can is applied when the tent is up; but whether that is sufficient test or not I must leave the future to decide. This is supposed to be a picture of the pitched tent but it is very crude artistry, I fear. The contraption on the right is a flap that can either be let down as a door or held up as it is to act as a sort of verandah.

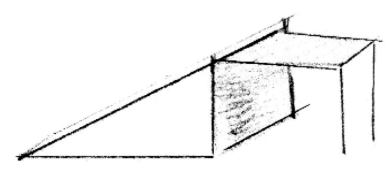

My other purchases to date have been an 8 mm Mauser with ammunition for it and my 9 mm; and three paraffin tins made up as food containers for flour and sugar. I had not originally intended buying another rifle, in fact it never entered my head until I started fooling about with the 9 mm again and trying to fix up an ivory fore-sight for it. That was a job! I knocked out the old fore-sight and in doing so the fore-sight block came with it. Then I got hold of a hippo tooth from a friend (H) and my troubles started. Hippo ivory is the very devil to work with and it took me the whole of one Saturday and Sunday's hard work to file out a sight to my satisfaction. After I had got the hang of it I made two in about half an hour, but then there remained the block to be put back into its place. It had been only soldered on in the first place, and I got the railway to do it for me. S was very obliging and had it done for me in no time, but unfortunately it came off again when I got back to the Estate, so I took it down to S to let him have a shot. I don't know yet if he has been more successful, I left the rifle with him a week ago and have just had a note from him (with a bill for 10*s*!) to say that he has done it. I will collect it in a day or two and hope it will be OK this time.

All this was very annoying but it has showed me the advisability of having a spare and anyway I think the gun a better gun. I took it out this morning to sight it. A, the Head Capitao, came with me and I think — though I say it — I made him think a bit.

It was carrying about five inches left at 100 yards, elevating OK. On tapping over the back-sight I just touched the left edge of my three inch bull. I again tapped over the back-sight and hit the right edge. A took this as being satisfactory when we inspected the target but I told him I intended getting my shots into the centre of the black. I had another four shots going left and right of the bull as I wound the sight too much in either direction; but finally hit it off square and put in three shots in the centre of the black, almost touching each other, much to A's delight. This is satisfactory, as I now have full confidence as to its shooting performance, which is half the battle in all shooting.

Another 'sair job' has been to get ammunition for the ·450. I anticipated my proposed jaunt last March and ordered ammunition from the Lakes who told me they would certainly get it for me by the end of July. I saw them last week and was told it could not possibly be here before the end of August, which is too late for me. I was lucky to find that J when I took my gun down to him last week had a supply of 500/450 bottle-nose ammunition. I had never heard of this before though, of course, the 450/400 is common. If necessary I can take as many rounds off him as I have soft-nose for the rifle myself and swap over the bullets. The number of different types of ·450 is amazing. ·400 No. 1, ·450 No. 2, 500/450, 450/400 and how many more I don't know. Mine — or rather Alan's is No. 1 and a hard hitting rifle even if it is a pretty old pattern and slow in working the hammers and under lever action.

My battery, then, consists of the 8 mm Mauser, 9 mm Mauser rifles, ·450 Rigby, 12-bore shot-gun by Crockart, and a B.S.A. airgun for collecting birds, so I am well set up. I shall not take the 250/280 rook rifle; it is pretty inaccurate now and the occasions are few when one would want it. My only regret is that I have not a bow to add to my battery; but there is no time now to think about that. I have been filled with a desire to emulate Pope and his confrères, but must leave it to some subsequent occasion. I have a trolling rod and reel, but have not yet succeeded in getting any tackle. The rod is the one I bought from Mallock for Mahseer, when I went to India and is the very thing for tiger fish.

A complication has arisen with Mrs. F who is a friend of W's paying Africa a visit to obtain copy for books and short stories. She goes home north to Tanganyika, Kenya, Uganda and the Nile and sails on the *Gwen* up Lake Nyasa on the 23rd. When she was here last month we thought we might arrange that I could take her from Mwaya at the north end up to Iringa or to Dodoma on the Tanganyika Central Line. I saw her in Blantyre last week and she now suggests my taking her right through to

Nairobi. I am not overjoyed at the prospect — the car is too small in the first place — and I don't look forward to the thought of possible break-downs. If I had a bigger car and was really a man of means instead of only pretending to be one, I should have greatly enjoyed it; as it is I think she would be wiser to seek other means of transport. We cannot possibly take sufficient luggage for both of us in the car without grossly overloading it and that to say the least is inadvisable when one is travelling over African roads. Frazer, my general factotum, must certainly come with us and there will be very little space for baggage in the dicky. Even alone I should be hard put to it to stow all my stuff, even travelling as light as I can. For the present we have left it undecided, and I have promised to do my best to get to Tukuyu by September 5th when we would meet again and further discuss the matter. I should like to help her out if I possibly can do so — but!

My main ideas for this trip are: 1. to shoot some elephant and thereby pay my expenses; 2. to collect birds and to make a more serious study of ornithology than I have been able to do before; and 3. to see the South Tanganyika Highlands and what propects there are for a settler. My idea originally was to make straight for Iringa, leave the car there and trek over to Mahenge and down to the Kilombuo where I could find Hassani, one of my old hunters, pick up my elephant there or thereabouts and then bring back Hassani with me to Nyasaland. Of course, everything may not turn out as I hope. I may find difficulties about licences as I am no longer resident in Tanganyika, but I think this ought to be wangled somehow. I should be able to take in North East Rhodesia on my way back, but I am making no plans, and will just proceed as my star seems to be leading me. Of course, I am just 25 years too late. I never cease to regret that I was not born 20 years earlier — Africa has changed so in the last quarter of a century and is no longer the country it was. I hate reading books of the Africa of that period, it makes me feel so envious of it all.

August 18th, 1928

Got the ammunition from J today and swapped the bullets over of my soft-nose ·450. This gives me 20 rounds which should last a considerable time. Collected the 9 mm from him also, with the foresight block fixed on, I hope satisfactorily this time. Have been spending the last few days getting my kit together and have wired Mrs. F that it is absolutely impossible to think of taking her in my car, it will be all that I can possibly manage to get my own kit on to the car. W arrived up from Chiumo yesterday and I am handing things over to him again by degrees and getting the baccy off

1

ALTITUDES

WATERLOW & SONS LTD. LONDON, DUNSTABLE & WATFORD.

(Ref:: Geological Survey Department, Nyasaland, 1931)

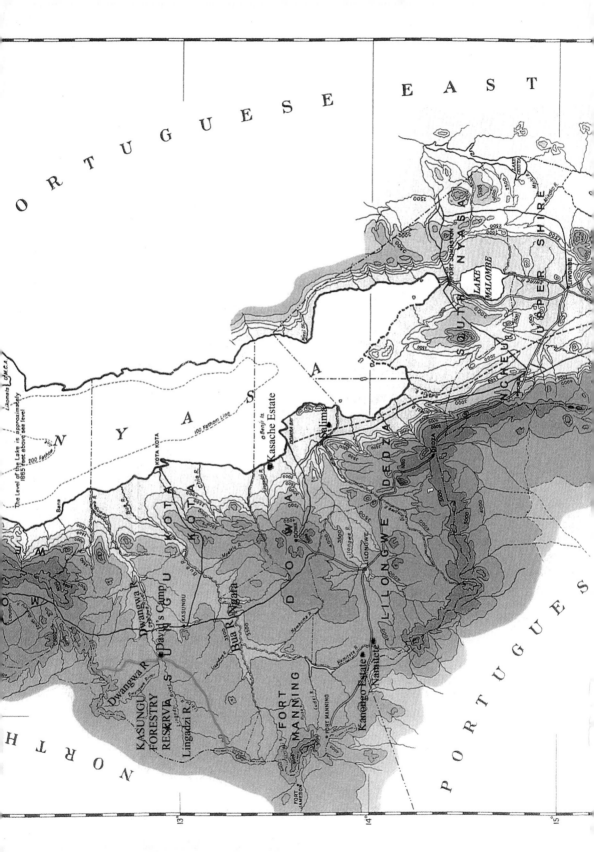

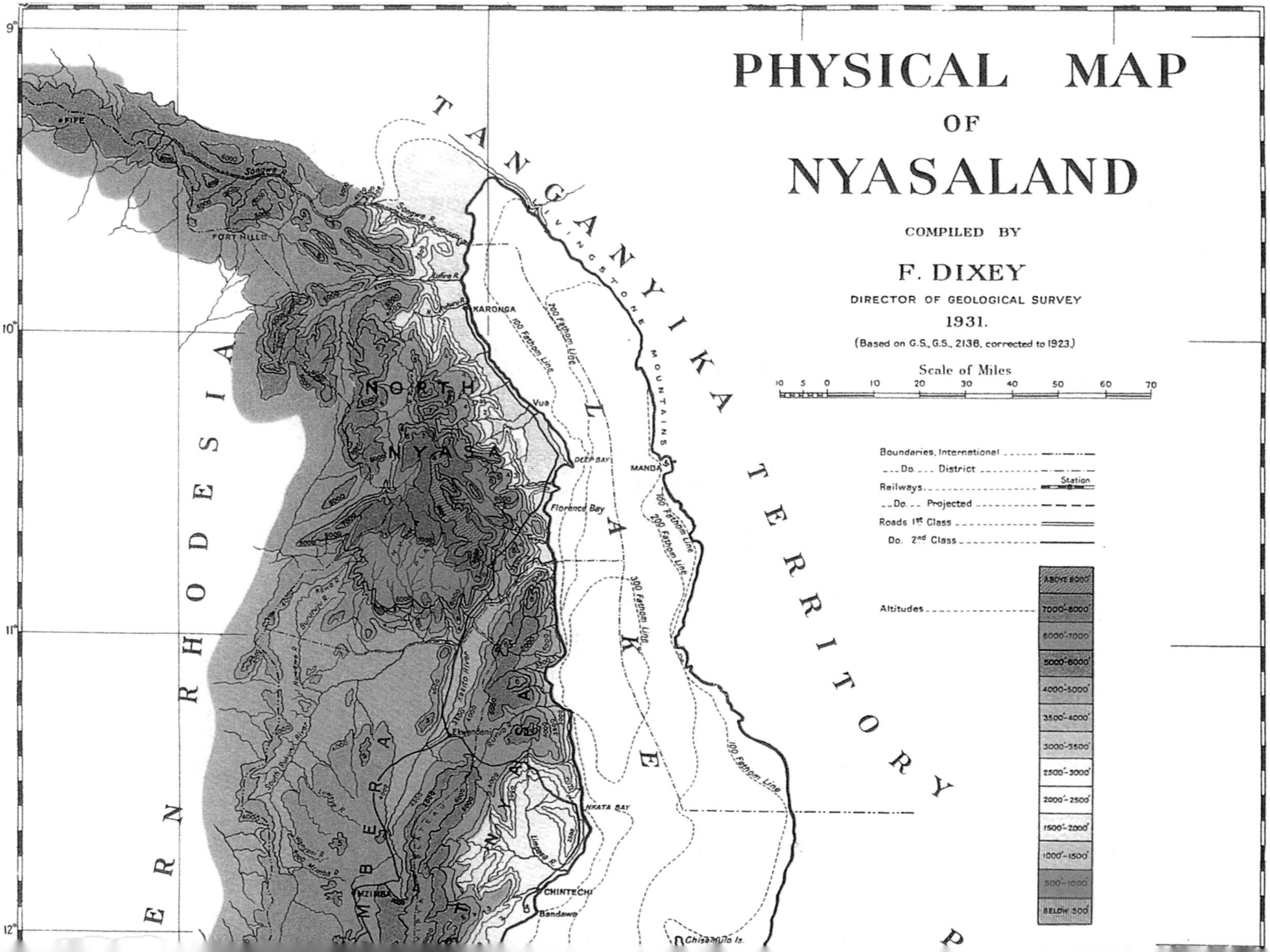

PHYSICAL MAP

OF

NYASALAND

COMPILED BY

F. DIXEY

DIRECTOR OF GEOLOGICAL SURVEY

1931.

(Based on G.S.G.S. 2138, corrected to 1923)

Scale of Miles

10 5 0 10 20 30 40 50 60 70

Boundaries, International _____
Do. District _____
Railways _____ Station
Do. Projected _____
Roads 1st Class _____
Do. 2nd Class _____

Altitudes _____

Above 8000	
7000-8000	
6000-7000	
5000-6000	
4000-5000	
3500-4000	
3000-3500	
2500-3000	
2000-2500	
1500-2000	
1000-1500	
500-1000	
Below 500	

TANGANYIKA TERRITORY

LIVINGSTONE MOUNTAINS

LAKE

100 Fathom Line
200 Fathom Line
300 Fathom Line

MANDA

NKATA BAY

CHINTECHI

Bandawe

Florence Bay

DEEP BAY

KARONGA

Rukuru

NORTH NYASA

SOUTH RUKURU RIVER

N. Chisamula Is.

NORTHERN RHODESIA

FORT HILL

SONGWE

MPIPE

down to Luchenza station. I did two trips today which leaves another three for next Tuesday. I shall spend Wednesday loading up the car and push off early Thursday morning. It is perfectly amazing the number of things that have to be seen to before starting on a trip like this. The car is at present in Blantyre having various gadgets fixed on to it. A Ford petrol tank just in front of the dicky, which, with a spare tin on the running-board should give me a total cruise of 400 odd miles. Foot-board and back-carriers are also being fixed.

August 21st, 1928

Finished the baccy today with three trips to and from Luchenza. In Blantyre yesterday buying many stores. Came to the lamentable conclusion that I'll never get half my stuff on to the car. Was packing up ammunition this evening, that alone must weigh the best part of 1 cwt. We'll know the worst tomorrow anyway, which I'll spend in loading up.

August 23rd, 1928

We started off from Majmbwa this morning, arriving in Blantyre about 11.30 a.m. Spent the rest of the morning and all afternoon doing various odd jobs which I just managed to finish by 4 p.m. By that time I felt so disgusted with civilization that instead of spending the night at Ryall's, as I had intended, we hauled out on the Matope road instead, and did the 35 miles to the Shire River arriving about dusk. Pitched camp by the side of the river; one tent rope to a tree and the other to the hood of the car. I am now happily ensconced at the entrance to the tent and writing this by the side lights of the car. I am wondering how Frazer will do in the 'thengo'. He has a lot to learn about camping but he is fairly intelligent and ought to learn. He is a good goer anyway, as I found last year; but I think he is rather frightened of doing such a long trip. He has confessed to me his fear of 'Jumbo' already, while we were coming along in the car and was in a great state when boys here told him that there were lion about. If he proves a real wash-out I shall have to send him back home down to the lake which will be darned nuisance as he is quite a useful lad.

A nightjar has just said 'chiwurawura' which I suppose means 'good-night' so we will comply with this order.

August 24th, 1928

Arrived in Dedza about 1 p.m., car going well; but sprung a leak in the spare petrol tank and spent all afternoon with Wood trying to mend it. In the end we weren't too successful, Mandala had made one of their usual jobs of it, fixing the cock in a position by the rim of the drum that was the very deuce to get at with the iron. I shall have to plug it with soap in an undignified sort of way. Found McGrath and Mrs. in the hotel, up for a holiday from Cholo. Played bridge with them in the evening and lost 2*s*. Vassili, the Resident here, made the fourth. This is an extraordinarily comfortable little hotel. It was just completed when I came through last year, but this is the first time I have stayed in it — the Angoni Highlands Hotel. Heard that Arundell, a Game Warden from Tanganyika was staying here at the beginning of the week and was saying the conditions of licences have been much changed since I was there. I may meet him at Kasungu, where he now is, and get firsthand news.

August 26th, 1928

Got to Lilongwe about 12 noon yesterday, one or two minor troubles on the road — nothing serious. Had lunch with Riddell of the P.W.D.; filled up with petrol and, as it was latish, decided to stay the night and not push on as I had originally intended to do. Lilongwe is 57 miles from Dedza and about 180 from Blantyre. Was told I might get through to Tanganyika, but it was very doubtful. Mike Calhane was down from Dowa and we spent a merry evening with Carey of the P.W.D.

Left Lilongwe about 7 a.m. this morning, following an excellent road for about 60 miles to the Bua River. There we branched off to the east to cross the river at the Ngara Drift, as the bridge is not yet built.

I asked boys at all the villages round Ngara and the Bua of news of 'Jumbo', but received nothing but negative information, so pushed on to Kasungu Boma, about 85 miles from Lilongwe. Barker is Resident there and as I arrived just at lunch time he very kindly asked me in. Arundell, of the Tanganyika game department was also hunting with him and Mrs. B and I heard a lot of news about Mahenge where he had been stationed. The elephant licence has been brought up to £50 for two Jumbo, which is not as it was a year or two ago. A explained that they had done it to clear the country of the 'stiffs'. I said I hoped I would not be included in that brigade when I got up, and refused a licence — but was assured I would not! If I ever do get up there I feel I should like to apply for a game ranger's job; It's a darned good one and would suit me down to the ground. Barker was not at all helpful with advice of where I should try in this district; not that I blame him. One hates outsiders who come and shoot up one's own hunting grounds. He told me I certainly could not get through further than Ekwandeni Mission, about 150 miles from Kasungu, which is really the first definite news I've had.

I took the road north again, however, at 2 p.m. and came on about 15 miles to the Dwangwa River which I had spotted as a likely place before starting on the trip. Stopped there and asked the usual question — 'Njobvu?' as we call Jumbo in Chinyanja and received the first optimistic answer I have yet had. The local chief came in to pay his respects and was extraordinarily enthusiastic. Any number of Jumbo with enormous tusks quite close — to the west. I had thought down the river, east, would have been the likely spot, but have been overruled by the enthusiasm of the 'Mfumu' who has promised me carriers for tomorrow.

In the hope of finding 'Nyama' I went out this afternoon just west of the main road and saw some roan, the first I've ever come across, and am ashamed to say, made bad work with them in failing light. I hit a bull, just about dusk and we hadn't light enough to follow him up. I hope to get him tomorrow but fear the lions will have him before I do.[1]

Back in camp I have been spending the rest of the evening sorting out loads for a safari or rather a 'ulendo', as we call it here, for a few days, to the place where there are, reputedly, such crowds of elephant. I want to get off at daylight, so must go to bed.

August 27th, 1928

My getting off at daylight wasn't exactly successful. I was personally up and ready shortly after 6 a.m. but the boys, whom I had enlisted as trackers, thought differently and failed to put in an appearance. The old trouble, of which one has so often had experience. So I left with a couple of other boys, about sevenish, Kasengeni, the Mfumu at the road, promised to see I had sufficient carriers for my loads, so I left them to follow on to Chitacko's after me. I went first to pick up the roan I had wounded — hateful word — last night, but, without the boys who had been with me at the time, failed to hit off the spoor so perforce had to leave him. Chitacko's proved to be only six or seven miles at the outside from the road. I arrived about 10 a.m. and was greeted with much 'Lillilooing' from crowds of women, who rolled about on the ground in their usual token of salute. One old hag of about 70 insisted on calling me 'Mwana wanga' — my son — much to my disgust. Chitacko himself is a merry old lad with swarms of children and the necessary wives. I amused them during the

1 Boyoli got him next day — joined me at Chitacko's.

next quarter hour by exhibiting my yard measure which is a celluloid bust of Lloyd George with a tape that pulls out from the mouth and flies back on a spring. It was a great success.

Went for a walk round to see what was in the country and found any quantity of elephant spoor about a month old and was told they had all gone off down to Mbanjan which is apparently 15 or 20 miles south-west — a deserted village; but the natives here are so bereft of grey matter that it is hard to extract anything reliable from them. Got back to Chitacko's about 12 o'clock and found Frazer and the loads had arrived, so rested till the evening when I had another walk round, but found nothing.

A lot of the grass is still unburned round here, which makes walking in the bush a wearying business. Frazer had to go back to Rasmjeni's in the afternoon to get the medicine box which we had left in the car and which we could not spare. He got back just as I was having a bath, so the distance direct cannot be more than four or five miles here. Dinner. And so to bed. The moon is nearly full tonight and the man in the moon showing up more clearly than I remember seeing it before. Hoping for a story I asked the boys who or what it was but was disgusted with their answer "Perhaps Jeso Kristo".

August 29th, 1928

A long tramp yesterday through country where the grass had not yet been burnt. Saw lots of elephant spoor but nothing newer than about a month old. Got to a village called Ngalika's, on the Lingadzi River and went out with a shot gun about 12 noon and slew four guinea fowl — saw nothing in the evening but small buck. On again today, up the Lingadzi, shooting a couple of reed buck on the outskirts of the village. I bartered most of the meat for flour and sweet potatoes, which the carriers brought along with them as this is the last village on the Lingadzi.

Came on the first reasonably fresh elephant spoor a couple of hours later, much to my joy and then for the next hour's walk continually came across yesterday's spoor, one 19 inch which is hopeful. Not much game about except a few reed buck and wart hog. Not surprising, really, when there are armed natives all over the place. I heard two shots from the bush as I went up the river this morning. A few yellow-bill duck on the river, but I had not got the shot-gun with me, I had taken the airgun in its place, with which I nailed a stone-chat which intrigued me. Frazer, of course, made a rotten job of its skin which is practically useless. I hope practice will enable him to turn out a reasonable skin, but he is at present a very poor hand at it. Saw more fairly fresh spoor in the afternoon up river from where I pitched camp and I am in hopes tomorrow will produce a track that will be worth following. Sat for duck at a pool in the river at dusk, but as the moon is practically full only three came, which I missed. A few spur-winged geese about; crowned crane; many hoopoes and two species of charadrius birds which I must take later to identify.

August 30th, 1928

Right and left at Jumbo! Both down to a single shot though the first tried to get to his feet again and had to be finished off with the 8 mm. The old D/B ·450 does excellent work, the second never moved after I dropped him. These are the easiest Jumbo it has ever been my fortune to bag, and there is little to tell in the getting of them. I had offered a prize of a shilling the evening before to the boy who found fresh spoor and brought me to it. I cut sticks 19 inches long and told two boys to go up stream and two down for about half an hour and if they found fresh spoor to measure it from the point of the toes to the heel and come back quickly with the news and on no account to delay after the sun had risen. My plan was most successful. The boys who went up stream found the spoor and were back first, showing me a length of spoor longer than the stick I had given them. Those who went down stream arrived a little later having found nothing. So off we went up stream and the boys brought us to the tracks. Of course they had measured up a double impression but that didn't matter as there was a fair bull in the herd and we followed up.

We had only been going about 10 minutes when we heard an elephant trumpeting in the bush on the south side of the dambo, and later, as we moved in that direction and picked up the tracks again, a tree coming down with a crash. The wind was chopping about all over the place but luckily there was so little of it — just a puff that came from any direction intermittently — that I didn't think it could possibly give us away.

We moved forward to try and locate Jumbo but by the time we had got to the place whereabouts one had trumpeted, they had moved on and we had to get back on to the spoor. The boys weren't anything too wonderful at tracking and I found myself doing most of it instead of them. We were quickly up to them again, this time in fairly long unburnt grass — we could hear them gurgling and crashing branches about, roughly 50 yards from us, but it was not until Boyoli, the head tracker, and I were within 15 or 20 yards that we saw them. One was plain to view, broadside on, with short thick tusks, so I took him without more ado with the sight of the ·450 at the ear hole. He went down to the shot and another came into view behind him a bit on the left and he took the other barrel in the brain; a pleasing shot which needed no backing up. By this time No. 1 was struggling to his feet so I changed rifles and put in a shot with the 8 mm which brought him down again. We then had to run back a few yards because a third tusker, which I had not seen before, got interested in us and made to come for us. I did not want to shoot him also, though I ought easily to have been able to do so, beause three is the limit of the licence and I had shot my first from Cholo last November. I came forward again and gave No. 1 another shot which finished him, and again had to beat a retreat because of No. 3. Finally he thought better of it and made off, which allowed us to come up and measure up our elephants. No. 2 was pretty small — No. 1 I reckon about a 30 pounder. I should have taken No. 3 instead of No. 2 — but then one can never be quite satisfied, and I was pleased enough with what was a pretty clean right and left. I took photographs, and hope I managed to get both elephants in together in one of them, which I climbed a tree to take, and received all sorts of flattery from the boys. 'Bwana njobra, Bwana mkuru', 'you are the big man, we are only children'.

What a terribly egoistic and boastful thing a diary is. I'm ashamed of reading what I have written. If in the future anyone takes the trouble to read this diary, I hope he will not put me down as the sycophantic egoist a diary makes one out to be.

I returned to camp shortly afterwards and had a meal then back to the elephants when we cut out the upper tusk of the bigger one after much labour. The man who is doing the job was not a highly skilled performer and the sun was low by the time we finished.

The natives here make no use of 'medicine' in elephant hunting — nor is the nerve of the tusk anathema and not to be seen by anyone for fear of blindness resulting, which is all more sensible than the more uncivilized tribes further north, but not half so interesting or amusing.

Made tracks for camp about 5 p.m., shooting a wattled plover with the airgun and which Frazer and I skinned on arrival. I can't identify him yet as my books are in the car and though I sent for them yesterday they have not yet arrived.[1]

August 31st, 1928

Visited the elephants this morning in hopes of finding lion at the carcases; but only vultures were in possession. Crowds of women and men

1 Later. *Lobivanellus lateralis* he turned out to be.

came in for meat and they spent the whole day bringing loads back to camp for smoking. I pottered round all day with the shot-gun and airgun getting a yellow-bill duck for the pot (*A. undulata*) and a babbler (*C. kirkii*) which I skinned in the afternoon with fair success. A pair of saddle-billed storks (*Ephippiorhynchus senegalensis*) in the river, queer looking creatures with their black and red bills and black and white bodies.

I expect hyaenas, 'fisi', will be round in crowds tonight to try and snatch meat. There is quite a little village camped round my tent, and meat smoking and fires everywhere.

September 4th, 1928

I had to continue this in pencil because that silly ass Frazer had gone and lost or at any rate mislaid my pen. I suppose I should really take the blame myself for not having put it away properly, but it is good to blame someone else.

Many happenings since the 31st. On the evening of September 1st, after a very pleasant day spent collecting birds and distributing meat to natives who came for it, there arrived a letter from the Boma to say that I was in or near the game Forest Reserve. The boy who brought the letter, on being questioned, told me I was right inside by several miles. From the Resident's letter I tried to make out that I wasn't, but he assured me he knew the boundaries well and that the Reserve began on the Lingadzi at Ngalika's. A rotten affair altogether. I, of course, packed up my traps immediately and started off back to Kasengeni's on the main road, before dawn the next morning. Very annoying as I had just built a grass hut and was settling down comfortably, not to mention the thought that there would be a case at the Boma and that the ivory might be confiscated!

I got into Kasengeni's about 9 o'clock on the morning of the 2nd, and went straight off to the Boma in the car to see what was to be done. It was Sunday morning and I found B in the house where we talked things over and I was told that there would have to be an enquiry into the matter and if I had been in the Reserve he would have to mulct me of a small fine. I promised to come in again next morning with the ivory and hear the worst. Camped that night at Kasengeni's, the load's arriving late in the afternoon and went back to the Boma on the morning of September 3rd with the ivory, Boyoli, the hunter, and Kasengeni, the local chief. I knew there was no doubt really, what the result of the case would be. I had questioned the boys beforehand and knew I must have been right inside the Reserve all right. Still I hoped I might wangle out of it from the wording of the Resident's letter to me. He had said west of Ngalika was the Reserve country and I had been due south.

The case went against me and I was fined £2; but I was allowed to keep the larger pair of tusks. I think I would have got them both if the smaller had been up to standard.

Boyoli was then tried for leading me into the Reserve and fined 5*s*., quite justly as he had made no attempt to tell me I was trespassing even when I asked him point-blank at my camp on the Lingadzi before shooting the elephants. The 5*s*., of course, eventually resolved on me. I was thankful, indeed, when it was all over with no worse results and I was soon on my way back to Kasengeni's.

I drove out to a spinney for guinea fowl in the afternoon, getting one. A pair of bush buck also came forward but went off in safety. There were bush fires all round the countryside and one narrowly escaped burning up the car at the village. I was away at the time sitting in front of another fire and watching the birds coming forward. Turacos of three kinds were the most plentiful. They came in streams over my head and settled in a tree about five yards off, so it was easy to distinguish them. It was only when I got back that I found that the other fire had been within three yards of my car when the boys had managed to put it out; it would have been a disastrous business indeed if the petrol had taken fire, as it would have destroyed not only the car but all my belongings, as well as the hut alongside.

Came by car today, back to the Bua River on advice from Barker. He told me it was quite impossible to go right north through Nyasaland and that my best chance for Jumbo was somewhere round a village called Kasangadzi, on the river. I found it after much search about five miles south of the Bua, but the natives there said there were no elephant, so went with a boy back towards the Bua and east to his village called Katangeza's, where he said there were Jumbo about. The last couple of miles was up a native path varying in width from two yards to a foot, but we arrived safely at the village with no mishap and there pitched camp.

I have to wait until the 7th before tackling elephant again, because I will not have a new licence until then. I have four carriers coming after me from Kasengeni's with the tusks and other loads I had no room for them with the extra weight of Boyoli — whom I have not sacked — remissly, I must admit. The chances of elephant here are not nearly so rosy; I feel I shall be extraordinarily lucky to get even one here. What to do next I find hard to decide. I have thought of making for Portuguese East down by Tete, where there is free elephant shooting in the Fly. An unhealthy district, it is true; but one must put up with that in these days of enlightened Africa. Tanganyika, I think, would prove just as much a wash out as this country, where there is hardly room to move without coming up against some barred area or reserve. In Portuguese East one would at any rate be able to breathe more freely. Poor old British Africa — thy glory has departed. You are ruled by missionaries and your lands are compassed and divided. Would P.E.A. treat a wanderer more kindly or would the Dago put him in jug, as well as mulct him of large fines?

September 5th, 1928

Went by car today about 15 miles up the Bua to get duck. Arrived about 11 a.m. on the dambo of the river where the car stuck in a deep elephant's foot mark and had to be shoved out and reversed. We were only about 100 yards from the river so started operations immediately. Saw some puku does in the distance, who fled at our approach and gave us a fine exhibition of long and high jump combined in their efforts to clear the river, which was very narrow just there. Even so they failed to clear it and came down with a splash sending up showers of water each time as they landed. A pair of yellow-bills came over just as we were starting off up stream and should have fallen an easy right and left but I missed my first barrel with ignominy. I then got one out of a flock of about a dozen which fell on the other side of the river and was collected by a boy who had come along to help; but further on, as we rounded a bend in the river, we saw the water at one point absolutely covered with duck. I hid in the grass at the side of the river and sent the boys on ahead to put them up. They came along in a solid stream, but I found that I was too far off in the grass on the banks as the duck all flew down the centre of the river. I only shot one out of the whole lot which was a knob-nosed duck (*Sarkidiornis melanotos*).

For the next hour or so I hid in the grasses of the river bed — knee-deep in water — while the boys went up and down stream to keep the duck on the move. I downed nine more making twelve altogether; but should have had many more. I only got one other variety — the South African pochard (*Nyroca erythrophthalma*) but as the duck and the drake of this species are so dissimilar, I thought they were different species.

The drake is a much darker-coloured bird with a rich dark chocolate head and neck, while the duck is a much lighter brown and has a brown iris to the eye as opposed to the drake's two rings of yellow and light red. It was this last that made me think they were separate birds at the time and the natives who also declared that to be the case. On coming up out of the water I found my legs were covered with leaches of a most voracious appetite and my legs were a mass of blood, however, I soon had removed the loathely brutes and the sun soon dried up the punctures, though I remained a gory sight for the rest of the day.

Back again to camp with an enormous appetite to find a new loaf awaiting me, which I devoured — every scrap of it — with about half a pound of strawberry jam and washed down with milk-less tea — one of the best meals of my life!

September 6th, 1928

Had another bang at the duck, getting four more species, or rather, three species of geese and one duck. The geese were: Spur-winged goose (*Plectropterus gambensis*); Egyptian goose (*Alopochen aegyptiacus*); and African pygmy goose (*Nettapus auritus*). The duck: Red-billed duck (*Anas erythroryncha*), as well as the pochard and yellow-bill of yesterday.

Saw puku and waterbuck on the river banks and had a bang at a bushbuck on the way home, but missed him. A pleasing day, but I shall never be a great performer with the shot-gun. I missed more duck and expended more cartridges than I care to think about.

September 9th, 1928

The pen is found; turned up in the car lying about behind the cushion, so all is well.

Got a buffalo yesterday, one of a fairly large herd which we hit while chasing oldish elephant spoor. I hadn't much hope of coming up with jumbo so took a buffalo for meat. Saw nothing else and no fresh spoor, so returned about midday to camp. In the afternoon I shot a parrot (*Poicephalus meyeri*) and some small passer which I could not identify. A black bird with a bold white slash across the wing, probably a funjellio of some sort. I told Frazer to cook the tongue of the buffalo for dinner, but he served it up after half an hour's boiling and it was still as hard as a lump of leather. I am hoping better things for tonight.

Today we started off as usual in the early morning and made a long circle round the neighbouring countryside, but found nothing fresh in the way of spoor. September 7th, 1928, incidentally which I see I have left out, was spent doing the same sort of thing, but then we met large herds of eland and a small herd of cow kudu both of which I left alone, but today was an absolute blank except for the sight of the usual small buck and wart hog — and of course a herd of buffalo which I almost forgot about. We barged into them in longish grass and they were off and away leaving a cloud of dust behind them before I had a clear view — let alone time for a shot. Boyoli did not accompany us today, he came to me yesterday evening about two hours after we got back to camp and calmly informed me that he had been bitten by a snake at the place where we killed the buffalo. There was certainly one small puncture on his ankle, which might have been anything, but he declared that only one fang of the snake had got him. I realized it was a try-on of some sort, but got my own back by scarifying the wound with my skinning knife and rubbing in Pot-permang. until he said he had had enough. He was perfectly OK this morning, but declared his inability to accompany me, so I left him behind in camp. He was no loss as my carriers have arrived from Kasengeni's with the tusks, so I took one of them in his place. The local guide is the first boy I've met in Nyasaland who has a pair of eyes in his head — he is not quite comparable to the old Wapojoro of the Mahenge district, but he can at any rate see game, which most of the Angoni or rather Achipeta cannot. The latter is the name of the tribe that inhabits these parts, they like to be called Angoni, because it flatters them — they are really a weedy branch of the 'Nyanja' natives.

I've just eaten the tongue, which has quite come up to my expectations. It took about 12 hours of boiling to get it into condition.

The Mfumu has just been in to say that the guide I've had these last three days — the one who can see — is 'hurt' and is not accompanying me tomorrow. They have no sticking power these people, or else are just lazy.

September 11th, 1928

Two more ineffectual walks round, yesterday and today, seeing no spoor of any newness or any worth following. There are darned few elephants in this spot and the boys tell me there is an 'Mzungu' about two miles north and another about the same distance south, both looking for Jumbo also. We are getting too much like Piccadilly here for my liking; I am going to give it another day or so and then buzz off. I think P.E.A. is the spot I shall make for, but am still swithering.

Birds of the last two days have been: *Lybius torquatus*, the black collared barbet — *Laniarius starki*, a Malaconotine bush shrike which we succeeded in making a frightful mess of between us in the skinning — a coucal, probably *Centropus senegalensis*, but there are so many of these which are so very much alike that it is impossible, except where features are exceptionally marked, to say definitely which species one conforms to — a fly-catcher, *Muscicapa caerulescens*, I think, and —a nightjar, *Caprimulgus fossii*, which I made a mess of. However, I am improving slightly in taking the skins and I hope before long we shall get really good results.

September 12th, 1928

Got a bushbuck this morning on the outskirts of the real thick stuff that we skirted looking for spoor. Pretty little brutes they are — it went to my heart to shoot him, but the boys are grousing because I don't shoot enough meat. There is not much pleasure in shooting up a lot of inoffensive game — the boys also get annoyed when I leave females alone. There is a herd of about half a dozen kudu cows that we meet every morning regularly, I got right up to about 10 yards of them one morning and watched them for some time. I'm afraid I shall have to shoot one for meat the next time I see them.

In the afternoon I made friends with a most engaging oriole (*Oriolus andersoni*). I went out shortly after noon about half a mile into the bush and sat down on a high ant hill to watch birds, there were one or two drongos about, glossy starlings and turtle doves. I heard an oriole whistling a few hundred yards away on my left, but forgot about him for the moment in my interest in two turtle doves who were courting each other and making love generally. When they had disappeared I remembered the oriole, who had been silent for about 10 minutes, so to try and interest him I whistled one of their call notes. I received an immediate response from the thicker bush two or three hundred yards off. I tried him again and again he answered, but this time from a tree much nearer to me, about a hundred yards away on the other side of the comparatively clear area where I was at the edge of the thicker bush. I again whistled the note he was repeating and this time he came straight out, crossed the clearing and settled in a tree some 15 yards off. I could see him plainly there, he was obviously listening and intent to hear my call again, and as soon as I gave it to him he came right up into the nearest tree to me, about five yards off. For the next quarter of an hour we whistled to each other, I trying my best to reproduce the notes he last had said, while the oriole flew from tree to tree all round the ant hill. It was most interesting to see his behaviour, he was obviously completely puzzled. He would whistle a note, then sit about waiting for my reply and when I gave it to him I could see him looking all round trying to locate me, his head turning first in one direction, then in another. Then off he would go to another tree and we would start again. The most interesting thing was the way he was obviously looking for me, or rather his mate, and turning his head to do so, up, down and all round about. I don't think he actually spotted me, because I kept stock still the whole time. Eventually he gave it up as a bad job and retired again to the tree from which he had originally come on the other side of the clearing and no further effort of mine called forth any response. Wretched bird, I wonder what he thought it was all about. I have often before tried to get an answer from this oriole, but this is the first time I have ever clearly succeeded, which makes it all the more interesting, because birds are just beginning to mate here and thinking of nesting time.

I saw one of the woodhoopoes, probably *Rhinopomastus cyanomelas* collecting something from a tree and making off with it, probably for nest building purposes somewhere through the bush, but could not locate the spot he was shaping for.

Later I collected a couple of woodpeckers, a flycatcher and a cuckoo falcon (*Baza verreauxi*), which last is the only one I have as yet identified. He was hawking locusts from tree to tree on the edge of the bush when I spotted him. I gave chase, but his movements were too rapid for me, he would only wait in one tree for a matter of 15 or 20 seconds before dashing on to another 50 or 100 yards off and I never got nearer than about the former distance, so I gave up hopes of shooting him and took a woodpecker that I wanted and had, in fact, previously been trying unsuccessfully to approach. At my shot the falcon circled round and came high up over my head and I was able to down him with my other barrel, a queer right and left.

Boys have just come in to say that they found spoor today in right the opposite direction from that in which I've been looking. That is elephant all over! Well, well, better luck tomorrow, perhaps; but I'm getting fed up with this spot. Have decided to give it two more days only and then shape for P.E.A.

September 14th, 1928

On this news I started off at crack of dawn yesterday and was several miles off in the bush before the sun had risen. We heard Smith in the direction of Mpali Hill, but needless to say struck nothing worth following. I believe the spoor seen by the boys on the 12th was that of a poor old cow with one calf who is wandering round the countryside and I have come across their spoor myself on more than one occasion. I shot a roan bull with 25 inch horns — rather a pleasing shot at about 250 yards with solid that raked him diagonally through the shoulder. There was no stalking the herd; they had seen us first in fairly open country and had our wind which was blowing strongly in their direction, so I had to take him from where I was.

Today was my Sunday morning. I felt heartily fed up with things when I woke up, so lay in and had a gentlemanly sort of breakfast at about 9 a.m. Feeling a bit better after that and a smoke, I went off down to the Bua in the car, about four miles away, and walked up the river for five or six miles taking Frazer with me for a change of companionship. I shot three duck — knob-nosed, pochard and red-bill, but didn't get any bird whose skin I wanted. I shot a young lily trotter (*Actophilornis africana*) mistaking it for some different species; but I see Sclater and Stark note that birds do not attain adult plumage until the second year, so it was that that misled me. Pretty late though in the middle of September it could not have been one of this year's brood as I can't make out that birds have yet started to nest and this one's wing quills were only just starting to sprout. I went up past the bridge over the river, a very ramshackle affair of rotten timber, but I see preparations in hand for a new bridge — there are brick kilns and iron girders ready for the building. I'm glad though I didn't try to cross with my car. Rested in the shade of a tree by the water's edge, a mile or two above the bridge, while grey turacos (*Corythaixoides concolor*) came and burbled overhead, and walked back later in the afternoon. Many cormorants on the river, of two sorts I fancy — could not make out a third species which I know exists, but there were really surprisingly few birds of much interest.

September 15th, 1928

The Mfumu came rushing to my camp in the grey of the dawn this morning to say that there were buffalo in the old maize gardens. I dressed hastily, swallowed some tea and rushed off but by the time I had got to the place where they had been — about half an hour later — they had disappeared, so we followed up through longish unburnt grass. It was not long before we came up with them and I went forward to try for a shot. I could get up to 20 or 30 yards of them easily enough, but that was no use, I could merely see the grass waving and black forms appearing now and again through it — quite hopeless to try a shot. I followed on behind them for a mile or two hoping they would go into burnt country, but they either saw or heard me on one occasion and crashed off, making a tremendous noise and split up into three herds.

I climbed up to the top of an ant hill to wait for the boys, coming behind, and from there could see one herd of 30 or 40 a few hundred yards off to my left while another of about the same number were moving off straight in front. We followed on again as soon as the boys came up making contact occasionally with the buffalo, first in the long grass and then in a patch of heavy 'msita', but eventually they moved out into a dambo. From this point I made a horrid mess of things. I hit one animal, taking a sight on the shoulder, but as it had no immediate effect, I fired at another and got him. He went down after a hundred yards dash across the dambo, so we then set about looking for number one. We could find no sign of him with the herd, so cast round to see where he could have made for, but with no success. Eventually I decided to give it up and make for camp, it was about 11 a.m. and getting pretty warm. We were skirting the 'msita' on our way home, when suddenly there was a crash in the edge of the thick stuff and we just caught a glimpse of something disappearing into it. We went up to the spot and found it was our first buffalo, who had been lying doggo there. He was hit all right and had been bleeding profusely, poor beast. We followed up, of course, immediately, as I did not think he would go far, having already been left alone for the best part of a couple of hours. He kept all the time to the 'msita', pretty heavy stuff it was too and hard to track in. Twice we came up with him, the first time merely to hear a crash ahead, the second time catching sight of him before he disappeared into the bush, but on neither occasion could I get in a shot. The second time this occurred I decided to give him another rest in hopes we should find him not so much on the alert.

So we sat down and made a fire by rubbing sticks and had a rest and a smoke. After about three quarters of an hour we tried him again, and had only been going a minute or two when we heard something ahead, approaching nearer, I at last made out a black form which eventually, when I could get it better focussed, resolved itself into the fore quarters of a buffalo. I knelt down and gave it him, drawing a bead for the neck which was the part of which I had the clearest view. He seemed to topple over backwards at the shot, but then crashed off again. However, I felt pretty confident that we now would get him, but to my disgust, when we got on to his tracks, we found he was a totally different animal. We saw that from the different blood spoor. I had made a confounded mess of things and felt thoroughly disgusted with myself. We sweated on for the rest of the day but could make nothing of it. The tracks were too puzzling with so many animals about and we never caught a glimpse of either animal again, so at about 5 p.m. we gave it up and returned to camp — I, for one, feeling heartily ashamed of myself.

I was pretty weary too after nearly 12 hours of it which did not help to mend matters and I feel like a novice at the game — spoiling two perfectly good buffalo like that. I shall, of course, have another go at them tomorrow, but do not feel in the least confident.

September 16th, 1928

No go. Found no further trace of the buffalo, so I will close the chapter on a very regrettable incident.

The boys at this village are the limit; they never even worried to bring in the buffalo I did get yesterday. When I discovered that this morning, I immediately returned and began packing things up for a move back to Blantyre. The only thing I got or saw on the way back from the buffalo was a hyena. We were crossing a pretty open patch between two bits of 'msita' when I saw something galloping in our direction from the other side. I thought at first that it was a lion but saw it was a 'fisi' when it got a bit nearer. It was carrying a chunk of meat in its mouth, obviously collected from the buffalo of the previous day and was now making a belated return to its home. I took it going at full gallop at about 75 yards holding just in front of its head and it collapsed at my shot. I thought he was done for but, when we got nearer, he started struggling and made off dragging his head between his front paws. I only had time for one shot more before he disappeared into the thick stuff and we followed it up easily enough over a heavy blood trail. It went a surprising distance but we eventually came up with him again in long grass and I was able to finish him off. How he had been able to drag himself so far was a wonder; but all African animals are the toughest of beasts and the will to live is strong in them. My first shot had smashed up his neck and the second ripped out the entrails but he had still managed to go the best part of two miles with these two crippling wounds. He was a big dog hyena and about as big as a lion.

Back in camp I've been paying off my boys and getting ready for tomorrow.

Some boys came in with a vulture which they had got at the buffalo — collared him inside the carcass they said. I can't quite make him out, he ought by rights to be ordinary *Gyps kolbii*, but he is very small, only measuring some 30 inches and his general plumage might be either that or *rupelli*, which is rare in Nyasaland. I think he is the latter, but cannot say so definitely.

I shot a bird that I've been wanting all the time I've been here, which

comes to feed on the seeds of a large tree standing in the village. I could not make out what it was at all, but now that I see its skin, think it must just be one of the glossy starlings.

A boy came in to say he had found last night's elephant spoor on a dambo close to the road, so I sent a boy off to see what sort of beasts they were. My informer told me they were three big elephants, but I suggested the poor cow and calf of whom I have written before, and so it turned out to be and I am not altering my decision to push off tomorrow which I would have done if the spoor had turned out to be interesting. I am going back to Blantyre, refit there and then push off to Tete.

September 20th, 1928

I'm writing at Ryall's Hotel at Blantyre. All went well on the trip south. I had lunch on the 17th at Lilongwe and dinner at Dedza. There I met the Governor and Lady B to whom I had to confess the iniquity of my conduct. However, he didn't think very seriously of it and began talking of trout, asking me to transfer some to the Nswadzi when I get back from my trip.

I left Dedza at about 12 midnight and driving through the night arrived in Zomba — after sleeping away a few hours of the early morning in the car drawn up at the roadside — at about 9 a.m. Had breakfast in the hotel there run by a fellow who had just taken it over from the previous owner. He told me his hotel was the best in Nyasaland — actually it is by a long way the worst — and that his one fad was cleanliness. I pointed out the cobwebs in the corners and asked if that was up to his standard. Unkindly, I feel. He was a queer bird altogether.

Another queer card I met on the way south was old Muirhead at Lilongwe. He is running the store up there, starting a new venture. I had lunch with him and he started talking. It turned out he was a fellow rather after my own heart, having spent his early years wandering round Africa — mostly in the Congo, as far as I could make out — and hunting elephant or trading in rubber. I think it was the fact that I had just been poaching elephant that got him going, as he had known a lot of that game in the early days. We found we mutually knew much of the old Lijede and we had a great pow-pow.

In Zomba I had my passport visaed for P.E.A. and came straight on to Blantyre. On the 19th I went down to Cholo to collect letters and deposit some unnecessary kit and have spent today re-fitting generally.

I've been having trouble with the car, it is only doing some 300 miles

to a gallon of oil, which is leaking out of the sump as soon as it starts heating. I can't go on like this, so got Mandala to look at it. They spent this afternoon fixing it up and assured me it was OK when I collected it at 3.30. Of course, it turned out to be one of their usual jobs and was leaking worse than ever, after standing a couple of hours in the shade here. They are going to have another crack at it early tomorrow and I've had a chit from B in answer to one from me to assure me that it will be satisfactorily fixed up. Personally I don't trust them one instant and expect I'll have to find someone else to fix things. I still hope to get off tomorrow but I daresay will find it impossible.

September 21st, 1928

Got the car back about 10.30 a.m. with no further sign of a leakage. I think it is OK at last, thank the Lord.

Spent a cheery morning in the hotel and started off after lunch, quite delighted to leave civilization and the fleshpots behind me again. Not that one doesn't enjoy a day or two in comparative comfort. I had really a very amusing three days. The brothers Farquharson were down from their place at Namitete and a lot of cheery people staying in the hotel. I don't think I got to bed before 2 a.m. any night. I tried to last night but was hauled out by KF who had the next room to mine and we spent the rest of the night yarning. I've half promised to go up there sometime later and stay with him and perhaps have a bang at Jumbo which are, by all accounts, numerous round his place.

Came in the 35 miles to the Shire as before, arriving about 5 p.m., on the Mwanza road this time and not the same place I stopped at on my way north. It looked like a nice enough spot, but the darned place is chock full of mosquitoes, which fact I might have anticipated. It's going to be damnably hot tomorrow and not only tomorrow but for the rest of the year as well in the country I'm shaping for. Hope to make Tete tomorrow and hear about things from the Portuguese. I have a hope that I shall be able to go up the Zambezi by canoe from there and then continue up some tributary coming in from the north. It will save a lot of porterage and difficulty of getting carriers if I can do this.

NYASALAND PROTECTORATE.

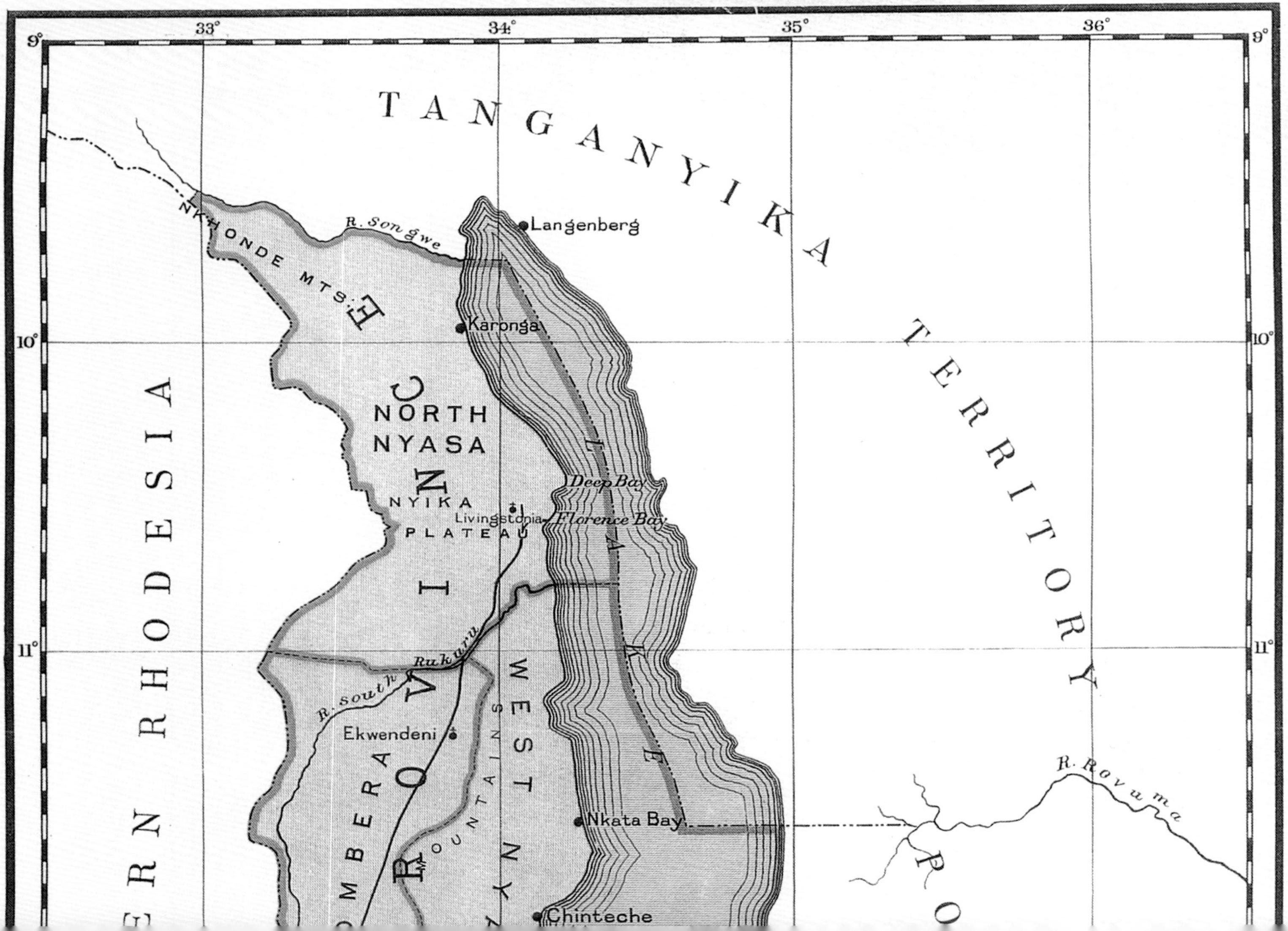

TERRITORY

TANGANYIKA

R. Rovuma

PO

R. Songwe

Langenberg

Karonga

E. Umonde Mts.

Deep Bay

L A K E

Florence Bay

NORTH
NYASA

NYIKA
PLATEAU

Livingstonia

WEST NYA

MOUNTAINS

N

Nkata Bay

Chinteche

Rukuru

R. Lwozi

Ekwendeni

MBERA

PROV

ERN RHODESIA

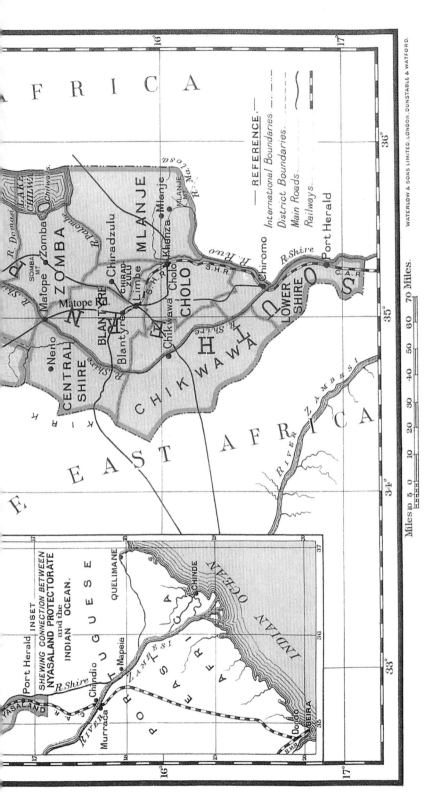

2

ELEVATION ABOVE SEA LEVEL OF PRINCIPAL PLACES (APPROXIMATE.)

Zomba	2948 Ft.	Fort Johnston	1700 Ft.	Luchenza	2500 Ft.
Blantyre	3500 Ft.	Dedza	4500 Ft.	Kota Kota	1800 Ft.
Limbe	4000 Ft.	Neheu	3500 Ft.	Chikwawa	127 Ft.

(Ref:. Geological Survey Department, Nyasaland, 1931)

Hassani in camp

David and Hassani

David and Hassani with 2nd elephant

David with ivory

340 lbs. of ivory

Making fire

Madewa with hartebeest 'nyama'

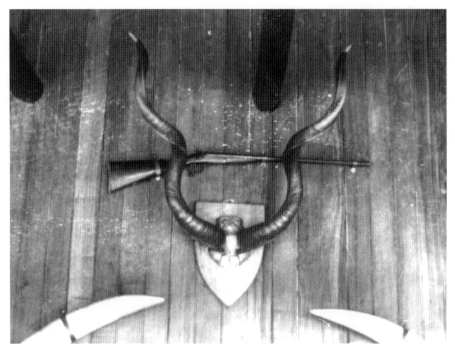

The ·450 displayed at Kasungu.
'In atonement for the right and left at Kasungu — 30th August, 1928.'

PORTUGUESE EAST AFRICA
North of the Zambezi

September 25th, 1928

I got to Tete on the 22nd, arriving about 3.30 p.m. The Zambezi crossing presents no great difficulty though it is awkward backing down the steep bank on to the little barge that takes one across. The owner of the ferry is a man named Gerard — an Irishman stranded in this part for I don't know how many years — I met him again in Tete yesterday. He was one who has obviously seen better days and probably owes his present circumstances, not so much to his fondness of elbow lifting as to the weakness of the top-knot. A decent enough fellow, anyway, as he offered to do me the double journey across the river for £3, the price generally being £2 for the single crossing.

I've been spending the last two days going from one government office to another in a vain endeavour to get licences, pass the customs and comply with a hundred rules and regulations that the Portuguese thrust on one. It is a thankless job. Most of it waiting and paying over money and trying to curb one's impatience. I wish I could speak Portuguese; it would probably save a lot in all these items. Still, I wave my hands a lot, which is effective and keep a broad smile on my face, which is even more so. Perhaps I shall get off tomorrow, but I'm doubtful.

Everybody is very pessimistic about my chances of elephant; they say the country was shot out 20 years ago and that I've not an earthly chance of seeing anything at all. As a matter of fact I'm rather encouraged by this; if they had said two years ago I should be less happy. I shall have to go to a boma called Muchena and announce my intention of shooting round there in the first place, after that I'm free of a good step of country and it will be a bad business if I find nothing in it worth shooting.

A man called de Beer came in yesterday with two pairs of tusks got south of the river, one was about 50 lbs., the other 18 lbs. or so. He said he had lost a real good fellow and had only seen vast quantities of cows. This is not so bad really, for a fortnight or three week's shoot. What a man with a name like that is doing shooting Jumbo for a living I don't know — but perhaps . . .

Met a young fellow yesterday, a Portuguese who spoke English well and was really quite a good sort. He has been trying his luck lately and told me he was waiting for the country on the Barwe River to be opened before going out again. This country had apparently been closed two or three years ago because people have been smuggling ivory out that way. On enquiry I was told the country would be thrown open again next May, so I daresay it may be worth while to think of approaching that quarter about that time, but another six months will show me whether it will be worth it or not. He came down here to the hotel last night and beckoned me out, from the table on the verandah, very mysteriously. I was wondering what had happened, but it transpired that all he wanted me to do was to go up and stop a roughhouse in a pub in the town. Poor old G had been making a fool of himself apparently and trying to scrap the Portuguese. I am afraid I wouldn't go along with him, I know what these shows are and generally the best thing to do is to leave them alone and you find things sort themselves.

Paid a visit to the bank this morning to get cash on a letter of credit and was given £20 more than the amount I signed for, half in Portuguese money and half in gold! I thought something was wrong and went back in the morning to return it. I couldn't make them understand for a long time what was up, but eventually they saw light and were very grateful. Perhaps an incident like this may be useful later, if I get down and out!

September 26th, 1928

Two hopefuls arrived up from Salisbury last night to see the Zambezi and spend a holiday there. I'm afraid Tete was not what they had expected exactly; but they were very optimistic if they expected to find a Ritz Hotel in the middle of P.E.A. Poor old Tete can't keep pace with the rate things have been moving the last month or two. I suppose formerly they had about two visitors a year, whereas now they come through at the rate of three or four a week. I spent today making my usual round of Government offices and I really thought everything was in order when I went to the Customs to collect my rifles which have been interned there since my arrival. But it was latish in the afternoon before I was in possession of the papers they needed and by that time the Chèf Departement, or what ever they call him was not there, so I have to go back tomorrow for what I hope will be the final formality.

I watched the river sternwheeler pulling out from the landing stage this afternoon in the midst of a great conglomerie of shouting natives and effusing Dagos. By the time those taking their departure had been hugged, kissed and slobbered over by the rest of the population of Tete they must have been truly insanitary receptacles.

The boat eventually got off, only to fetch up on a sand bank about 100 yards off, where the rag-time performance started again. I hear from our two visitors from Salisbury that they are now stuck again on another sand-bank a mile or two down stream. They saw them there on their way back from a trip in a dug-out to look for crocodiles.

September 27th, 1928

Got off today about 11.30 a.m. I had been promised that all should be ready by 8 a.m., so that was not so bad. I had to pay out more money at the Customs because my ammunition hadn't been left there originally. It was only inspected and left in the car; another catch of these people. Recrossed the Zambezi, but like a fool hadn't realized that the road to Muchena didn't join on to the Blantyre road. The fools of ferry boys told me it did and it was not until I had gone about six miles up the Blantyre road that I found out they had misled me, intentionally I think, to save themselves a two mile pull against the current. The only thing to do was to come back and board the ferry once more, which I did, much to the boy's disgust, and eventually got to Nynagwe where the road starts, after another two hours or more on the river. I could not cut across the thengo because the Revubwe River comes in just between and it is too broad and deep to ford. From Nynagwe, after a good deal of trouble getting out of the boat and up the bank, I found quite a fair road in front of me and came along about 20 miles and am camping tonight by an Indian store. Not much in the way of creature comforts, though I was offered the usual Senhora on arrival! They tell me there are plenty of elephant round Muchena, which I hope will prove to be the case. It will need one or two Jumbo of a fair size to repay me the amount which the Dago has taken from me. £20 deposited with the Police in case I am D.B.S.'ed or other-wise cleared out of the country — £28 deposited for the car — £12 for the rifles — about £60 altogether which they say they'll give back to me when I leave. Besides this I have had to pay about a fiver for ammunition and 15 or 20 quid for stamps to stick on my wretched applications for *Billets de Residence*, shooting licences, etc. This includes a few pounds for two blokes who kindly stood surety for me. What that meant, exactly, I couldn't make out, but I suppose it was merely another wheeze to extract an extra quid or two out of me. I am I suppose £100 out of pocket since first seeing Tete. If there are no Jumbo here I certainly shall be D.B.S'sed! I don't know why one enjoys doing this sort of thing. The two fellows up from Salisbury thought me quite balmy I believe. Still I am happy — how happy anyone else would find it is hard to realize — and have still the greater happiness to look forward to. Is it Schopenhauer who says the greatest happiness is that of anticipation and memory? Who ever it was hits somewhere near the bull's eye alright. Lion about but a good distance away, I don't suppose they'll trouble us. (They didn't.) But he forgets the anticipation of the memory, which should also be included.

Frazer summed up the Portuguese rather neatly this morning as we were coming along in the car. I was talking of the waste of time in Tete and he said:

"chifenkwa wakuda wambiri" — "because they are very black".

September 29th, 1928

Yesterday I went first to Muchena Boma where I met a 'very black' Portuguese who looked at my licences in a very self-important sort of way. He had little news to give me of elephant and so I pushed off as soon as I could down the road again, some 10 miles to a point where I had turned off to go to Muchena, there I took another road that joined at that point and forged ahead pretty well north for the rest of the morning, stopping occasionally to try and get news of elephant. Needless to say, I once more had only negative information, until I got to a place where a footpath joined in from Furancungo. There I was told there were elephant at F about two days off — no road for a car — and that there were also elephant beyond Matenji where the motor road ended. I had heard of F in Tete as the place to shape for, so decided to give it a miss as I knew there were other people hunting round there, and went straight on down the road eventually arriving, much to my surprise, at a beautifully cared for plantation away up in the Matenji hills.

I was greeted by a young Portuguee who spoke good English and soon afterwards met his father, sister and two more brothers. They were all very kind to me and treated me with great hospitality, putting me up for the night and looking after me generally in a manner in which I can only hope would be returned were they to be travelling in British territory. The father is a big man in these parts — Bivar,[1] I think, by name. I understood

1 Rafael de Bivar Pinto Lopes who in 1922 rented from the Zambezi Company the vast lands of Macanga and Angonia. [Ed.]

him to have been Governor in Tete some years ago. I had to carry on conversation with him through the medium of the Senhora — quite a pretty girl of — well it's hard to say but certainly not much over 20 and more probably 18 or 19. She told me her grandfather had owned many properties in P.E.A. and her father had selected this place to stay at and improve. It was certainly a charming place — good buildings, a very comfortable house, apparently wonderful soil and an excellent climate. One could travel a good many hundred miles in Africa before striking another place like it. Very well watered, with little streams running as brown and clear as a Highland trout stream. In fact I altogether fell in love with the place — if I could only have done ditto with the Senhora, I would seek no further and cease from wandering. But the 'Heavenly Spirit' wasn't singing its best, so in the evening I collected porters for a move on today. Had quite a lot of trouble collecting them and walked round several villages tempting boys to come along with me.

I finally collected 12, whom I beguiled with promises of 'nyama' and an English sixpence apiece and they promised to turn up next morning to take my loads. It requires a lot of tact to get boys to go with you always. Load carrying is not a popular business and one has to get on the right side of these boys somehow. The general procedure when one arrives at a village is to call the headman and make him produce the boys; but that is rarely successful. As soon as one puts in an apprearance all the able-bodied men run off into the bush and hide until the danger has passed. So the best plan is to make a circuitous approach, rush into the middle of the compound and pull the boys out of their huts before they have time to run away. I was fairly successful in doing this. Once one has got hold of them cordial relations are easily established by the most child-like behaviour one can possibly think of. Keep joking the whole time about their personal appearance, about the number of their wives, their sexual relations with them — this last is most important — and perhaps a final injunction that they are not to sleep with their wives that night or they will be too tired to carry loads next day, and one can be fairly sure that one has made a good impression and that they will not let you down.

Back to the house when it was already dark to find that my Portuguese friends had a room all ready for me and gave me an excellent dinner. We talked tobacco most of the time and I hope I was able to put him up to one or two dodges which we find successful in Nyasaland and which they had not heard of before. I also talked elephant and was told there were any amount of them on the Lingove River which I understood was about 20 miles off over the hills. They were wildly optimistic of my chances, if what they told me were only half true I have indeed found a little Paradise. However as they had never been to the place themselves, of which they talked so rapturously, I knew one couldn't believe one quarter of what they said. I think they were carried away with delight by a couple of my elephant stories and also because I worked in a mention and praise for the Portuguese poet Camoens who wrote the *Lusiads*. I did this last rather neatly — I felt I had to show off my knowledge of him and pretended to mix up his name with 'Camion' the French and Portuguese word for 'lorry' when we were talking about cars, anyway it went down very well.

This morning the boys, wonderful to relate, all turned up and I sent them off, about 7.30, following on later myself after a good breakfast and many goodbyes and mutual good wishes with the Bivars. I am not sure that is really their name, I didn't extract it from them until the last minute and then had not the wherewithal to write it down.

Today I have come a very long and tiring march right over the range of hills and down to the foothills on the other side to the Lingove. The first part was a very stiff climb, but the beauty of the places we passed and the grandeur of the views made it worth while. We stopped once at a little burn reminiscent of the upper reaches of the Blackwater. It certainly should have been full of trout but alas, such was not the case; but that loss was almost atoned for by the countless hundreds of beautiful tropical butterflies flying all round us in the dappled shade of the trees whose greenness was almost comparable to that of an English spring. I don't often rapturise about scenery, but this place has entirely won my heart and I would not complain if I were to spend the rest of my life here.

From the watershed we dropped down a matter of 1,500 or a couple of thousand feet, I would reckon, to a little village called Msatwe. We did not arrive until 6 p.m. and some of the carriers have only just put in an appearance, 9 o'clock at night. I reckon it is nearly 30 miles from Matenji House, because we were going fairly hard most of the day. It is disappointing at the end of a hard day like this to hear the usual discouraging replies to questions about elephant, but some of the sting is taken out if one remembers to be prepared for this. The elephant is the wiliest and hardest of creatures to hunt and he who is foolish enough to go after him must be prepared to lead a very hard life and go through disappointment after disappointment before any success is attained. The day of exploring new country is nearly over — quite over in so well known a country as P.E.A. There may be an odd corner of French or Belgian Congo or even north-east Angola where few people go, but even that is doubtful. Here I am told that there was a Portuguese Senhor looking for elephant a month or two ago unsuccessfully and that perhaps I shall be more lucky on a small river called the Bandi, 10 or 12 miles further on, I make out. Anyway I am going to let the carriers have a rest tomorrow morning and I will explore the neighbouring countryside with a couple of local boys, when perhaps I shall come to some decision as to where I should make my headquarters. This village itself, is obviously not the place for that. We are still in the foothills and though, as Aloysius Horn says 'the elephant is a bit of a mountaineer', he prefers flatter country as a rule — that, at any rate has been my experience of him up to date.. Well — must go to bed *A la belle etoile* tonight — it is not worthwhile pitching a tent when there is no chance of rain and one is dog weary.

September 30th, 1928

Walked round this morning seeing a couple of waterbuck only, at which I failed to get a shot. I found elephant spoor about a week old, apparently making for this Bandi River so it was obviously the place to make for first. I did not stay long out because there was very little game about and though I want meat badly to make the carriers happy, there is not much chance of getting it here. The Lingove River here is a beautiful clear stream running between rocks on a sandy bed and I had a most gratifying bathe in a little pool before getting back to the village where I rested until the afternoon.

The carriers then came up in a body and said they were not going any further. They had nearly died on yesterday's march and they were now going home. I made suitable remarks to them and told them they would anyway see me as far as the Bandi. I then told the Chief to bring in flour for which I gave money to Frazer, and leaving things to simmer down a bit I went off with a rifle to look for game. I saw no signs at all, though there were some interesting birds about — some sandgrouse and a type of nightjar, which is new to me being the most interesting. I did not take anything as taking skins when one is on the move is a nuisance. I shall be thankful when I get into some semblance of a permanent camp again. It is one thing to toddle along a road as a government official with good carriers, askaris and the local chief at one's beck and call, but quite another to try the same game as a nonentity trying to make a living by hunting. How I'm going to get back again up the hill the Lord alone knows. My present carriers I will certainly not be able to keep much beyond tomorrow. In this village there are about two men and a boy only and on the Bandi — nobody. They tell me there are plenty of villages on ahead, somewhere beyond the Bandi with many boys, so I must just trust to that. Anyway that's looking a long way ahead and sufficient unto the day.

October 1st, 1928

Much to my disgust we heard shots this morning coming into the Bandi and on arrival there found a Portuguese bloke already in possession. He is a fellow shooting for the Government and though very black, with a completely native brother, turns out to be not a bad sort really. He gave me some maize coffee in his hut, which was really extraordinarily good, and insisted on taking me out hunting this afternoon, although I would much rather have gone alone. He made a desperate noise tramping through the bush in hobnailed boots, but he could certainly see game. I slew a wart hog quite close to camp and gave him a fore-leg when we got back, for which he expressed his desire. All the same I hope he doesn't stay here long. He tells me he is going away north-west in a day or two, which I hope will prove to be the case in reality.

I have been at war with my carriers since getting back and though victory was in the balance for a period of about two hours, I think it is eventually mine. The same troubles as before, of course, but the boot is now on the other foot. Yesterday I was completely in their hands, but now, having arrived at this place I intend making a permanent camp and being in possession of meat, I can afford to lay down the law.

The point turned on the meat. I sat in my chair with the wart hog about 10 feet off when I got back from the hunt and waited for them to make the first move. This was not long in coming, a deputy came up to ask for meat for their evening meal, I said yes and told them to cut the animal in half. Then as this was about to be done, I stopped them and said on second thoughts, that it was now my turn to be 'wobruta' — difficult — and that not any man would receive a bit of meat until they agreed to do what I told them. I wanted a good sized hut built tomorrow and four boys to stay with me until I had no further need of them or collected others in their place; their answer to this was a sheepish sort of 'no' and that they were all going back up the hill tomorrow.

"Very well", I said, "No meat, and certainly no more money",

and I went and had a bath while they talked things over. Then I sent for their head man and explained things again and told him to go back and select four boys to stay with me. That was no go; so I had dinner and talked in loud tones about the excellence of wart hog soup. This may have had its effect, anyway after dinner I sent up Frazer and told them this was their last chance of getting any meat as I was now going to bed. I could hear them talking things over and at last Frazer came back to say that they all wanted to stay! This wasn't exactly what I wanted however, so I called them all up again, made my pick of four stalwart boys to stay, harangued them all about their evil ways and told them that from now onwards they were to do what I wanted. They climbed down all right, so I gave them their half wart hog and we are now, I hope, at peace again, with the victory mine. I'm going to have a Sunday morning tomorrow and build huts and admire birds.

October 3rd, 1928

Yesterday I shot three hartebeest on a dambo a couple of miles from my camp in order to have plenty of meat with which to barter for food-stuffs from the neighbouring villages and to pay off the boys who are going back to Matenji. I got them about 4 o'clock in the afternoon but when I myself came back to camp an hour or two later, I found my boys had not yet gone to bring them in and that the one I had sent back to tell them to go and collect the meat had lost his way and never arrived. I sent them off, post-haste, but it was not until about 10 o'clock at night that they arrived. I thought that they also had lost their bearings and we kept a big fire going to guide them.

Today I've been finishing off my grass house which is quite a palatial affair as these things go and will make me fairly comfortable. I found two nests also with eggs in them. One was a red-eyed dove (*Streptopelia semi-torquata*), the other a kite (*Milvus aegyptius*) who had made a nest in a tree very easy to climb. I blew the eggs with a cigarette holder which was the only thing I could extemporize as a blower, but it was not very satisfactory. I have now, however, gone and spoiled that like an ass. There was an old bit of baccy or something stuck in the tube which I was trying to get out, it wasn't really doing much harm but would have been better away. Now there is a large darning needle down one end of the tube, a nail down the other and a chunk of wood in the middle — all firmly fixed and the tube is blocked entirely. It's wonderful what one can do if one only tries! I've also taken a notch out of one of my front teeth in endeavouring to pull out the needle.

October 4th, 1928

Our friend the Portuguese departed yesterday leaving me a clear field here. He promised to send me a hunter and food from the village he was going to today, neither of which have arrived and we are sorely in need of both. I shall have to send a boy to find the village tomorrow and see what he can do in the matter. Went for a long tramp round today seeing nothing except some hartebeest which I left alone. Nor were four boys whom I sent off early in the morning to look round any more successful in finding spoor. Jumbo is being chased round so much in this part that I don't expect any success for a very long time, if at all. I think my friends in Tete were not so very wide of the mark after all in saying the country was no use. However, I'm quite content to spend some weeks at any rate here; life is full of interest even if one is not doing any good with the elephant.

I sent off carriers in the morning, each with a goodly supply of meat to take back to their homes and am keeping the four boys I picked out only.

This afternoon we were also unsuccessful in getting any birds or eggs; we spotted a vulture's nest on a tall tree close to camp and a boy succeeded in climbing to it only to find a young bird in the nest fully-fledged and almost ready to fly. I was about a month too late, which is surprising so early as this in the year. I also cut out a woodpecker's nest but there was nothing inside. Fly has been pretty bad all day today, I wonder if a grey cloudy day makes them more active. One would have thought the reverse would have been the case.

October 5th, 1928

Two of my remaining four boys ran off in the early hours of the morning. I don't know what the trouble is or why I should find it so hard to get boys to stay with me here, but I suppose the answer is the old chestnut 'Cherchez la Femme'. If they had their wives with them they would probably be quite content.

This morning I took one of the remaining boys with me and went off in search of the nearest village to get supplies. We were right out of flour and the boys were eating meat only last night. We hadn't the foggiest where the nearest village was but took the first path we met and followed it. It led us north-west over the Lingove again, whereabouts I shot a hartebeest out of a herd of about a dozen, and then on over some hills for about 12 miles in all I should reckon, eventually arriving at a fair size

PORTUGUESE EAST AFRICA
NORTH OF THE ZAMBEZI RIVER

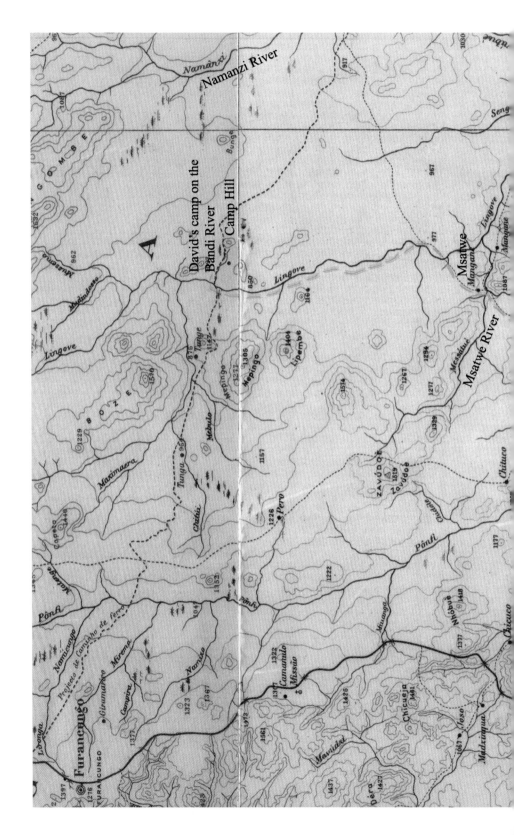

MATENJI HILLS

Matenji House
where the Bivars lived

Msegwe River

Ponfi River

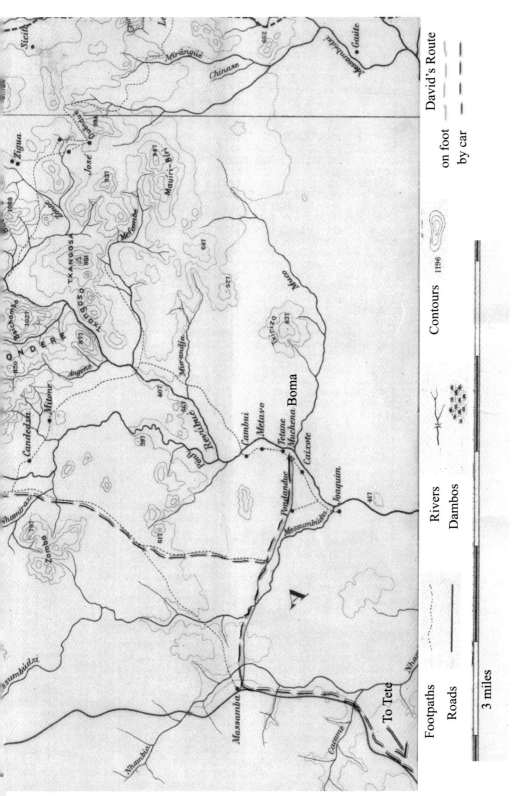

3

David's Route

on foot

by car

Contours   1196

Rivers

Dambos

Footpaths

Roads

3 miles

(Ref.: Carta Da Colonia de Moçambique, Ministerio Das Colonias, 1935)

village called from the name of its headman Macheso. I found M at home and he turned out to be a very decent sort of fellow for a change with some idea of command of his villagers. When I had explained what I wanted and told him there was a hartebeest for him in exchange for flour and what other foodstuffs he could produce, he set the women of the village going and in an hour or so turned up with a goodly supply of the much needed 'ufa'. I also extracted a cock and two hens out of him, which I promised to return to him when I leave as I only want them for eggs. We left the village greatly rejoicing in the afternoon followed by quite a safari of women and children to show him where the hartebeest was, where I left him to deal with the meat as he wished, only taking some for our present use. Two boys from his village came with me, each with a fair sized load of flour which will keep us going for a long time. I got a wart hog close to camp, which will also be useful when and if boys come in from the other neighbouring villages.

I was given news of a couple of elephant at Macheso's, reputed to have been making south two days ago and of a herd that went north-east about the same time. I shall go out tomorrow and see if I can't hit the spoor of the former which may prove to be bulls, but these brutes move about so much that they may be to hell and gone by this time. Personally I saw no sign of elephant at all during the whole day, though we must have gone the best part of 25 miles. The only thing of interest we struck was a pack of hunting dog about five miles from camp. My two remaining boys from Matenji on being told that they were to go tomorrow to bring in the wart hog came out with the information that on the contrary they were now going back home. Altogether the boy question is a serious one. If I can't get hunters or boys to stay with me the whole of my chances of elephant are ruined. I really don't quite know what to do about it all. The hunter promised me by the Portuguese has failed to put in an appearance and I fully expect that one day soon I shall find myself alone here in the bush with Frazer and a piccanin who is the only stalwart one from Matenji. The two boys from Macheso's may or may not stay, I scanned their faces anxiously when I first saw them and wondered to myself whether our acquaintance would be of any duration. I suppose I shall have to make a trip to another village in a day or two's time to look for boys, but I'm still hoping that some stalwart will turn up of his own account, as a volunteer is always worth twice as much as a boy who has been induced with promises of 'nyama' and money and cajoled into the business in a manner which I have never found necessary before. What would I not give for one or two of my old hunters from Mahenge, the poor old weedy Wapojoro who everyone despised, but who were the best hunters I have ever come across. Of course, I refused to listen to the Matenji boys utterances, but the remedy is in their hands as all they have to do is quietly to disappear as did the other two.

October 6th, 1928

> Far and few, far and few
> Are the lands where the Jumbos live
> Their heads aren't green and it's I who am blue
> For I can't follow up in a sieve.

There was no call for such a tale of woe after five days ineffectuality only, and perhaps with more thought and at a later date the Muse might have heard more readily, it would have been wise to have kept this for a later lamentation.

October 7th, 1928

Nevertheless I did find elephant spoor two days old only today, two bulls, I made it out to be, one quite a good size. No use to think of following, of course, but I daresay we'll hit them off again before long. I went for a fair walk out to the Lingove, west of my camp, and found the river there ran through very broken country, fairly thickly wooded, and it seems a desirable sort of place for an elephant to take a midday siesta, there is no actual 'msita' that I could make out, so that if I do get up to elephant there it ought to be quite an easy affair, so long as one holds one's rifle straight. Coming back in a circle and approaching camp from the north I came over many little dambos. A dambo, incidentally, is just low-lying marshy ground, or rather what might be marshy ground in the rains; at this time of the year they are perfectly dry generally, but full of beautifully fresh green grass beloved of all game and one is pretty sure of finding some-thing in them early in the morning and in the afternoon. On the dambos I found this morning was much spoor of many kinds of game and even at 11 a.m. I found a hartebeest and a couple of wart hog on two of them so they will be well worth a visit when we are again in need of meat, which is tomorrow. I have just eaten my dinner and though I pretended not to notice it, there was was a distinct odour in the curry which was not of any of its usual ingredients. A young bushbuck that I bagged yesterday evening with a shot-gun while looking for nests, had not stood up to today's heat as well as it might have.

I have taken two clutches of nightjar's eggs in the last two days. The standard wing (*Caprimulgus vexillarius*), also eggs of a weaver, the red-headed cardinal weaver, I think, but cannot identify him. I have got the cock bird for identification. I'm afraid it is a nasty business blotting a wretched bird because you have its nest and want to know what it is. What humanitarians at home would think of a fellow who went about blotting songbirds at nesting time I don't know, but out here it is a very necessary performance. It is worse than useless taking eggs if you don't know what the kind was who laid them and only leads to further puzzles in the future. All or nothing is the only way, the time is not yet in Africa for the one egg humanitarian business. My weaver had three eggs of a beautiful verderer blue laid in the usual retort-shaped nest, made of twigs and lined with grass, hanging on the very end of a tall bamboo by the side of a dambo. I had three shots for the hen bird which was not a very skilful performance as I missed each time, but am more pleased to have taken the cock who is a far more beautiful bird with a brilliant scarlet head and neck which the hen lacks, I made out, being far more sombre coloured, brownish above and white beneath.

October 8th, 1928

I am out of luck; if I'd only gone yesterday for the tramp I went this morning I would have found elephant all right. The brutes had been further down the Lingove than I went yesterday, and though I followed up for a few hours this morning, it was a hopeless task. Tracks of the night before last of elephant going hard and not feeding means an affair of a couple of days or so and we were without food of any sort so I could not think of it. Never mind, we are at any rate getting a bit warmer on the trail. The Lingove once again changes its character where I was this morning. Here it runs through pretty flat sort of country and has about 50 yards of sand and mitete grass on either bank. This pass is full of bushbuck, I suppose I must have seen or heard a dozen or more while going along the banks. It is also full of francolin, I had of course not taken a shot-gun with me so we met them in crowds, also guinea fowl. The francolin I made out to be the common kind in Nyasaland (*Pternistes humboltii*). I have got a real gem in the boy from Macheso's, he is as good a tracker as I want and really comparable with the very best. In other things he is a great fool but that doesn't matter. The way he followed up Jumbo this morning put me back to school once again, which is as it ought to be. I was beginning to get rather a swollen head about my own capabilities as a tracker after being out with Nyasaland natives only for the last two years; but I remember now what a real hunter can do when he tries and it makes me go green with envy. In other directions Jasmine, that is his name, does not win such high marks. As we were following up the spoor he on one occasion suddenly stopped dead and pointed out some perfectly harmless waterbuck on the other side of the river to me which, incidentally, I had been observing for the last five minutes and said in perfectly calm tones, as if it was the most ordinary thing in the world, 'Njobvu' (elephant). I told him not to be a fool and get on with his job, much to his chagrin. About midday I realized it was no good going on with the spoor and we came back to camp finding a couple of nests of Jardine's babbler (*T. jardinii*) on the way. Untidy sort of nests they build of unlined grass placed in the fork of a tree about nine feet from the ground. The egg is about the size of a starling's but of a glorious hedgesparrow blue. Went out in the afternoon to look for game as we were out of meat but, of course, on the afternoon that we wanted meat badly we found nothing at home on the dambo I mentioned yesterday. That is always the way; but my jaunt was not altogether unsuccessful because I collected three green pigeons (*T. delalandii*) with the shot-gun. They were coming in vast quantities to feed on the fruit of a wild fig tree standing in a dambo three or four miles from camp and would have given fun if we were out for sport with plenty of cartridges as they have a very rapid flight and swoop down out of the blue before you know they are coming. I am afraid I — being a hungry man without any dinner — waited for them to settle in the tree in an unsporting manner before taking my shot — but they taste no worse for that — I have just dealt with them, one boiled down into soup and the other two as a stew and very good they were.

October 9th, 1928

I went south this morning for my walk round. The first mile or two over a big dambo which lies in that direction only half a mile from my camp. I found it full of game at this early hour, 6 a.m., and counted the best part of 60 head including hartebeest, kudu, reedbuck, bush pig and sable antelope. I got a bull of the last named as they were the first we came upon —an easy shot through grass at about 100 yards. His horns went 39 inches, which is fair to moderate. Besides the game I have mentioned, we also found fresh eland spoor and buffalo not more than a day or two old, so that this dambo might really be called a veritable hunter's paradise. One could have murdered enough stuff to feed a battalion of men, if that is what a hunter's paradise means. I think the Portuguese bloke who was here before had not discovered this place, as when I asked him if there were any dambos lying to the south he told me there were none of any account. Either that or else he was putting me off on a false scent, but more likely the former or game would not have been there in such numbers. The kudu I saw were two goodly bulls and one cow, but there must be many more as I saw their spoor in great profusion. Continuing south through the bush we again saw vast quantities of spoor everywhere, but alas, no fresh elephant tracks, though we made a long sweep round, not getting back to camp until the afternoon.

I dug out a kingfisher's nest in a bank, the bird had flown out of the hole as we approached, but unluckily we were too early as it had not yet laid its eggs. With other nests I was more fortunate, collecting what I think is a bulbul (*Pycnonotus layardi*) in a small tree on the Bandi River, fairly close to camp; a nest I had marked down previously as a nightjar's, whose eggs a boy brought to me which he had found when bringing in the meat; and a babbler's (*T. jardinii*) which I found myself in the evening. I took the bird of the last named as I was in doubt about Jasmine's identification of the nests we found on the Lingove yesterday, and so it turned out. They were not the Nyamtambwe at all but the ordinary Jardine's babbler. My nest had six eggs in it which I think is more than the normal number. The nightjar that the boys brought to me I make out to be not the same as the one we got before and I am puzzled to know just what it is.

After I had spotted the sable this morning and was stalking them, a nightjar flew up from my feet which I saw was not *Semeiophorus vexillarius*. I looked round for the nest, but as the sable were getting excited could not waste much time and did not manage to hit it off. I am sure that this was the bird whose eggs they found later — it might be either *Caprimulgus rufigena* or *Scotornis fossii* — they are much smaller than those of *Semeiophorus vexillarius*, darker in colour and have no gloss. It is unfortunate that I did not get them myself, but must trust to be lucky enough to find another nest later.

October 11th, 1928

Nothing much doing yesterday, I went down the Lingove in the morning but saw nothing of interest except a vast herd of waterbuck, 40 or 50 of them at least I should think. In the afternoon, strolling round with a shot-gun I shot a bird which I can't exactly identify in Sclater and Stark. I think he is a *Campephagid* and should be *C. caesia*, but doesn't quite work out. It is quite a common bird and I'm pretty sure that a bird I got on the Lingadzi in Nyasaland is the same thing.

Today I went south again over the dambo where I had seen so much game two days ago, but though I found the sable and kudu at home, I did not get a shot at them and it was no use continuing up the dambo as the wind was wrong, so I pottered about looking for nests all morning and found three more of the standard wing nightjar, which makes quite a nice series. After I got back to camp Jasmine came up and said he wanted to be paid off as he was going home; when asked what the trouble was he said he was afraid because I wanted to shoot him! I could not make out what he meant as it is not my habit to threaten a boy with a gun or anything so foolish, in fact beyond calling him a B.F. on one or two occasions, I don't think I have as yet tongue-lashed him even. For a long time I could not make out what on earth the trouble was and thought he was just talking nonsense to make up an excuse to leave me. He kept on repeating that I was going to shoot him with a rifle but I got the truth out of him at last. He is such as ass he couldn't explain things properly, so I called him up and made him sit down beside me while I was skinning a bird and had a quiet talk. The trouble was that as we went through the bush single file, my rifle slung over my shoulder, covered him following up behind me and he was afraid it might go off at any moment if a twig were to catch the trigger. I showed him how it was quite impossible for the rifle to go off as I always keep the bolt and striker in the 'fired' position even though it may be closed on a live cartridge and he at last came round and saw light. It was really quite a just complaint. I don't think I actually do cover the man behind when I have my rifle slung over one shoulder. To do so I should have to carry it in nearly a horizontal position which would be most uncomfortable, but it would be disconcerting to the man behind if he thought that the rifle might go off at any moment unintentionally. I hope J is more happy about things now, anyway I've heard no more from him about hopping it.

Yokania, my other boy from Macheso came back today; he had gone off home for a day or two to bring back his cooking pots and things. He was a day late in getting back but to appease me he brought with him an egg which he declared to be that of an 'Nsio-nsio'. I had not found it before so was greatly pleased, but his description of the 'Nsio-nsio' does not take me a very long way on the road to identification. It is an egg very like the English blackbird but a little smaller and more pear-shaped. I think it will turn out to be a thrush of some sort if he is able to point out the bird to me on some future occasion which he says he will do.

October 12th, 1928

I went out north today over a succession of dambos, many with game still on them. I found a 'sounder' of wart hog on one and was greatly entertained by their behaviour. We came suddenly on to the dambo's edge and the wart hog were feeding close to the bush about 50 yards from me. I came on quietly for a further 10 yards before the big boar spotted me, whereupon I stood stock still, calling softly to Y to do likewise. The boar had seen something moving and now as there was no further sign he got very interested to know what it was. None of the others had seen us so they paid no attention to the old fellow's half-hearted alarm snorts and stamps, but the old man kept his head turned in my direction, looking for me, then began circling round gradually approaching, followed by the rest of the sounder, some four or five in number. Eventually with many false alarms they all came right up to us until the old boar was only five yards distant when he began to snort and stamp his feet and play about generally, rather like the antics of a dog inviting his master to came and play with him or do something he wanted. The others of the family, not having seen us originally, were not interested in the least, but stood about looking in all directions and swinging their tails about with an air of complete boredom as if they were just letting the old man have his way but wished he would get a move on and let them return to their food. I gave a 'view halloo' to finish things off, when they turned tail and fled, nearly falling over each other in their excitement.It was a better variety turn than I have ever seen staged at the Coliseum or paid ten bob to look at, but then Nature beats Artificially every time — all round the ring and then some — if one only has the temperament to see it and look for it.

Another pretty picture I see every day is the bathing of a little kingfisher who haunts the pool beside which my camp is. I can't quite make out which he is, I haven't the heart to shoot him and besides I am hoping that he will nest around here before long. My pool is only some seven yards wide by about 15 yards long. There are two trees standing on the opposite bank which have clusters of a round red fruit and there are bamboos over-hanging the pool on all sides. I have my chair and table taken down there every afternoon and sit and watch the birds that come to feed on the fruit. There is a bunch which is just ripe now and hangs about 10 feet from me. To this come glossy starlings in great numbers who talk and jabber to their heart's content; bulbuls also and occasionally a black-collared barbet. I have noticed that the starlings always try and drive away a bulbul if they think he has got hold of a particularly lucious fruit, but the bulbul is a great warrior and will not put up with this but succeeds in holding his own and driving away any starling that makes a surreptitious attack on him. My kingfisher comes and perches on a bamboo overhanging the water and from there dives down with a splash on to the surface, turns and hurries back to his perch all in a moment, and then sits and preens himself, jerking himself about in a most comical way until he is ready for another dive. He is only about four inches long and a most sedate individual, nothing sems to disturb him. He just sits there wagging his tail even if I try a shot with the airgun at a green pigeon who often comes also to feed on the fruit. I've often heard people complaining of how wretched they are in the bush if they run out of reading matter, and can quite see how terrible this would be if the last Edgar Wallace shocker were finished and they were of the kind who take no delight in nature. My bush library consists of three volumes of Sclater and Stark's *Birds of South Africa* which are worth more to me than all the books that were ever written, and I never seem to have enough time to do half the things I want to, let alone feel the need of a library of shockers.

October 13th, 1928

Saw sable and kudu this morning but could only have had a shot at cows of each, so I left them alone as we were not wanting meat. I have rarely been in such bad fly country as that lying to the south and south-east of my camp. In other directions they are not nearly so bad but in those quarters they fairly swarm. Parts of the Matenji area were as bad or worse but I know of no other part where I've met such quantities. I don't think there's much danger of sleeping sickness, though this is supposed to be an infected area; as long as one keeps away from villages one ought to be fairly safe but it would be a bad business if one were to go down with it. I was taken up by a fellow the other day at Dedza — Major G, O.C. the Nyasaland Volunteer Rifles, incidently — because I said that a tsetse would bite through a thick flannel shirt. If I had need of further proof that this was the case I've got it all right here, they continually bite me through my shirt on the back and shoulders. I notice they are far worse on the dambos and water courses even when the latter are quite dry and one doesn't meet nearly so many in the higher bush lands. I suppose they like living in long grass and thickish country generally better than the open bush.

Skirting the foot of a small hill about 250 feet high while coming home this morning, I looked up and saw what was ludicrously like one of

Edward Lear's *Nonsense Botany* drawings. There were five kudu cows all standing together round a small tree right on the sky line above me looking absurdly large and out of proportion generally to their surroundings. *Kudulilia Hilsidtopia* would have been a 'Learian' remark to have written underneath them, if one could have transposed them into one of his books. Y brought me another egg of his 'Nsio-nsio' this afternoon, also two young birds which he had found in another nest, but I have not yet been able to shoot the old bird as he failed to refind the nest from which he had taken the egg. We went back and replaced the young birds in their nest and I saw the bird that he pointed out to me as the parent. I think it is *T. libonyanus* but cannot yet be sure. Y is going to be a useful lad. He is young, quite intelligent and keen about my bird and egg collection madness. I had to explain to him gently today that he was not to bring me young birds from nests that he found and that it was only eggs that I wanted. He is enthusiastic too about our chances of getting elephant here later. He says they have all gone off just now to the north but are certain to come back before long and that a month or two ago this country was full of them. That at any rate was certainly the case, as I can see for myself by the quantity of old spoor wherever I go for my tramps. I cannot but think that they will return here soon, but I may have a longish wait before I am successful. One must not be impatient about things, I wouldn't care if I knew they would certainly be here in numbers before the end of the year, but as the old jumbo is the only thing that brings in the money one can't help being anxious for success quickly, however full of interest life may be.

October 14th, 1928

Paid another visit to the Lingove where I had seen fairly fresh spoor earlier in the week, but found that the elephant had not been back. I shot a bushbuck for meat but saw no other game. Only these and the water-buck live down there; the other game seem to stick more to the higher ground and dambos away from the river. Today I've taken eggs of three different sorts of weavers. One lot down in the Lingove, building on bango reeds overhanging the river; another which builds rather an untidy sort of nest for a weaver on the Bandi; and a third building on high thorn trees on a dambo close to camp. I've only got birds of the last as yet, but will have to take the others later to compare them. I had a difficult job in getting the eggs from the nests in the thorn trees. The trees were impossible to climb. I had to tip up the nests with a long bamboo and try to catch the eggs in my shirt which I made a piccanin hold stretched out underneath the nest. I'm afraid we broke more eggs than we got whole, which was disastrous. I think I know of another colony of the same bird which may be more easy to get at. I shall look for Jumbo in that quarter tomorrow and take the eggs on the way back. I've gone and blistered my feet like a silly ass, through wearing badly darned socks and may have to take it fairly easily for a day or two until they recover. It is annoying, but I must be thankful that it is the first trouble I've had. The vexed question of footwear in the bush I think I have solved to my own satisfaction. I find that either crepe rubber Veldt schoen or rope-soled canvas shoes, with a combination of ankle-high puttees, are the very thing for these tramps, the only trouble is I wear out vast quantities of socks; I wish I could do without them altogether but I begin to blister my feet if I try this, perhaps a hardening process would enable me gradually to discard them altogether, I think I must try it as the time is rapidly coming when I shall have no more socks to my name.

October 15th, 1928

Sunday morning today, though I actually think yesterday was the Sabbath. One is apt to lose count of the days of the week leading a life like this and I know I would not have the slightest idea of what the day of the month was unless I kept a diary.

I attacked another colony of weavers in the morning about four miles from camp but I'm finding it very hard to take a representative series of these eggs; it is nearly always impossible to climb up to the nests and all one can do is to tip them up with a bamboo which is not satisfactory as hard set eggs and youngsters are already in a good many of them and the heavier fresh eggs are smashed more easily. I also got one of the helmeted shrikes (*Sigmodus tricolor*), not the nest but the bird itself and I see they are not yet breeding. In the afternoon I at last shot the nsio-nsio of Yokania at a nest a few hundred yards only from camp. It turns out to be the ordinary *T. libonyanus*, which I had rather expected.

Crowds of women came in today with baskets of flour to barter for meat. I wish they'd bring in some other sort of foodstuff for a change. We now have enough flour to keep us going for a long time and I would much rather see a few fowls and potatoes coming in. These women were still only from Macheso's village, I don't think the other villages can possibly know that I'm here except the Msatwe-ites, of course, who would be wiser to keep away. If they come in for meat they will go away again with their ears bung full of fleas only, unless they pay for it with the money I spent at their village buying flour at most extortionate prices. I shall have to try and slay something large tomorrow for these women. Today's bag was another bushbuck only, which will not go very far.

October 16th, 1928

Went out very early this morning but was unlucky to find no game on the dambos I visited. All I managed to bag was a bush pig. He was a fine old hog and seemed far more greyish in colour than the bush pig are further north. I've noticed this fact in the other bush pig I have seen in my tramps, there is not nearly so much red hair on them as I think is usual. I stayed all day on a dambo about six miles north-east, in hopes I would get something larger in the evening, but was unlucky. I spent a most pleasing day, though, as I took eggs of a kingfisher, a weaver and some *C. heuglini* small 'passer' which I had not got before. This last had eggs of a dark brown colour laid in a beautiful moss-made nest on the bank of a small pool of the river at the dambo. It took me a long time to obtain the bird also as the pool was densely overgrown with bushes, trees, etc. and it was very hard to see just there in the dense shadows. The kingfisher too was very wary and I had another long wait for him also. There were many more interesting birds about so I must pay another visit to this dambo in a day or two. Today I sent back for Frazer to come along with tea and food, which he did, arriving about midday. I also sent a message to him to bring along the shot-gun and cartridges for it, and I was deeply incensed when he produced three cartridges only, however, as I collected three birds with these it didn't matter. The last bird was some small finch which had made a nest in a dead tree beside the river. I tried to send a piccanin up to it but he got frightened and we had to push the tree over to get at the nest, only to find that the eggs were already hatched. Coming home with Jasmine in the evening, we lost our bearings completely as darkness overtook us before we were near camp, and we spent an hour or so wandering about. J was quite frightened and asked me to lead saying he had no idea where camp was, neither had I for the matter of that, but we pushed ahead as best we could until I eventually saw the light of a fire somewhere ahead, which, though J thought otherwise, turned out to be the bush burning in places where Frazer, like a sensible lad, had touched it off to guide us on our way, so we arrived home about a couple of hours after night fall. It seemed a very long job to skin my birds after that, but it was finished at last and I'm thankful enough to get to bed tonight and not have to spend a night in the bush, which at one time I quite thought we should be doing. I'm going to run out of paraffin for my lamp in a day or two so must economize.

October 17th, 1928

My lucky day of the month has passed and gone with only another bush pig to mark it. It is curious how when one wants game badly one is never able to find it and when not in need of meat one sees stuff everywhere. The common-sensical point of explanation of this fact — for fact indeed it surely is — is of course just the good and bad luck of the game; but sometimes it is so noticeable that one seeks for some other reason. It is of course how when game abounds as it did on the flats of the upper Rufigi, they know by a hunter's actions whether he is after them or not, and when they see that there is nothing stealthy about his coming they just stand round and watch him go by, knowing they have nothing to fear. It had often been noted also with lion that game know well enough when he is hungry and when they see by his actions that he has already had his meal they pay no more attention to him than if he were the most inoffensive of animals. All this is true enough and perfectly logical, but does not explain my point. Why is it that when one wants meat one often arrives at dambo after dambo seeing by the signs that game was on it five minutes before but has now disappeared! Whilst on other days when one does not want meat one finds the game still on them. Naturally I am not generalizing on this or else one would never shoot anything — all I say is sometimes — and I'm going to offer a very bold explanation for it. In all seriousness, I like to put it down to a telepathic sense of danger that animals I think undoubtedly have to a more advanced degree than human beings. When a hunter is tramping through the bush, all alert, rifle at the ready and every sense doing its utmost to find game he may be sending danger signals ahead of him, and it is these wireless danger signals, this malignancy in the atmosphere that the game picks up by some means unknown to us, or at best little understood by us who have lost this finest of all senses.

We know little of telepathy, we even doubt that such a thing exists at all, and prefer to put down to coincidence the few queer incidents of our every-day life that might be called telepathic. But there must be few indeed who have experienced no such incident, even in a workaday life in a large city; out in the bush where one is close to nature incidents repeat themselves incessantly. The sense of warning one gets as one is about to put one's foot on a snake is one, the most common, and I think realized by many who live in tropical countries. The atmosphere is here again malignant and it makes one stop and look before taking that last step, else the cases of snake bite would not be so extraordinarily few.

The other day when I was waiting for duck, hidden in the grass on the banks of the Bua, I had another case. An unaccountable urge seemed of a sudden to take hold of me to get up and look behind me — no there was not a lion stalking me — but a boy whom I had sent down stream to put up the duck was just 20 yards off, coming back to me. Now it may or may not have been running in that boy's head 'I hope the Bwana doesn't suddenly get up and fire at a duck in my direction'. I'm afraid I didn't ask him and he wouldn't have understood even if I had. But those are two very minor cases in point to show what I mean. Others could doubtless think of some more remarkable.

But if it can be granted that a human being does occasionally get these premonitions, these danger signals, call them what you will, how much more likely is it that an animal whose life is so much more often in danger is more often moved by them, and urged far more strongly than we who have few things to harm us, can possibly realize.

October 18th, 1928

(Sounds pretty good rot, but there may be something in it.) I got my meat at last today, a couple of hartebeest and a reedbuck, which will make them happy and buy us as much flour from the women as we want. Next time I shall refuse to take any flour or at least give them such a small quantity of meat that will make them understand I want something else. It's no use just talking to them, they will go on trying it on until they realize it's a failure

Found a nest on a dambo with young birds in it, and as it was a similiar nest in a similiar position to one I found a few days ago with eggs in it, but whose bird I failed to see, sat and watched it for a sight of the parent birds. It turned out to be a bulbul all right, as I had expected — the ordinary *Pycnonotus layardi*. But I'm glad to know for sure that this is the case. I'm expecting rain before long, today was pretty hot and thundery and I think there was rain up in the Matenji hills. I hope it does come before long and fetch the young grass up, as I think the pachyderms will then at last remember that there is such a place as the Lingove and Bandi rivers. At present they seem to have fogotten all about them. Not very successful with birds today. I got a swallow which I have not yet worked out, which

F spoiled. I skinned it myself, as I always do now, fairly successfully, I thought, but when F produced it after sewing it up it was a most wretched looking object. I also shot an oriole, but when I picked it up I found its head was a mass of blood which always spoils a skin, as it is the very devil to get off to make it look OK again. I tried though after skinning it to wash it off with some warm water and then dry it quickly with some warm wood ash and I hope it may turn out fairly well.

October 19th, 1928

I got another kingfisher on the Lingove, in fact two more nests there were, which was the reason for my sending back for F and the shot-gun. I dug them both out, finding one nest well incubated, and the other I fear the same, but I took the eggs of this as there was in this nest in addition to the five round obvious kingfisher's eggs, a sixth oval white egg which must be either a cuckoo's or a honeyguide's. J says it is one of the latter's which may well be so as they too are parasitic in their habits; but I suspect a cuckoo as the egg looks too large for a honeyguide's. I think I shall have to write a monograph on the breeding of *Halcyon swainsoni* as Sclater and Stark state that its habits are not known and I have plenty of opportunity of observing them here. It is the only kingfisher that I have found here in any number.

I had another little 'mlandu' on the Lingove today. I had shot a water-buck right on the path on which the women were returning to their village at Macheso's, so I thought this would be a good opportunity to extract an odd fowl out of them in exchange for the meat. I waited for them to put in an appearance which they did before long and they proceeded joyfully to cut up the buck, delighted to find that I'd got more 'nyama' for them and fairly close to their village. Then the fun started.

"Now", I said, "what are you going to give me in exchange for this."

All they could think of, of course, was flour, which I refused and said that I wanted fowls. They said they had none, an obvious lie as I has seen chickens in plenty at their 'mudzi' myself and they had brought me in eggs when they arrived two days ago. After a few more words and many lies about other people having fowls but they themsleves none, I said that rather than give them the meat for nothing I wanted, I would burn it all here in the bush. Frazer had joined me by this time so we proceeded to stack firewood in a mighty pile all round the buck and collected dry grass to set it off. When all was ready I produced a box of matches and said this was their last chance as I was now going to set it off. At this the women who were sitting all round much concerned at my intentions, began to climb down somewhat. One said she had just one small fowl which she would give me in exchange. I said NO, I wanted a laying hen of large size. They denied ownership of such a curiosity as that, so I then lit the grass and my funeral pyre began to blaze up. When they saw that, excitement became intense and with many ridiculous speeches about the difficulty of bringing me a good-sized fowl, they said they might find someone in the village who was the possessor of such a thing — so I let it go at that and kicked off the fire and let them have their meat. I don't know now whether they'll bring me my fowl — one fowl in exchange for a fair-sized buck isn't much of a bargain but I shall be thankful if I even get that.

(Later — I got it — they were honest.)

October 22nd, 1928

Rested in camp on the 20th and spent today seeing to my specimens. Jasmine has run off. I went off yesterday north-east to find another village lying some nine or ten miles off I would reckon. I slew an eland bull close to the village and hoped it would be an easy matter to pick up boys there with that inducement. But on the contrary, I was given the cold shoulder. I pushed on over the hills in the direction of Macheso's again. Coming into another village later in the afternoon I was lucky to get a wart hog just in the village fields and there I found boys of a totally different character. I was told that their chief had just left that morning with three boys to pay me a visit in camp, bringing me rice and other food stuffs and that the three boys were wanting work. They expressed great concern when I told them what straits I was in for the lack of boys and said that they would see I did not lack them in future. How far I can trust them in that I don't know, but it was pleasing to know that there were three in my camp though I cursed myself for having given myself an unnecessary tramp.

I spent the night in that village and slept pretty well considering I had only a blanket with me and my dinner had consisted of very tough wart hog and boiled rice which had not been boiled enough. I paid for that today all right as my inside has been complaining loudly and painfully, but I got back to my camp at about midday coming by Macheso's and over the Lingove again.

I ran into Jasmine just outside Macheso's and he ran off in great alarm when he saw me. Yokania even, gave him the rough side of his tongue and told me afterwards that he was full of shame, not having expected to see me in that quarter. I explained to Macheso the circumstances and he too told me that Jasmine was a great fool, and that he would do his best to find a good lot of boys for me. So I must rest content with these assurances. Now in camp I find the three boys from the village I spent the night in and have told them they are to stay with me. They don't look an especially bright lot, but perhaps I'm making a mistake. They'll have to wait here for a day or two anyway as I am pretty weary and don't intend to go out and shoot game for anyone until I feel like it and I know there are no elephant within a hundred miles .

October 25th, 1928

I found a pair of treecreepers building a nest on the topmost branch of a tall thorn tree close to camp. I have marked it down for a visit in a few days time, but how I'm going to get at the nest I don't quite know yet. Took eggs of another weaver and found a green pigeon's nest in a position impossible to get at. I could see the eggs through the bottom of the few twigs laid across a branch which was all the nest there was, but broke the eggs getting them.

Yesterday I spent the whole day on the dambos where I had been so successful with nests about a week ago, but this time only got a weaver there and the parent bird; however, I found a flycatcher's nest on the way back which pleased me. It was the paradise flycatcher (*Tchitrea perspicillata*) and its nest was a most absurdly small construction for the size of the bird and I would never have found it if it hadn't been for the excited calling of the female who flew round my head in a great state of nerves. I bagged a hartebeest also which has already disappeared in bartering for foodstuffs. Today I made bad work trying for a herd of hartebeest in the dambo south of my camp, missing a couple of shots absolutely clean, so as I was still not feeling too bright, came back early to camp. Something I'm eating is disagreeing with me badly. I've now put it down to native millet which I've been mixing with flour for bread, and have decided to stop that to see if that is the trouble.

October 26th, 1928

Got a hartebeest this morning about five minutes walk from camp. The boy who was with me nearly gave the show away by moving about in full sight of the herd and playing the fool generally. Altogether it was very nearly he that died and not the hartebeest. I saw plenty of game afterwards on other dambos I visited. I got the bird and eggs of one of the puffback shrikes, *Dryoscopus hamatus*, he, or rather she, turned out to be. The nest was very obvious for a bird of such skulking habits of whom one so rarely catches a sight. They attract attention more by their call, which is a harsh gutteral 'Kreeeee' from the female immediately answered by an even deeper 'Kraw' from the male, coming so quickly that one thinks they are one and the same bird, if one is at some distance from them.

Came back early to camp having as usual seen no sign of elephant, and I heard from a boy whom I had sent down to the Lingove to have a dekko round there that he had met with no better success. If I hadn't my birds to interest and comfort me I should be in a most despondent condition. As it is I've so much to do that I'm content to trust the boy's definite remarks about the numbers of jumbo who will turn up as soon as the grass comes up.

October 27th, 1928

Yesterday evening I got of one the golden cuckoos who ought by rights to be *Cuculus cupreus*, but she doesn't quite work out as she ought to and may be something else. She was hanging round a sunbird's nest — my treecreeper, incidentally, of a few days ago, I suppose the curved bill misled me in a too hasty diagnosis — and I daresay had marked it down to deposit her egg in later, as there was a fertilized egg or beginning of an egg in her ovary.

After that episode I had one of the most wretched evenings of my life. I had my bath and sat down in my chair to wait for dinner for which I was very ready, being very hungry and feeling perfectly fit. Suddenly a coldish wind sprang up and I immediately donned a heavy blanket dressing gown and again sat down impatiently, when of a sudden I felt intolerably sick and proceeded to get rid of what food I had inside me in the approved style. Regaining my chair I felt quite fit again and could even tackle a little dinner when it came along. I had some soup and a couple of eggs out of the curry, leaving the rest alone. Hoping all was well I went to bed quickly but soon had to forsake that retreat and from then for a period of a couple of hours or so I was retching incessantly in a most painful manner. Finally the bowels moved in a manner which I can only describe as torrential and I at last felt better though in a very weak condition.

Today I'm pretty well OK again, but shall take it very easily for the next day or two as it would be disastrous if my complaint were to turn into anything serious.

A letter has just come in from Furancungo Boma to say that I ought to have reported there when coming into the district and asking me to go in there now. I have replied that I have no carriers to take my loads and have enclosed my license for endorsement and asked that this may be sufficient. I hope the bloke in charge there is a reasonable individual and will not demand my presence as it would mean a four days' trek which I am not keen on undertaking at present.

October 28th, 1928

Full moon tonight and I'm able to see to write this by its light except when it disappears behind a cloud which is fairly frequently. There was rain last night and it still looks as if there may be more shortly. This has been an annoying sort of day; I've found nests of three birds with youngsters in them, eggs of which I have not yet taken. They were a sunbird, *C. collaris*, I fancy, a shrike of some sort and the fork-tailed drongo. The last was the most absurd and inadequate apology of a nest that I've ever seen and I would never have seen that it was a nest at all if the bird hadn't suddenly swooped down into a tree under which I happened to be walking at that moment, and begun feeding it's wretched youngster at a place where there were a couple of small twigs and a few cobwebs stretched across the fork of a small branch. My only consolation is that now I know what sort of a thing to look for another time, and also that these three birds are fairly common ones.

My three new boys have come to me with the suggestion that I should try for elephant at a place some two days off, I make out, where there is some heavy msita. They say they think elephant may be there now and I don't know that their suggestion isn't sound. It will mean about a week's absence from this camp to give the place a fair trial and I shall have to go very light, with a blanket and cooking pot only. I shall take it easy again tomorrow to give myself a chance to be perfectly fit again and then perhaps give it a trial. I ought really to wait for an answer to my letter to the Boma, but don't know that this really necessary.

October 29th, 1928

Today after an ineffective walk round in the morning both as far as game and nests are concerned, I took eggs of *Bradornis ater*, the black flycatcher, close to camp, which pleased me. This is the bird that so closely resembles the square-tailed drongo (*Dicrurus ludwigii*) in appearance that I doubt whether it is possible to tell the difference without shooting the bird and counting the number of rectuaries which are 12 in flycatchers and 10 only in drongos. I know of no other way of telling the two birds apart, and I'm quite sure they must be freqently mixed up. I think *Dicrurus ludwigii* is the rarer of the two and that the bird that one so often sees and thinks to be it is really the flycatcher. In the afternoon as the larder was empty I waited for green pigeon by a wild fig tree to which they were coming in large numbers and got four. I also shot a cuckoo (*Cuculus solitarius*) who had been worrying me for some days past to know just what he was. I never saw him as he kept hidden always in the tops from where he called incessantly through the day and often in the night as well, a piercing whistle of three notes each in a lower key to the last. I don't know what words one could put to them and I see Sclater and Stark were beat to find a phrase for them also. All I can think of that suits is quite unprintable. Curious how often it is that the most apt wording to put to a bird's call could not be printed even by a most broad-minded firm of publishers. I've heard other people complaining about this fact so that I do not feel that I am laying myself open to accusations of a depraved mentality in admitting that I, too, find myself putting the most lowdown remarks to many bird-calls. There is one just printable that I can recall at the moment, that of a thrush[1] of some sort who repeats 'castrate the beggar, castrate the beggar' so clearly that one simply could not frame other words for it. But that is mild to some other birds' remarks which are in such bad taste that I wonder how they can have the face to say such things.

October 30th, 1928

A hawk today which simply will not work out to anything it ought to. I don't dare hope I have found anything new, as that would be too much to expect in this type of country which has been worked by so many people before. Not that this particular part of P.E.A. has been worked before, I should be very much surprised if it had, but similar types lying north and south certainly have. I think the only sort of place where one has any real

---

1 Later. This is not a thrush at all but the alarm call of the bulbul when he finds a snake or other noxious animal. He prefaces his remark, too, with the word 'snake' most plainly, so that his full sentence is 'Snake — castrate the beggar'. It is such a sensible remark, given that, I make no apology for writing it as he sings it, though I have changed the syllable of one word to appease the censor.

hope of picking up something is the mountain tops where there is thick primeval forest. I got the egg of my hawk also, in a large unwieldy sort of nest, about 30 feet from the ground, set in the fork of a tall tree. Unfortunately it was very well incubated and I had to smash in most of the side of it before I could extract the youngster. It's annoying when one has to spoil an egg in that way, and when just as one finished spoiling one egg a boy brings in three woodpeckers with the youngsters almost squalling inside, one really does get peeved. I got a small heron also this afternoon whom I've not yet worked out, I think he must just have arrived on a migratory flight, as his crop was practically empty and I've not seen anything like him before here, though I pass the pool where I shot him every day.

We were right out of meat so I went out in the afternoon to look for game and found one solitary hartebeest on the large dambo about a mile east. He was in a splendid position for a stalk and I got right up to about 40 yards from him, when I proceeded to miss him blatantly. The trouble, I think, was that I was really keen on bagging him, thoughts of going hungry to bed were troubling me and so I was too careful — anyway the hartebeest went away laughing at me and I had to trek off to another dambo another mile on, where I managed to slay a reedbuck — doe rather — which was the only thing on the dambo. She hadn't a young one with her but she was full of milk that has given me my first taste of luxury for over a month. There was not really a great deal of it but it was very rich, more like thickish cream in consistency — and very good to taste again in one's tea.

October 31st, 1928

Since childhood I've been vaguely aware of the tale that a bird will remove its eggs if they are touched by a human hand but never having seen it in print as a fact, I relagated the whole story to the limbo of childish fables where it has lain mouldering all this time unheeded and only slightly pricking my conscience when after having removed eggs from the nest of a bird I wanted I've replaced them to wait for the bird on some subsequent occasion. Last week it gave me a painful reminder when eggs of a weaver bird I wanted, mysteriously disappeared in the night. As my picannins in camp denied having taken them, I put their disappearance down to some marauding animal, bird or beast, and thought no more of it. But today the old story has again come out and this time to remain out, burnished up brightly, by what almost amounts to proof positive of its truth.

I had found a small cup-shaped nest in the fork of a little tree, containing one egg, pure white with a few purple spots on it. Having no idea what the bird was I waited on the spot, but only saw some orioles flying about, which I could not think could be the bird of the nest. I walked off a short way and hid myself by an anthill and there waited for some twenty minutes with no success. Then realizing I was too far away to be sure of getting or even identifying the bird when it should return, I got up and went off for a short walk round to look for other nests, meaning to come back from a different side and hide myself in a better position. I first had another look at the egg which I removed from the nest to see if it was incubated or fresh. Then, replacing it, I went off for my walk, coming back in about 10 minutes and hiding myself well about 15 yards from the nest. After a further short wait, a shrike (*Telophorus senegalus*) came with a swoop into the tree and then proceeded to climb on to the nest, so that there was no doubt that this was the bird I wanted. It soon got off again however, and flew off, in a manner that struck me afterwards was a laboured sort of flight, only to return again shortly and take up its position on a branch close by the nest. I then fired and got it but on going to collect my egg, I found the nest empty! I don't think there can be any doubt about it; that bird took away its egg and hid it somewhere because it knew that its nest had been found. Of course some marauder may have found the nest and removed the egg in the interval that I was away, but it is most unlikely as my absence was certainly no longer than a quarter of an hour, and I was never more than two or three hundred yards away, so that I would have seen any hawk, at any rate, that might have been in the neighbourhood on the lookout for such food. No — I think that bird was the culprit and though I've lost an egg I wanted, I have gained what is far more — another atom of knowledge about these fascinating creatures. I found the bird contained an egg in the oviduct, which though well formed its shell had not hardened, and I lost that also and spoiled the skin in removing it. Talk of Nature and pitch forks, it's certainly come back on me a hundred fold this time!

November 1st, 1928

I was lucky to get a sable today as I wanted meat badly. Women came in yesterday with news of elephant spoor seen making in the direction of the Nabdimabo River, two days ago, and so I'm off tomorrow after them, going as light as I can. Yokania came back today so that gives me four boys and three fair sized piccanins to carry my loads and I shall be able to take a bed and be fairly comfortable. There remain here one old man and a piccanin to act as watchmen. I intend being away a week or so, but have hopes the jumbo may be making for this country at last, in which case I should be back earlier, however, I'll just proceed as they guide me. We shall be quite independent of villages and only pay one a visit to get news. We can then push off anywhere and sleep where we find water. I make out though, that the Nabdimabo River is a goodish distance away, so I daresay we'll sleep there tomorrow night.

November 5th, 1928

The whole thing was a leg-pull, I believe the women were just chancing their arm with their news of elephant. I went to the spot where they said they had seen the spoor and found absolutely nothing. I also met a party of boys coming from the north, where the women had come from and even they said they had passed no spoor on the way. So I made a sweep round and got back to camp today coming in from the north-east. Anyway I now know pretty well that there is not such a thing as a pachyderm within a radius of 25 miles of my camp which is all the good my little trek has done for me.

I have broken my luck with the 8 mm rifle also, which is a bad affair, as I wounded an old sable bull. I can't make out where I can have hit him for I was well forward on him as I could see by his action when he dashed off after my shot. He went miles after that and I eventually had to give him up as we lost the spoor of the herd with which he was keeping up, though bleeding profusely. I think it must have been just a flesh wound through the brisket, which would not trouble him very much. I did get one sable, however, out of another herd which I met yesterday on the way back to camp, so that keeps the larder going. They were on a dambo a good 10 miles away and I did not envy Yokania his tramp back with the boys to bring in the meat. I thought they would sleep at the spot and told them to take the tent as it was looking like rain, but they weren't believing in that game and all got back about dusk with the meat. I found a couple of boys awaiting me with three fowls and eggs in exchange for meat, which are very acceptable.

They are the first comers from the village lying to the east and they tell me that a boy is on his way to my camp who wants work as a hunter. They say that he is making a sweep round to the south first to see if there are any elephant in that quarter. This is good news if it turns out to be true as a volunteer hunter appears to be a rarity in this part of the world. But I now take all good news 'cum grano sallis'. 'Cum granis multicimis' I should say, as the native always tries to put one in a good temper by telling one things he knows one wants to hear whether they be true or false.

As far as eggs were concerned my trip was very successful as I took clutches of the southern bee-eater (*Melittophagus meridionalis*), the fork-tailed drongo (*Dicrurus adsimilis*) and some warbler which I was unable to get for identification, none of which I had taken before. The eggs of the bee-eater were of a beautiful pink colour before they were blown, even more so than those of a kingfisher. They nest, like the latter bird, in a hole in the river bank and lay four eggs to the clutch. I found another nest, a flycatcher's, when I arrived back in camp which had the prettiest of eggs — a light green ground colour spotted and streaked with a rich red brown. It was a difficult nest to find; I was walking through a fairly open bit of bush when I noticed a bird in front of me which looked as if it had just flown off its nest. It's action gave it away, a hurried flight of some 10 or 11 yards only, and it then settled in a tree, where it began preening itself in a most innocent manner. I looked round in the direction it had come from, but it was some minutes before I spotted the nest, cleverly hidden in the leaves of the top of a stunted bush sapling. I took the bird also which I know fairly well but have never been able to work out satisfactorily and beyond saying that it ought to be of the *Muscicapa* genus of flycatchers I can identify it no more definitely.

November 6th, 1928

Great trouble today in paying off the boys who brought in the fowls. They weren't satisfied with a fore-leg and the whole of the ribs of the sable which Frazer had given them, so I went out to see what the matter was and told them to take away their hens as I didn't give away meat for nothing. This quieted them so I then gave them 6d. for the cockerel I had already eaten and told them to push off. When I got back to camp after a short walk round, looking for nests, I found them still there as I had expected and I then purchased the two remaining hens for about one quarter of the meat they had refused in the first place and they went off quite satisfied, like a couple of real fools.

I found a nest of one of the *Laniarius* genus of bush shrikes with fully fledged youngsters in it which annoyed me greatly as I had often visited the spot before and never seen the nest which was a very insignificant affair, nor did I find anything interesting in the afternoon though we spotted several nests that will be of interest later on, when the birds have laid.

November 7th, 1928

Went out with 'Dulai' this morning and found lots of hartebeest close to camp which we both failed to spot until after they had seen us. I cursed D heartily for this as after all it is the boy's job to spot the game for his 'Bwana' and I think he was just wandering along behind me, lost to the world. We wanted meat, so I was determined to give him a long trek as some atonement for his sins and we went right out to the dambo about seven miles away with the little stream running through it. There again he failed to spot a couple of reedbuck until it was too late. It was just as well, however, as just as we were topping a slight rise in the ground to have a look at another part of the dambo I saw the horns of a sable down on the lower ground and a short detour and a crawl up an ant hill brought me within easy range of two bulls which I downed. This gives Master Dulai a real good trek to teach him to use his eyes, as he will have to go all the way back again with the women to show them where they are, whereas if he had spotted the hartebeest in the first instance he would have had an easy day.

Coming home again we heard a honeyguide calling in a great state of excitement a few yards off our path so I determined to follow him up. I'm ashamed to say I had never before taken the trouble to do so, though often summoned by them to come and find the bees. We followed this one for about half a mile whistling occasionally in answer to his excited chatter to show him we were coming and encourage him. He flew on straight ahead in short flights of about 100 yards, waiting in a tree to give us time to catch up and calling to show us the way. Finally, for the first time he allowed us to come right up the tree in which he was perching and there, sure enough, in the tree nearest to him, which we were passing, were the bees. A goodly swarm which the boys will have to cut out when they go for the meat. We could not do it at the time as we had no axe. This annoyed our bird and he followed us home for a least a couple of miles until he eventually got fed up and left us, I hope he is still hanging round this afternoon as I have told them to leave him a good supply of wax and young bees which is the food he wants. I could not make out which honeyguide he was and of course hadn't the heart to shoot him after his kindly action.

I found another glossy starling's nest nearer camp, again with youngsters in it. One of them fell out of the nest when Dulai climbed up to it and I have brought it home to try and bring up. I'm afraid it will die, as it is really not quite old enough yet, but it would most certainly have gone out if we had left it where it was.

Came across a curious bit of superstition the other day which I have just had propounded to me. It was the day I went with Yokania to look for boys when that blighter Jasmine had deserted us. After leaving the first village we came to, where we had drawn a blank, and were making over the hill in the direction of Macheso's again, I noticed Y suddenly stopping and picking up a white pebble which lay on the road. I thought nothing of it just then, but when later he proceeded to fix this pebble in the fork of a small bush we were passing, I grew interested. I asked him what he was doing and his answer was that the sun was getting low and something about being late on the road. I saw I was up against one of their superstitions, but was feeling too weary to investigate it further just then, so I told him to remember to tell me all about it some other time. Today I remembered the occasion and got him and Frazer to expound.

The superstition, apparently holding good amongst the Wanganga also, is that when one is late on the road and the sun is getting low and you still have a goodish bit to travel, you pick up a stone — any sort of stone will do, but a white one is preferable — and fix it in a tree at the same height the sun is at. This will keep it from going down quickly and benighting you on the road. Sort of Joshua ordering the-sun-to-stand-still idea. I asked them if they really believed in it and they said 'no' but that they still did it out of respect to old times. Same as we chuck salt over our shoulder to prevent bad luck when we've spilt some on the table. It's a curious custom anyway, which will rapidly disappear under the sway of our 'Down with all folk lore' missionaries.

The boy has just got back with honey from the swarm we found this morning. He tells me that the honeyguide was there and he gave him his food all right. The bird did not apparently show him the way again but came up while he was cutting out the tree.

November 8th, 1928

Nothing much to write of today — the boys did not get back until long after nightfall yesterday evening — it's a long tramp to that dambo — and they spent today cutting up and smoking the meat. I have just been pottering round lazily and unsuccessfully though I've marked a couple of shrike-like nests for further visits. The scarcity of shrikes round here rather distresses me as they are most interesting birds. My glossy starling has disappeared, she was not able to fly so I thought she would be quite safe in an old biscuit box filled with grass for a nest, but when I got back after a stroll this morning

I found she had gone. A pity, because she would have been quite easy to bring up.

Very hot and thundery again all today, I hope we haven't long to wait for the rains to set in.

November 9th, 1928

Found any number of hartebeest today feeding in one large herd right at the end of the long dambo which starts about a mile from my camp. It's a little patch cut off from the rest of the dambo to which I have not often been before, which I suppose accounts for the large numbers there today. I nailed one out of the herd which was the sign for a general exit. I have never seen anything else but hartebeest on this dambo which is uninteresting of it as I often go to it, close at hand as it is, and if it produced a kudu or an eland occasionally I should like it better. Both these two species are rare here, the latter surprisingly so. I can generally find kudu cows to the south but have only once seen bulls since I've been here. Eland I've only met with on one occasion, the solitary bull which I got about a fortnight ago. I think I saw a cow in the bush nearer camp on one occasion but couldn't be sure as it was slipping away through the trees when I caught a glimpse of it.

Found a nest of another *Cossypha* today which contained two very well incubated eggs. I waited for the bird and saw it on several occasions, I think it was *Cossypha heuglini* — the same bird as I have already got — but its nest was rather different from the last one, being in a small tree raised a couple of feet off the ground. The eggs were not in the least similar, either being much smaller and not nearly so brown in colour. The actual nest though was the same, so I don't think, on the whole it was another specimen of the genus.

Quite heavy rains fell today, at about midday.

The morning was very hot and stuffy and one had no energy for a long tramp but it is now quite cool again, though the dampness in my grass house is not so desirable a quality. I must not grouse about it though, because after all it's what I'm waiting for and what we hope and believe the elephants are waiting for also. The frogs, anyway are happy tonight. They've turned in now for their nightly chorus. Their favourite remark is 'Schnaps' and if very happy they make it 'Schnaaps-ah', assuring their statement so to speak, even 'Schnaaps-ah-ah' which must mean the height of bliss.

November 10th, 1928

Spent the day sorting specimens of birds and eggs and writing up notes. I also completed a short story which I began earlier in the month of a pleasing sort of day's sport in the bush. I don't know that I'm really quite satisfied with it, somehow it didn't quite work out as it should. *La recherche du mot* just wasn't meeting with any great success.

I wish these brutes of jumbo would turn up; I've spent nearly six weeks with no success and as far as I can see I am quite liable to spend another six as unsuccessfully.

November 11th, 1928

Armistice Day once again, it doesn't seem like 10 years since the end of the war. I foolishly also proclaimed an armistice with the game and will suffer for it this evening as meat will not keep for two days in this thundery weather. I spent a pleasing sort of morning down at the Lingove getting the eastern roughwing swallow (*Psalidiprocne orientalis*) and a sandpiper which turned out to be the ordinary common sandpiper we get at home in non-breeding plumage. There are a few duck on the river also which rather puzzled me and I couldn't get a shot at one to find out what he was. They may have been *Anas sparsa*, which is a rare bird as its name would indicate.

November 12th, 1928

Went out east this morning in search of game, but found nothing except a solitary hartebeest on the dambos who was very wide awake and not to be caught napping

After that I tried to stalk some bustards who have recently been in residence, but they also were too wary for me. There were two specimens which I must certainly circumvent somehow later as I don't know exactly what they are. After that I spent almost an hour or so investigating the Nyamtambwe. The call notes of this bird are the most beautiful music one hears in the bush and would make any song thrush go green with envy. One often hears them especially in the early morning and at evening, but I had never actually seen the bird who gave them before, which is not surprising as it turns out to be my old friend *Cossypha heuglinii* who always keeps hidden in the thickest parts of the tangled bushwood and grasses on the banks of small streams. From there it gives vent to this beautiful music which rises and falls in the sweetest of cadences. A clear flute-like whistling, so faint at first that it seems to come from the clouds but which swells in volume until one realizes that it is being uttered right at one's feet. But it is a long time before one can actually see the bird who lures you on to a clear approach and then flies off unobtrusively and its next burst of song will be heard from the next thicket 50 or 100 yards away. I am glad I at last know what it is as I've always been puzzled by it before thinking the Nyamtambwe of the natives was only *Turdus libonyanus*, as I had been informed was the case.

November 13th, 1928

I chased those duck down on the Lingove today, but was defeated in my attempts to get one. On the very first occasion I saw them I might have had the easiest of shots as a pair flew straight down stream within 10 yards of me, but I was examining a bird at the time with my glasses and failed to see them until they had passed. After that I merely caught occasional glimpses of them on the river and they slipped off each time without giving me a shot at any reasonable range. I got two kingfishers, though, which I had not taken before — *Ceryle maxima* — the giant kingfisher and *Alcedo semitorquata* — neither of which appear to be breeding.

When I got back to camp the boys told me that a herd of hartebeest had come right into camp a few minutes before, so I went out and slew one on a dambo a couple of hundred yards off only. Two of my boys came to me today and said they wanted to stop work and go home. They gave all sorts of reasons, but I think the true one was that they were scared of me! I think I have been cursing them a bit too frequently of late, but at times they do get on one's nerves when the absolute non-existence of jumbo makes one anxious about things. However, I hope things are satisfactorily settled now, they are not a bad lot really, and I must curb my temper if I don't want to lose them.

November 14th, 1928

Went out this morning to look for the bustards again with three boys to put them up and send them the right way over me, but of course today got no glimpse of them at all. I shot a reedbuck close to camp and a francolin also which got up at my feet on the way out, so we have enough food to last us a day or two anyway and plenty to buy flour with yesterday's hartebeest. I have so many boys now that they eat more flour than I could have conceived possible. So many are really unnecessary, we were really a happier party when there were only a couple of hunters and a boy to collect firewood. I shan't mind if the two 'fearful' boys of yesterday run off one day soon as I am expecting them to do. A boy who is afraid of me I've got no time for, what will he do if he sees an elephant if the ferocity of my countenance frightens him.

November 15th, 1928

Yesterday I was trying to think of some subject of interest to try and write about, but failed to think of anything of which I wanted to write just at present. I woke up in the night, however, with the idea that the sounds one hears in the bush and fails to see both by day and night would be a fitting subject to try my hand at, so I have today composed a short essay of perhaps 3,000 words on this subject. I wish I could truthfully say that it has turned out a success. I quite enjoyed writing it but don't suppose for a moment that any firm of publishers would look at my half-baked efforts at short stories. Unless a subject is of real excitement or of interest in some other form to a reading public it takes a better pen than mine to make it saleable. I'm wondering greatly what luck we've had with a few stories I wrote of encounters with elephant which are being sent to an American magazine for their refusal — I don't suppose one can expect much from them, even if they are accepted.

November 16th, 1928

Went out latish this morning over the dambo lying to the south where I found a herd of buffalo feeding. It was the first time that I had actually come across buffalo here though we have occasionally seen their spoor. I got right up to them and killed a large cow, that I thought as a matter of fact was a bull. However as this is not looked upon as a crime in Africa I was pleased enough to get her, not being after heads.

After I had been back in camp some time and getting on to midday the boy whom I had sent off earlier in the week to look for elephant some 15 or 20 miles south arrived in camp to say that he had seen no spoor there, but that coming into camp that morning he had seen an elephant standing under some trees only a short distance away. On being questioned he said that he hadn't been able to see what his tusks were like as its head was hidden, but that it was a large elephant. On this news I hurriedly collected solid bullets for both the large and small bore rifles and lost no time in getting under way. We soon arrived at the spot where Jumbo had been, but he was of course no longer in evidence. That did not surprise me, what annoyed me was the fact that we could find no spoor and I was beginning to think that the whole matter was a leg-pull and a flight of fancy on the part of Madewa, who after an unsuccessful tramp of two or three days had let desire out run consideration for the truth. But in the end he took us up to the actual tree where he said he had seen the elephant and there at last we did find traces of Jumbo and began to follow up. It was a filthy sort of country to walk in; long unburnt grass cut short by a network of old elephant spoor which made tracking a hard business. But the difficulty was so great that at the end of about five minutes it began to dawn on me that it was quite impossible for an elephant of any size to have left so few traces of his passage behind him, and so it turned out, for we finally found what one could distinguish as the impression of a forefoot of a very small calf. So much for Master Madewa's idea of a large elephant, but I was not too disappointed as it is a sign at anyrate that there are such things as elephants in this country and others may come along shortly. The return of the buffalo to the neighbourhood is another good sign, so altogether things are looking up.

Frazer and the piccanins have gone off to bring in the buffalo. I let Frazer go as he wanted to see what a buffalo looked like, and I am left alone to keep guard on our belongings. My fowls are rather alarmed by this strange state of affairs and when I left camp a few minutes ago for a stroll, kept up an incessant crowing until my return. All the same I hope they get back soon as I want my bath and dinner.

November 17th, 1928

Very hot and thundery all day; in the evening great banks of black clouds rolled up from the east, just as the sun was setting in the west, and spread over the sky, giving a queer sort of light effect. There has been much lightening since but as yet not any rain to speak of, it still looks very threatening so may fall tonight. I hope it does come and cool things down a bit.

A lot of boys and women in camp today to get meat of yesterday's buffalo which is just as well as we were very short of foodstuffs. It's been too hot today to be very energetic, besides, what with people going all over the countryside, coming into my camp, going out to the buffalo, etc. I should get news quickly if elephants turn up.

I shot a big crested cuckoo in the morning which turned out to be *Coccystes caffir* and is quite a good skin, but otherwise had no successes. I thought I had found a nest of the Cinnamon roller as I saw one of these birds flying out of a hole in a dead tree, in fact it was my approach that seemed to have disturbed her off the nest and when I saw there were bits of grass protruding from the hole I thought I was in luck, however, the boy I sent up the tree to have a look told me there was nothing but an old nest which was annoying as Sclater and Stark give no description of the eggs of the bird or its nesting habits.

November 18th, 1928

Visited the long succession of dambos east this morning and for the first time found eland spoor there. Also for the first time I did not see a solitary head of game on any of them which shows, firstly, that game are without doubt coming into the neighbourhood, and secondly, that with the new grass just sprouting they are keeping more to the bush. In the afternoon I had two successes with birds that pleased me greatly. I first found eggs of *Telephorus senegalus* in a nest that I'd been watching for some 10 days and got the bird after about an hour's wait. This is the bird that so unkindly took away its egg on the first occasion that I found its nest so I am glad to have found another. Then, shortly after I got back to camp I shot a bird that has been worrying me for five years. It turned out to be a black cuckoo, *Cuculus clamosus* by name, whose note one often hears but who is the very devil to see. I first noticed its plaintive three-note whistle in Tanganyika when I first arrived in the country and I've been trying ever since to see the bird who made it or to find someone who could tell me what it was, in neither of which I have had any success. In my camp here, I have often heard it but as usual when I tried to stalk it, it had immediately stopped calling and cleared off without giving me a sight. Today for the first time a pair of the birds came right up to the camp, I quickly seized my gun and managed to shoot one. For a long time I had thought it was a cuckoo shrike, one of the *Campephagidae* but am glad to know now that this is not so. This is about the last of the really striking calls that I did not recognize — in this district that is to say.

November 20th, 1928

Yesterday the 19th we walked the sun round in our efforts to come up with a pair of elephants whose spoor we hit at about 7 a.m. It was by far the longest day's trek that I have ever had in my life for a single day and I don't suppose we were far short of 50 miles. I suppose at this time of the year in these latitudes the sun rises at about 5 a.m.; we left camp at about 5.30, heading south in search of game. When Yokani and I arrived about the place where we got the buffalo a few days ago, we came upon the spoor of a couple of elephants that had passed during the night and we immediately proceeded to follow. They led us back at first in the direction of camp, and at about 8 a.m. we came within a half hour's walk from here, so I sent Y back to bring the heavy rifle and more solid ammunition for the 8 mm. I have lately not been taking the ·450 with me as a rule, elephant have been so scarce that it has not been worth while to give a boy its tiring weight day after day. Also Y had not fed so this was a good opportunity to let him do so. So off he went and got back to me at about 9 a.m. — an hour later — with Madewa, my other hunter, and the various things I had sent for, including a loaf of bread and some honey. I spent the interval wandering round looking for nests and followed up the spoor for a short way to see how it was going, but this was my only easy time for from then onwards, from the time we started following up the spoor again until about two hours after nightfall, we were continually on the move except for two halts of about 10 minutes each at the most, one about mid-day when I ate some bread and honey and the other about 5 p.m. when we realized we were beaten.

The elephants were trekking indeed and travelling for most of the day along their paths, so that we had an easy job following up and swung along the whole day at a good 3½ m.p.h. I hated the idea of giving them up, the first decent sized fresh spoor I've ever seen since arriving here, but there was nothing else to be done, we hadn't gained a fraction on them throughout the day, in fact I think we were further behind than when we started. They were making for a barren country, bare of all villages and are probably still going ahead at that speed. If we had had food with us for a couple of days we might have carried on, sleeping on the tracks but one gets fagged out on that game, and it is really not worth while when elephants are on the move, as these two were, for they may go on for a week. We gave them up, as I have said, at about 5 p.m. and turned our heads for camp.

There is a little hill at about three miles from my camp which we have found very useful in showing us our position when we are far off, but it looks nearer than it is in the distressing way a large thing like that always does and though we put on speed it was another three hours at least, at a 4 m.p.h. rate, before we were home again at about two hours after nightfall. I estimate my 50 miles in the following way, two and a half hour's walk to the time when Yokania went back to collect the heavy rifle — say 10 miles altogether, taking into account a mile or two pottering round while waiting for him to get back. Eight hours actually following up the elephant after that, 28 miles; and 12 miles slogging back to camp again when we were going as hard as we knew. Anyway it was a trek that I don't want to do every day and I am taking things easy today to make up. We came across a herd of buffalo, but they were too far off camp to make it worthwhile to shoot one, but besides that we saw very little game the whole day. On the way home I shot a hawk which intrigued me and wished I hadn't as it was a nuisance to carry in the dark — I couldn't give it to the boys as they had found some honey which they insisted on bringing along.

In the evening I told a couple of boys who had come in for meat and who were going back this morning, to start off very early and look for the spoor of these elephant on their way home, as I had an idea they might find it again in that direction. Nor was I mistaken, and if they had only done what I told them, I might have come up to those elephant today. But they, in their confoundedly unbelieving and lazy fashion, did not leave my camp until after 8 a.m. and came back to me with the news that they had found the spoor as I had said, a couple of hours off at the Lingove. Feeling sufficiently rested by then, I pushed off immediately with them, but luck was not with us. They had come across the spoor on the river, but we found it at a point about a mile or two before we arrived there and we thought and hoped that this was fresher than when they had seen it. We followed for a couple of hours, only to find that the brutes had swung round and that where the boys themselves had first found it was the fresher spoor. We arrived at that place two hours later than we might have, following the spoor up the Lingove and I once again realized it was no go. The elephants were still trekking pretty hard and not feeding; if we had gone straight to that place in the first instance we might possibly have come up with them, but now it was a hopeless task and I perforce had to give it up again. Heavy rain was coming on also which would have made spooring on hard ground next door to impossible, so I turned my face home again and got back to camp about 4 p.m., absolutely drenched to the bone.

I have often written of the disappointments of elephant hunting but this has been the worst spell of luck that I have ever had. I don't know in the least what to do, those elephant were making up stream and may go anywhere. I think I shall cut across country tomorrow, starting early and have a look on the Lingove further up, where it swings round to the north of my camp.

November 21st, 1928

This I did and found absolutely no sign of Jumbo, so he has not gone in that direction. Where he has gone I'm beat to know unless he has turned round again and gone back to the country over which we chased him two days ago. The whole trouble is that elephants do not stay round here at this time of the year, they may walk through this country searching for food, but not finding anything, go off somewhere else. But then I have no reason to suppose that they will find better feeding anywhere else; I've been turning over in my mind the advisability of leaving this spot and trying elsewhere. I would do this if I only knew where to go. The boys first say one thing and then another; at times I think I shall never get up to elephant here, at others I think I am bound to do so when there are any elephant to get up to. After all, a couple of solitary jumbo is not all that this country can produce. I have seen enough old spoor to believe that, and I've spent long enough at the game to know that the native knows just as little about the elephant as anybody and he certainly is not the fountain of wisdom of the fauna of his country that he likes to pretend to be. On the whole I think I would be wiser to stay where I am. I will anyway have to go and see about the renewal of my licence at the end of the year and it will be then time enough to give up this spot if I then see no hope at all of getting anything. But its a wearying game when one is out of luck — at times I wish with Kipling to be able to 'lie down for an aeon or two'.

November 22nd, 1928

It's funny that I should have been complaining about the scarcity of shrikes a day or two ago as since that date I've taken eggs of two more species and seen a third, two of these birds I had not seen before in the district. They were nothing out of the common, any of them. Those whose eggs I took were the Senegal bush shrike of November 18th and *Laniarius sulphureopectus* whose nest I found yesterday evening, the third shrike I noticed was *Lanius collurio*, the red-backed shrike which breeds in Europe and only visits these parts during the northern winter.

There is little to write of today. It's been confoundedly hot again and working up for more rain. A walk to the south-west in the morning produced no sign of those jumbo who must be by now somewhere in Angola I should fancy, if that is the direction in which they were moving. I shot a couple of guinea fowl who stood obligingly in line for me at about 30 feet range — what crimes we commit from the sporting standpoint when we are out for the pot — but beyond that saw no game at all. In the afternoon I went out south-east and found a little dambo which I have never visited before. There was not much sign of game visiting though, so I have not missed much by not going there. Madewa — his real name incidentally is Chikamadewa but I have cut it short as the other is too long to be saying constantly, — came to me and asked leave to go down to the Lingove soon after he got back in the morning, saying he wanted to see if he could find spoor. Greatly surprised at this unlooked for enthusiasm, I of course gave him leave straight away and he departed. He has just got back with a couple of good-sized barbel and three or four roach-like fish which he netted in the river and showed me the real reason for his energy. Must try and get some game tomorrow, there are women waiting for meat, who want to get off home, but it will be great luck if I strike anything within reasonable distance of camp, game is not easily to be found now that young grass is springing up in the bush as they no longer find grass only on the dambos.

November 23rd, 1928

Got a reedbuck this morning, close to camp while skirting the side of a dambo. He had a good head, going 14 inches from the beginning of the horny substance on the skull. I don't remember offhand if this is the right place to measure from or if measuring actually from the beginning of the horn it was about an eighth of an inch short of 13 inches.

After that I followed up another honeyguide, *Indicator minor*, I'm practically sure it was, as I had it under observation through my glasses for a long time while we were cutting out the honey. It's actions were very similar to *Indicator sparrmani* but it has not quite such a noticeable 'twitter' nor does it fly so straight to the spot where the bees are, which makes it harder to follow. I had no matches with me, which fact I only discovered when we arrived at the nest so we had to make a fire by rubbing sticks, at which game Madewa proved himself a great hand. My other three boys, by the way, have all run off — which I was expecting and half hoping for — they were not getting enough work to keep them happy and always quarrelling, which combined with their timidity, made them really undesirable.

November 24th, 1928

Spent a very pleasing day at the Lingove netting fish, we got three kinds, a barbel, the roach-like fellow of the day before yesterday and something else, more reminiscent of a small chub, if that is the fish whose mouth opening protrudes in a round ring. I also shot the largest tusked wart hog I've ever seen in the flesh. I don't know what the tusks actually measure yet as they have not brought him in. I got within 10 yards of a whole family of them as we were approaching the river. I did not see any sign of my duck this time nor did I get any kind that I wanted particularly and the only bird I shot being a rather common sandpiper, whom I mistook for another bird of that family that I was chasing. I've seen him every time I've been down there and failed to get a shot.

Fried fish tonight — the first I've tasted for many a long month — I can only wish I had some potatoes to fry along with them!

Later — not much of a success — too bony!

I've been able to renew my supply of wheat flour, though which is great luck, as if that had run out it would have been a bad state of affairs. I should have been reduced to eating maize flour only and you can't make bread with that. At present I'm living largely on bread and honey and I generally have rice boiled with whatever meat course I have in the evening. As a treat about once in 10 days, I allow myself wheat flour cakes and plum pudding. I've got a few raisins and currants which we mix up with flour into a steam pudding and I sprinkle it freely with honey which makes it very good. The only thing I really want badly is fresh fruit and vegetables.

Later — I've got badly sunburnt. All my back and shoulders, the price I'm paying for those fish and the result of sitting for about half an hour completely starko on a log in the river. I began a gradual descending process when we arrived there; my socks and shoes coming off first as we were wading about. Then I went in over my shorts so they came off and finally, having fallen down on one occasion and barking my shins incidentally on an unseen log, my shirt went to join my other articles of attire to dry on a bush on the river bank. I felt much happier then and more able to assist in un-netting our fish arrayed as I was in a double Terai hat only. But I am now, in the patches which are generally covered, the colour of a boiled lobster.

November 26th, 1928

The 25th I made out was a Sunday, so I had an easy day, visiting marked nests in the vicinity of camp and seeing to specimens. I found a weaver's nest and that of a sunbird, both of which contained eggs. I could not make out what sunbird it was as the cock bird never put in an appearance, though I waited until it was dark, having found the nest just about sundown. Beside these I found a drongo's nest but the eggs were too well matured to be of any use. Boys came in from the Namanzi River wanting work, in company with a lot of women to get meat. They tell me there has been a herd of elephant seen there lately, the spoor that is to say, but that they do not stay around there. One of the boys who ran away the other day had the cheek to come back pretending he had heard I had sent for him and wanting to finish off his month's work. He got it good and strong and departed forthwith. I explained to him that he was both a liar and a coward and that I had no time for either.

Today I went out to try and get game but only saw a herd of kudu cows slipping off in the bush. I got eggs though of another sunbird and also the Senegal bush shrike, the latter too hard set, unfortunately, to look at all pretty. I have kept one though as it is unlike the last lot of eggs I took of this bird. The sunbirds may be the same as yesterday's as they were in a very similar type of nest, but they are not in the least alike in size or colour. Again I could not get a sight of the cock bird though I shot the hen on the nest and though I waited at the spot while I skinned her, the cock never put in an appearance.

November 28th, 1928

I got a hartebeest this morning at last and in doing so gave as bad an object lesson in poor woodcraft as one could want to see. I spotted the herd at about 150 yards in fairly open bush through which we were going. We had just come on fresh spoor so had been keeping an extra wary eye open. We dropped to the ground and I began crawling back to get behind cover for my stalk. When I reached the place where Madewa was, some 15 yards behind, he pointed out to me that one of them had spotted us; I looked and saw that one animal was very interested in something in our direction so I made up my mind not to risk further delay and took my shot from there at the beast who was looking at us. It was standing facing us so I reckoned there would be either a kill or a clean miss. The thud of the bullet told me I had hit all right and the animal dropped to the shot, but as we were starting to walk up to him he got up again and made off. When

I got to the place where the herd had been I saw there were still two hartebeest in view which had not run off with the remainder and were still hanging round undecided which way to go, so I again stalked these and killed one, an easy shot through the shoulder. Neither of these two animals were quite full grown, but I had to take one since my first animal was still an uncertainty. Then, having inspected our slain animal, we went back to pick up the spoor of the one I had fired at originally. We soon found the place where he had fallen down to my shot and there were tracks leading from that spot, plain to view, so we lost no time in following, which was an easy matter as the ground was soft from recent rain; I was surprised though to find no sign of a blood spoor, though we came on one occasion on a place where we thought he had been staggering and wanting to fall down. We followed that animal for about half an hour, when I realized he could not be very badly wounded. There was still no blood and the tracks showed he had been going strongly. We then circled back and picked up the spoor of the herd and followed them for about the same time but could find no trace of a wounded animal with them, so I decided to go right back to the place where we knew the animal had fallen to my shot and start again. This we did and looking more carefully this time we saw that the tracks leading from there, which we had followed originally, were not absolutely fresh and had probably been left five or six hours before and that in the same spot there were other tracks also — not quite so obvious as they were smaller and left by a much lighter animal. It was only then that it dawned on me that the first animal I had fired at might not have been full grown either. He looked large enough, but he was standing on higher ground than I was and there was no other beast standing close to him at the time with which to compare him. But if that was so, then it must either have been the one I shot on the second occasion, or else the other one which ran off. I did not think the latter could have been the one as we had seen him bounding off in that queer canter that all hartebeests use and he seemed to be going strongly. Then by elimination we should find two bullet wounds in the one I had killed and sure enough it proved to be the case, as a more careful examination showed. My first shot had entered at the brisket and travelled upwards, coming out at the withers so had not raked his vitals, while my second had gone in at the shoulder and come out at the other side. What asses we had been, wasting an hour or so in a fatuous attempt to find an animal that was already lying dead, when a little closer observation in the first place would have told us the whole story and later a little bit of woodcraft would have told us long before that we were on the wrong track.

November 24th, 1928

Heavy rain fell last night and again this afternoon. The first 'planting rain' of the year I should call it. My roof leaked on both occasions, so I shall put the tent over the top of it tomorrow which may keep things dry I hope. I went out with Madewa in the morning but saw nothing I wanted except a thrush which I first took for the ordinary *Turdus libonyanus*, but as it seemed much bolder than that thrush usually is, allowing us to appraoch more closely, I shot one and found that it was something totally different. I can't quite work it out but think it is some *Monticola*. Frazer has been sick for a couple of days, so I have had to do the stuffing and sewing up of my specimens myself. The first two I made a mess of but got quite a good result with this thrush which I showed him when it was completed, as he had recovered from his malady, and told him that I expected results in future to be up to that standard. The whole thing is easy enough as long as one takes time to do it and trouble. Master F gets bored with the business I fancy and does not treat them 'tender' so that skins which look good enough after I've done my part of the business come back to me often in a pitiable state of bedragglement. Cursing him is no avail, he just looks sorrowful and goes and does the same thing next time, so that really good skins are few and far between in my collection.

November 30th, December 1st, 2nd, 3rd, 1928

Nothing much to write of but must make some entry or I lose count of the date. The mornings were all spent tramping round in various directions. Total bag: one wart hog and one stembuck, both got yesterday near the Lingove. It's just about all I saw on all three days together. I think the game is deserting this part of the country as the elephant have, following their lead. There has been a lot of rain lately but things keep pretty dry with the tent over the roof of the house. I shot a shrike today which I can't work out, at least I suppose it is a shrike, I can't conceivably see what else it could be but it will remain a puzzle until a book is brought out taking in birds north of the Zambezi. (I worked it out in the end. It turned out to be a red-backed shrike *Lanius collurio*).

December 4th, 1928

Struck elephant spoor yesterday, a couple of days old, fairly close to camp, which annoyed me exceedingly with the thought that I ought to have found it before if I had been more energetic, but one can't do a complete circle of one's surroundings every day and elephant have been so scarce that it's not been worthwhile sending out boys to have a look round first thing in the morning in all directions. I must start this again now however, as there seem to be more signs of elephant about once again. Yesterday and today were two more blank days as far as game was concerned, seeing nothing except an odd wart hog and a few small buck disappearing in the bush ahead. I've just got back to camp after another walk round this afternoon, which was also a failure though I tried to stalk a couple of reedbuck who had seen us long before we were anywhere near them.

Today I found two green pigeon's nests with eggs, one in the morning and the other this afternoon. I had a great time getting the eggs of the second one. Yokania climbed the tree, but as the nest was right at the end of a long horizontal branch he could not reach it and the eggs would have fallen out with his weight bending down the branch. We succeeded eventually when I had the brainwave to think of attaching my Terai hat to a long bamboo and holding it underneath the nest when Y poked the eggs into it from above.

December 5th, 1928

A perfectly foul morning spent getting seen by buck and then following a wounded one. My 8 mm badly needs a rest having had the odd round fired out of it for the last three months every day or two, so I've been taking the 9 mm recently with the result that I wounded a hartebeest, breaking a foreleg. I got up to it again on several occasions but simply could not get a line on him. The wretched animal could not go far, but travelled down wind the whole time and always spotted us before we were up to him. I eventually left Y to deal with him as it was merely a question of time before he could get him. But he, like a lazy young devil left him without a serious effort — either that or he was afraid of the rifle, I don't know which. I shall send him out again tomorrow to try and finish it off. Later: Hopelessly heavy rain has fallen which will wash out all spoor. I went down the water course of the Bandi for a walk in the afternoon with the shot-gun — of course the first thing I saw was a bushbuck which would have given an easy shot with the rifle at about 40 yards. Too far off to try with the gun. I then found a most pleasing nest of a lark or a pipit of some sort containing two eggs of a greyish white ground colour thickly spotted and streaked with brown. I could not get the bird, though I waited at the spot for the best part of a couple of hours. She came back twice but was so wary that the first time I failed to get a shot at all and the second time I had a bang at the grass where she landed that had no effect. To my disgust when I got back to camp I found that the eggs were too hard-set to blow. It has been a wretched day altogether, my only success was in shooting a guinea fowl which I heard calling from a tree on my way back to camp. It was practically dark and the wretched bird was roosting for the night when I shot it in the poaching style. I tried to get its mate also but couldn't see it in the dark — what crimes!

December 7th, 1928

Still short of game, though I got a guinea fowl yesterday evening, which keeps the pot going for myself at any rate. I also found a pipit — No I didn't though — I'm quite wrong in my calculations — both these events are already recorded for December 5th — shows how easily one forgets the odd day.

Yesterday was spent writing letters for a boy to take into an Indian store about couple of days off, I make out, with the hope that he will post them and not collar the money I enclosed in payment for stamps.

Today it was raining hard in the morning so I remained in camp and mended the cleaning rod of the shot-gun which I had just broken. No sign of elephant was the report of the three boys who went out in the morning and also the report of Madewa, who came in about noon after two days' tramp towards Msatwe, where he had heard that elephant had been seen. He said he had found week-old spoor of the two elephants who gave such a long tramp about a fortnight ago and that was all. I wonder if I'm ever going to see anything here.

December 9th, 1928

I got a duiker yesterday evening at the end of a long tramp, morning and afternoon. It won't go very far in the way of buying foodstuffs or to keep the boys in supply, but it will last me anyway for a day or two. Today I sent off Yokania with the 8 mm to let him see what he can do. I gave him a little instruction in the art to begin with and couldn't understand his awkwardness, for he is on the whole an intelligent boy; but I discovered in the end that the damned fellow was left-handed which explained his pervesity in not doing things the way I did.

December 10th, 1928

Another gameless day except for a francolin which I got this morning when I went out to look round. It rained hard part of the morning and most of the afternoon as well. I sent off Y again with the rifle but he was as unsuccessful as I was. Yesterday incidentally he came back late in the afternoon saying he had found a herd of waterbuck at the Lingove and had had two shots both of which missed. Not surprising seeing that it was the first time he had ever fired a rifle. I found some small flycatchers' nest this morning with hard-set eggs but had better luck this afternoon with a hawk's nest that one of my piccanins spotted and acquired much merit thereby. Another day or so and I would have been unable to blow those also, but he got them just in time. Egg collecting is a most annoying game; when one's luck is out one finds nest after nest of birds whose eggs one has not yet taken with hard-set eggs or youngsters in them. It is not so bad when there are youngsters; one is resigned to one's fate but when one finds perfectly good eggs seemingly and then smashes them in the blowing, language has not yet invented words suitable for the occasion.

It's just four years today since I shot my first elephant, I think fate might have been kind to me and have let me repeat that performance on the anniversary of so notable an event but Dame Fortune has deserted me entirely I begin to think. Of course the whole trouble is that it is my thirteenth elephant that I'm after. Once over that obstacle perhaps she will again remember me.

December 11th, 1928

Went down to the Lingove and for a long tramp over the other side seeing absolutely nothing the whole day. I don't know that I would have been able to shoot anything anyhow. My eye is almost out of action, the result of a bee sting I got yesterday while cutting out a hive in the afternoon. He got me right on the eyelid and it has swollen up so much today that I can hardly open the eye.

December 12th, 1928

My eye was still pretty well bunged up this morning so I sent off Yokania to see if he could get anything, of course with no success. About 10 a.m. Madewa rushed into my shack to say there was a duck on the water pool — camp was very silent, the piccanins were away getting honey or following up a honeyguide at least and Frazer was out of camp at the moment also, so only Madewa, who has hurt his foot and I were present. I had just noticed that the fowls were making more noise than usual when M arrived with this news so I walked out in my pyjamas and slew the black duck which I have been wanting all this time and have chased so many times unsuccessfully down on the Lingove. It was very clever of the fowls, I think, to draw our attention to this strange arrival in that manner. I, at any rate, would have noticed nothing if it had not been for them. We are today very short in all departments of the commissariat. We have no meat in camp. We have no meat, the boys' flour is almost finished, I am on my last loaf of bread and have no rice. Honey is no longer so easily obtained as nests we cut out now only contain young bees in the combs — the hens are no longer laying as they did last month and today's duck did not go far as I wanted the skin and so had to sacrifice the legs and wings. A poor state of affairs altogether. I've been expecting the boy I sent off to the Indian store to arrive back here for the last day or two; if he doesn't come tomorrow with the much needed flour I shall be annoyed to say the least of it. It's a toss-up though whether he has managed to get any flour or not; ten days ago I sent to the place where I had previously managed to get flour only to find that the native Portuguese from whom I had bought it had gone off on a jaunt to Tete. My dinner tonight consisted of most of that loaf of bread.

December 13th, 1928

I shot a couple of reedbuck this morning so we are all happy again. After I had got them I told Y who was with me to go off home with a leg of one of them and tell Frazer to start cooking my lunch while I stayed round a bit to look for birds and eggs. This he did and I started wandering back slowly also up the centre of a large dambo that I knew well getting a corncrake, the ordinary European variety. After I had got to the end of the dambo and was entering through the bush to the west, which is in reality the source of the Bandi River and leads to my camp, I suddenly found that this second dambo was in quite the wrong position and when I went down into the open on to it, it was absolutely strange, also that I was going in straight the opposite direction from my camp. As I have mentioned before there is a little hill two or three miles from my camp which gives us our position when we are far off, but there is also another one which is very like it in shape lying ten or twelve miles to the east of it and in the direction we took this morning. The only difference between the two is that one is completely covered with bush whilst the other has large boulders towards the top. It was this latter one that I now saw in front of me whereas I ought to have been making for the former which was not then to be seen. I could not understand how I could have switched right round like this as I knew well where I was when I left the large dambo where I had got the reedbuck. I tried to think away the boulders on the hill in front of me and to recognize things on the dambo on which I was, which is the right thing to do if one wants to get lost; and so, realizing finally that I should be on my way to that if I didn't pull myself together I again turned about and went straight back on my tracks to find my first dambo and start again. I then realized how badly askew I must have been going when I left it as it also was not where I was expecting it to be — but as from the top of the rise up which I was going I could see our own little hill, I wasted no more time and made for it joyfully, getting home without further mishap. But it just shows one how careful one should be not to wander along in the bush lost in thought unless one has a boy with one, or one's bump of locality is considerably better than I can ever hope mine will be.

December 14th, 1928

Rained hard the whole day. I spent the morning taking my binoculars to pieces. I had let them get wet, like a fool, by leaving them under a leaky part of the roof with the result that one couldn't see through them. Drying them by the fire didn't improve matters much so I took my courage in both hands and took them down and polished up the lenses and object glasses. All went well and I thought I had made a job of it but I find now that though I can see out of either glass perfectly the two images don't hit it off together and though I have tried to correct this, must confess I'm beaten. Still, they are serviceable again now which is more than they were before, so I register a partial success.

A boy came in this morning with a basket of beans much to my delight and I have bought them at an extortionate price, but anything for a change in diet.

December 15th, 1928

Took a skin of another kind of francolin, *Francolinus shelleyi*, which I have noticed from time to time here but as yet had not been able to procure, but beyond that had no success. I've a very good mind to give things up and struggle home to Nyasaland if the roads are at all passable. I rather fancy that Jumbo will not turn up here now until the grass is well up, somewhere about February or March, they certainly have made no sign of their presence to date, as I was hoping they might with the rains; so now it means that the only time they are here is when the grass is right up and not when it is just starting to grow. If I had carriers I would beat it, I think, and try again next year to the south of Fort Manning in the country towards Zumbo on the Zambezi. But now the question is how to get carriers to take me to Matenji and if I can get down that road again and up to Blantyre. I hate giving things up like this but is it worthwhile to hang on when Jumbo seems so problematical. I'm bothered if I know what to do; I wouldn't mind sticking it for another month or two but is it worth it and what success might I have? Then, on the other hand, if I do go back to Nyasaland I shall be at a loose end again there and regretting that I didn't hang on here for a bit. It's hard to make up one's mind — why don't we find some portent in the skies, or throw bones, or have some sort of oracle to consult on such a thing. I know just what I shall do, I'll take a week to make up my mind one way and then change over and swither about from one to the other in a lazy kind of way. Anyway I've only got a fortnight left of my licence and though I've written to Tete for a renewal I don't expect an answer to my letter within the time unless the 'pork and beans' gets a most unusual move on. I think I would be wise to go into Furancungo boma about the 20th, try and extract porters from the bloke in charge there and come back here and beat it. What a rotten business the whole thing is, if I had only a pair of tusks or twain to show it would be so different.

December 16th, 1928

I told a boy from Macheso's today to go and get me carriers to take me back. He said he would be able to find boys and be back here within a week. I wonder. Still I may be pessimistic. I have offered him a 'prizie' for each able-bodied man or stalwart piccanin he brings me. My boy arrived back from the Indian store today without any flour so I shall have to subsist on 'chimanga' for the rest of this little trip. It's not so bad really but I wish one could make bread with maize flour. I have got nothing I wanted today, bird or beast. I'm not really so fed up and miserable as anyone reading my writings for the last few days might suppose — only disappointed at having to give things up with no success with elephant.

December 18th, 1928

Shot a duiker yesterday morning which a piccanin described as a wart hog when he came to me with news that he had seen it close to camp in the early morning. I would have been more pleased if it had turned out to be that because I have no fat for cooking — and the old wart hog generally produces a fair supply of lard. But beyond that my other anniversary — when I got three elephants on this date four years ago — passed without event. It's time I was off, I'm only waiting for boys for my loads and hope they'll turn up without my going to look for them myself. I want a day or two's easy to let a septic ankle get right. It's not in the least bad yet but I don't want it to develop that way. Another day or two also and I'm hoping Madewa's foot will be serviceable again. He has had rather a nasty place on the sole which is taking a lot of healing. He's a stalwart boy and I want him for a good load. I think our friend at Matenji will have given me up for good by this time and think me killed by an elephant.

December 19th, 1928

I have been reading John Locke's 'Conduct of the Understanding' in a little book about four inches long and about two inches wide sent me from home to take on this trip. It is dated 1825 and Bacon's 'Essays' form the second part of it. These I love and get great entertainment therefrom but if an elephant hunter dare criticize an eminent philosopher I should say life is too short to follow the ramifications of Locke. There is no short cut to wisdom and true knowledge and it would be only a very serious-minded adherent of pragmatism who could spend so much time in such self-introspection as Locke advocates. But then there is far too much of the hedonist in me to think of pragmatism in any other way than incidental in life, and true knowledge gained otherwise than by the experience of years. Before tackling an enterprise let us weigh our actions, analyse our thoughts, think all round the question by all means but let us be quick about it or there will be little time left for the undertaking or the difficulties we perceive will make us relinquish the thought of it altogether and we will lose the knowledge that the experience of it would have given. Nor is that all, for after years it will be a subject of regret and where will our happiness lie if we cannot find it in our memory? In the present, perhaps, but that is an indefinite state, full of little cares and worries that we soon forget in memory. In the future? In anticipation of some particular time undoubtedly but not generally, as a rule one has more fears for the future — as unknown. So if we have in our heads a preponderance of passed regrets also we shall have cause indeed to call on our 'Beloved to fill the cup' and happiness only lies for a short distance along that road. Not that I do not agree with Horace in his sympathy for the fair Neobuli:

'Miserarum est neque amori dare ludum
Acque dulci mala vino lavorare'

On the contrary, I think he has put things very concisely and neatly but we must have recourse to these in the natural exuberance of spirit and not because we are wretched; our 'mala' must be really of little moment and not call to be washed away repeatedly and if I am further to criticize the poet — our 'ludum' must be play indeed and not allowed to develop into anything more serious. What Locke would have to say on such a question is not apparent but I can't help thinking altogether that pragmatism is so realistic a creed as to render it quite unsuitable for any but the most sober-minded of philosophers to whom worldly desires make no appeal. Will must be subjugated to brain and that is a task to which the ordinary man is not well fitted by nature. We know what happens if we try to cast out Nature too suddenly, so that if we would subjugate her with our brains it must needs be a slow process, only possible to future generations with the brain's evolution. The brain of man has only been a force for a few thousand years, whereas Nature has held sway since the beginning of time and still has a store of secrets for the brain of man to tackle before she can be under his yoke. Thought of in this fashion I would liken the brain to an interesting but precocious child who, as such, should be left in its place and not taught to meddle with things that are not good for it until such time as it can duly assimilate them.

Heard today that the native from Macheso's who was looking for carriers for me is coming in tomorrow with two boys and four women for my loads. This ought to be sufficient with the boys and piccanins I have got here, as long as I don't have to be carried myself. My ankle has swollen a bit and is anyway going to be a darned nuisance on my way back.

A boy has just rushed in to say that there was 'nyama' close to camp, he said that he had heard something running in the bush close by, so I told him to go and see what it was, but a moment later, hearing some loud barking, I went out and caught a glimpse of a few hunting dogs going through the bush, apparently tracking some wretched animal. I wish I could have got a shot at them, but they were too far off and it was only an occasional glimpse of them one had through the trees.

Africa is on her worst behaviour today. My hunter, a new boy who knows how to handle a rifle a bit, failed to find game — Yokani had no success in netting fish on the Lingove — Madewa whom I had sent to a colony of nesting swallows came back eggless — a piccanin that I told to go and inspect a nest we have been watching of some warbler was unable to find it even — while I, confined to camp to give this ankle a chance, have found little better to do than write the foregoing nonsense.

December 20th, 1928

No sign of those carriers today so Y went off by night taking a rifle and a couple of piccanins with him to bring them in without fail tomorrow, which I do not expect him to do. I found another egg of *T. senegalus* in a nest I've been watching close to camp — very different in markings from any I have previously taken. Every nest of this bird that I have found has had different shapes and colouration of the eggs which makes it very puzzling to deal with.

December 21st, 1928

Some difficulty getting carriers — what a 40–50 mile walk will do for my ankle remains to be seen. Kill or cure I should fancy.

December 22nd, 1928

Got to Msatwe this afternoon — very heavy loads because a boy ran off in the night — the new hunter fellow whose services I had enlisted about a week ago. That is typical of the African native to leave one in the lurch and make things harder for one whenever he can. I didn't leave the Bandi until about 9 a.m. as loads had to be continually disarranged and re-sorted. They tied up a load for this man who deserted and didn't discover it until we were just off — if I had gone on ahead I think they would have left it there, for they stood about looking at it and saying there was no one to take it until I suggested untying it and distributing the load amongst them. I was sorry for the smaller piccanins, poor little brutes, with loads I wouldn't like to hump myself half a mile, but they managed somehow and we have got in here dry, which was lucky as rain came on just after we arrived. Tomorrow's march is about twice the distance and we'll never do it in one day unless I can pick up some boys here to help. My ankle held up well so long as I kept moving but whenever I stopped it was a bit stiff moving off again. I was lucky to have with me a rubber anklet which I spied this morning as we were rearranging things and remembered having chucked it in at the last moment at Cholo. It was lucky that I did so as I think it helped a lot. I find here that there is a native shooting game, with some success too, to judge from the quantity of meat smoking on grids in the village, which explains the scarcity of game on the Bandi lately. I had meant to push on for a few miles this evening to cut off something of tomorrow's march, but the piccanins are too tired and as rain is still threatening must give up the idea. We were not without casualties coming in today as two of my noble hens died of exposure — sun stroke really I suppose, on the way. They have done me royally the whole time I was at the Bandi and even in their expiring moments each produced an egg. It was a poor return that I made to them to kill them off in that fashion.

December 23rd, 1928

Great difficulty in getting the loads off this morning but we managed it at last having roped in a couple of boys and the same number of women to help. Camping tonight at the top of the hill, cutting the distance in half and leaving a fairly easy walk for tomorrow.

December 26th, 1928

I arrived at Matenji on Christmas Eve thinking my greatest difficulties were over and hoping that the road to Tete would still be passable but on enquiry from the Bivars I was told that it was quite impossible to get a car along the road at all; they said that they had got back for the last time this year at the beginning of the month but only with the greatest difficulty and with the help of large numbers of boys — now, they said, it was quite impossible. However, having arrived so far, I decided it was up to me to have a dash at it so I started off on Christmas day, fairly early — the car was going well after its long rest and for the first ten miles I thought that the Bivar family had enlarged on the difficulties for I found very few places that gave any trouble, but after that when I had arrived at the foot of the hill my troubles started in earnest. Three crossings of the Msegue River I managed somehow, one in pouring rain and a thunderstorm, working like a navvy shifting stones and hoeing out the perpendicular bank on the other side. I must have looked a wonderful sight arrayed in a pair of shorts only and grimed with mud all over. The last one was the worst; when I arrived about 2 p.m. I thought we should never manage it. A few stones of the piers were all that remained of the original bridge and the water was running a foot or two deep for a span of some 15 feet. I had collected some boys by this time so we set to work shifting stones and boulders to make a drift passable. I thought of cutting four long and straight trees which I could lash together, two by two, to make a bridge to climb up the further bank but I gave up the idea as impracticable owing to the difficulty of fixing them at such an angle. All we could do was to hoe out the bank and build up the drift until the ascent showed a slope which would be possible for the car. Thus we set to work and after a couple of hours or so I thought we might manage it and brought the car forward for the attempt. If I could have rushed it I might have managed, but it was necessary to crawl along by inches over the boulders and even here we stuck once or twice and had to stop and lift the car, bodily, out of holes between the stones displaced by the two front wheels. When we started the climb on the other side I realized, as looked at from the car, how steep it was. It didn't seem so bad when we were looking at it before but I could tell from the angle at which the car stood that even if it had been a flat hard surface I would not have been able to manage. We got about half way up with help of boys pushing behind and pulling in front but then we stuck fast, the back wheels finding no hold in the soft earth and digging themselves worse and worse each time I let in the clutch. We tried everything I could think of, filling up the holes with small stones, pushing others underneath the wheels to give them a flat surface to start on, but nothing we tried had any effect and I thought we were there for good and all.

About 5 p.m. I sat down for a rest and sent a boy off to try and find others to help to pull the car bodily up the hill. With 20 boys pushing and pulling it would have been a simple matter but I had only some half dozen and a few children who were not nearly enough. While the fresh recruits were being summoned I sat down to think it out. My great fear was that no boys would come and that those I had would run off and leave me there on the bank of the river to be swept away by the next flood. In the position I was I could go neither forwards or backwards. After half an hour's rest I decided on one last attempt; night was falling, the boys were grousing and wanting to go back to the village and no others had come to help. I started them working once again; we lifted each back wheel in turn and pushed stones underneath to heighten them, then I started the car up and amidst loud cheers we gained an inch or two. Heartened by this little success the boys began working better, though I still had to cajole and even plead with them to put their backs into it. Each time we stopped we had to lift up the back wheels and heighten them again and it was wearying back-breaking work. A jack was no use at the angle we were standing nor could I manage a fulcrum on which to lever up the car with a large pole; but little by little we managed it at last, gaining an inch or two at a time, and I was delighted enough when the car eventually took hold and dragged itself the last yard or two in one burst.

But our troubles were not yet over as only a hundred yards off was yet another stream to be crossed; this did not present the same difficulty however, as there were still traces of the original bridge and all we had to do was to make the approaches passable. We were over that at about 7 p.m. and I had a clear road in front of me to the Ponfi River, so I gave the boys 6*d*. apiece and they departed to their homes saying — some of them — that they would come again next day to help at that river, so we loaded up the car again and moved on.

The drive down to the Ponfi River I will not dilate upon — we arrived about an hour later — it was only about five miles — the reason for our slow progress being that my lights were not working well as the accumulators were not yet properly charged after the car's long inactivity. But when we had eventually arrived I realized that here I had met my Waterloo. There was no vestige of the bridge left, only the remains of the centre pier in the middle of the river, which formed an island and the water was swirling down on each side, deep and swift. The first span I might have managed all right; it was only about 15 feet to the pier but on the other side the span was at least three times that distance and the river flowing like a millrace right up to a perpendicular bank on the other side.

I waded out to the island only with great difficulty as the strength of the current nearly swept me off my feet and there I sat down on a boulder and looked at those 15 yards of the swirling Ponfi between me and home. It was a bright moonlight night with the moon nearly full so that everything showed up as clear as daylight; on the other side I could see the start of the open road to Tete with no more difficulties ahead. But how to get there unless the car grew wings overnight! I sat there for an hour or two in the warm night thinking things out but could only come to one conclusion, which was to go back to Matenji and start off again on another hunt until the end of the rainy season. If I could have collected 40 or 50 boys I would have managed; that number would have been able to lift the car right across, but I was afraid that with fewer they might give up the attempt half way across and leave me to be carried away by the flood. It was a lamentable conclusion to come to after overcoming so much

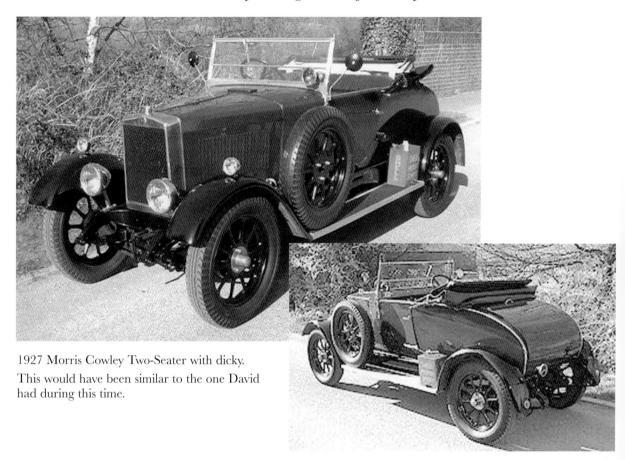

1927 Morris Cowley Two-Seater with dicky.
This would have been similar to the one David
had during this time.

already, but I was forced to it; there was no way round the difficulty unless I could collect the large number of natives I wanted. So back I went to the car, fixed up my camp bed and had a meal of bread and jam and tried to go to sleep at which time mosquitoes and hippo-flies tried to attack me through my mosquito net which I had swathed round my head. I gave up the struggle for sleep about midnight and walked down to the river with a rifle on my shoulder and sat down on my boulder to rehearse things in my mind over again. But there was no way out of it. Two canoes lashed together might have got me across, a raft — it was a risk I was not prepared to take in that current, so at last I walked sorrowfully back to the car and slept until broad daylight when the local native chief came up to pay his respects. He told me he could collect 15 or 20 boys to help and that if I wanted more I must write to Muchena where there were plenty. But would they come? I asked — to be told that if the Senhor of the Boma told them to they would have to come. Now the Senhor of the Boma was on a visit to Tete I knew as I had been informed so by the Bivars at Matenji and even had he been there, would he have stirred a finger to help anyone so unimportant as myself? What about canoes? I asked him but he said there was only one small one there and no other on the river nearer than Tete.

So there was only one thing to be done and at about 11 a.m. we loaded up the car again, turned round and started off back again to Matenji, getting in at 2.30 p.m. The river crossing gave us not much difficulty this time but we were not without hard work getting up the hill and sticking on dambos wet and sticky from recent rain. Every time we had to stop we had perforce to off-load to help the car and hump our heavy kit over the bad parts and I was heartily sick of it by the time we reached the last hill. There disaster nearly overtook us completely. We had stuck on the very worst slope of the hill, a gradient of about 1 in 7 I should think, so I put stones behind the back wheels and started taking off the loads. As the car grew lighter its centre of gravity changed and just as I had taken out the last box it jumped the stones I had put behind the wheels and started going backwards. I made one frantic rush for the brakes but was too late and the car, rapidly gaining speed, ran down the hill backwards. I shall never forget that moment as long as I live. There we were, Frazer and I in the middle of the road with our loads all round us and our only hope of transport back to Nyasaland whirling to destruction before our eyes. It was a long hill and steep with a river at the foot and if the car reached that it meant a fall over the drift to be smashed to pieces on the boulders of the river bed. Just as it was nearing the river, three hundred yards away, some inequality of the road swung round the front wheels and, going at 30 or 40 miles an hour, it leapt the small embankment of the roadside and disappeared into the long grass of the bush where it gradually bumped to a standstill.

I went forward to see what had happened expecting to find the car smashed to bits but by the most wonderful luck it hadn't even turned turtle and there we found it swathed in grass but still standing on its wheels. I didn't dare look for damage just then but went straight to the switch and when cranked up — the car started, I climbed into the driving seat, put the gears in — it answered and began moving off. We had to hoe out the embankment to regain the road but once there the car took the hill like a bird. It was absolutely unhurt in any way and a thorough inspection at the top showed me no sign of any damage — what wonderful luck and what a testimonial to the strength of design of Morris cars.

That was our last excitement. From the hill top we could see Matenji House a mile or two off, so we loaded up the car for the last time and made our garage a few minutes later, tired out, hungry and covered with mud from head to heels.

What an O.D.T.A.A. Christmas to have spent! I have been writing this at odd times on the 27th and 28th which I have spent resting and making preparations for my move back to my camp on the Bandi. Perhaps luck will be with me this time and I shall yet shoot my 13th elephant in Portuguese territory. I am not going to worry any more about my licence; I have done my best to procure it and on advice from the Bivars will carry on until it arrives. I can do nothing else, anyway, as it is unthinkable to stay here until it should arrive.

December 29th, 1928

Still at Matenji trying to find carriers and enjoying the rest and change of climate up here. I tried to get the Bivars to allow me to make my own commissariat arrangements as I do not wish to trespass on their hospitality more than I can help but that they would not allow, so I am living in their office and having my meals in their house, very comfortably. They instructed me in a childish card game one evening which they dealt and played 'widdershins' in which fashion they told me all round games are played in Portugal.

Bivar himself is an interesting man and we discuss all sorts of topics, from astronomy to world politics, through the medium of the Senhora who must get very bored at our conversation. All the same I want to get off again as quickly as I can and back to my little grass shack. I suppose I shall have about four months this time and am planning to send a boy to Blantyre to renew my stock of necessary supplies. Socks and shoes are the most important things I need and I must just do without the luxuries of wheat flour and jam which I had before.

'BUF'

KUDU

WATERBUCK

PUKU

'NYAMA'

151

1929

January 5th(?), 1929

I've lost count of the date! This is somewhere about right and must suffice. I failed completely to get porters at Matenji — my own fault because I went the wrong way about it. I was fed up with cajoling Brother Blackman and took the other line of telling the chief to send me boys for my loads and writing down their names as he gave me them. I was, I confess, hoping that Bivar would help me by ordering them to come in as he is authorized to do by the Portuguese Government; but he made no offer to do so as I still think he might have, so about the 31st I went off again with Frazer and a couple of boys and one piccanin who were all who had volunteered service with me. I took a different line this time to avoid the steep climbs to Msatwe and am writing this at a little farm belonging to a two anna Portuguese where I've been since the New Year. He is named 'Chipazi' — Big Foot — by the natives because he walks about in hob-nailed boots and leaves his tracks all around the district. It was here that I renewed my flour supply a few weeks ago and I find that he has also all sorts of other foodstuffs for sale at quite reasonable prices, so I'm going to send regularly for them when I get back to the Bandi. My delay in returning there is of course the carrier question still, but I'm not in any hurry this time so am not impatient. I shall get the boys eventually. I'm on a pretty strong wicket with friend Chipazi or Signor José Fernandez as he informs me is his real name. I've promised him 25 rounds of Mauser ammunition and six photographs of himself, wives and progeny if he gets me to the Bandi River with my loads.

This is a most appealing bribe to him and he lost no time in fetching my traps from Matenji when I had come to that arrangement with him. The boys who fetched them arrived yesterday and of course refused point-blank to go any further but José Fernandez is not going to lose his photographs or his ammunition if he can help and I expect he will produce boys in a day or two. I had a touch of malaria the day after I arrived here but managed to shake it off easily with large doses of quinine. It was just one of my usual spells which I have been wonderfully clear of for the last year or two. A slight fever one day rising in the evening; a head-aching

153

and bone-aching sort of night, disappearing completely next morning to reappear greatly reduced next evening and the third day OK again. My ankle, by the way, is now on the mend I hope. It burst on the last morning's walk into Matenji leaving a largish septic ulcer which I've been treating ever since. It is not in the least painful now so does not inconvenience me. I think the walk did it more good than harm as it brought things to a head more quickly. Today I've been strolling round looking for nests and had great luck in taking four clutches of eggs — three species — all of which were new to me. I found a pipit nest this afternoon — yet another variety of 'Prinia' warbler of some sort but my luck had by then departed as it contained youngsters and one egg which I took in hopes that it should prove to be addled, but I found that the youngster was just about to hatch out so returned it to the nest. The boys brought me in some fungoid growths today which they announced to be good food. They were like the tiny little toadstools one often finds round dead trees at home growing in great numbers. I didn't think they were yet sufficiently hating me enough to want to kill me off so I tried them for lunch and found them very good indeed. Another mushroom I ate on the way to Matenji also looked evilly poisonous, but as the boys were all eating them by the handful and appearing to relish them greatly I told Frazer to cook a few bits of the smaller ones for my supper, they too had a fine flavour even better than an English mushroom, which one would not expect from a fungus the size of one of these double sheets of paper, grey, darkening into brown on top and pure white underneath.

January 8th, 1929

Friend Chipazi informs me that this is Monday the 8th so I was only one day out. He has promised to let me have five boys this morning for my loads, but we woke up to a drizzling rain and the worst sort of weather which delays me once more. I shall be very glad to see my grass shack on the Bandi again and be able to get comfortable. I've bought some potatoes, beans and onions here but have been unable to buy rice or flour owing to this man's dilatory sort of way of doing business. I told him I wanted these the first day I arrived here but he has been so slow in sending for the rice and in drying out the flour on these only two fine days that we have had that I shall have to move off without them. His excuses were that he was very worried as one of his labourer's wives had died. I asked what was the cause but he didn't know. The death occurred the night before last, there was much tramping about and lighting of torches towards midnight so I went out to see what was wrong to find Senhor José and his boys hunting for something on the ground by the light of their guttering torches. Asking what was lost, I was told they were searching for the 'excrement of dogs' as some medicine for this poor woman or her husband who was also sick. Next morning after much thought he came to me and said that he could not understand the cause of the poor woman's dying and asked me if I thought leprosy could be the trouble. It turned out that the husband was sick with this complaint so the supposition was more than likely with the combination of the remedy offered.

What joy it will be to get back to more civilized sort of food. I refuse to buy hens here at enormous prices, so my diet consists of beans and potatoes which is a very indigestible substance to live on and though I eat vast quantities of them feel always that some vitamin is missing though I am full internally to the brim. It is better that way though than to be always hungry as I was at Matenji. There the menu was not very different, but their meal times were strange and I never seemed to have enough to eat. I think I outwore my welcome there and I know I was glad to depart.

I wish I could remember some of the priceless gems of speech and phrase which the Senora let fall but I have a bad memory for such things and can only remember her description of a tetse fly which has 'a bloody belly — something dreadful' after feeding on you. That and a harrowing tale of how a father and big brother slew a wretched hippopotamus confined in a small pool of the Ponfi River whilst daughter and little brother stood round in admiration. How dangerous it was and the hippopotamus was a really dangerous animal — did I know? I'm sure I heard this tale when I arrived there first and will bet I hear it again when I leave for Tete.

The funeral cortege of the woman who died the other night has just passed with much yelling and beating of drums. It seemed more like a marriage ceremony than a funeral.

January 11th, 1929

I moved out of Chipazi's leprous establishment on the afternoon of the 9th and got into Msatwe in the evening. My carriers were my three own boys and six others given me by Chipazi to see me to the Bandi, so he got his ammunition all right. At Msatwe I bought some fowls, but with difficulty because I'm getting short of small change and the Portuguee native is wise enough to dislike his own coinage; but as it is their own filthy money anyway they have no right to expect always to be paid in good British silver. I believe, strictly speaking, one is not supposed by the Portuguese authorities to pay natives in anything but Portuguese paper money but it is a law more observed in breaking than compliance.

I arrived at my camp on the Bandi about midday yesterday, much to my satisfaction; it was really quite like getting home again after the discomforts of the last three weeks and I woke up this morning with that pleasant feeling of satisfaction with life that one has the first morning after one arrives at home for a holiday. I shot a reedbuck close to camp in the evening and didn't it taste well after a diet of beans?

Today I've been cleaning up guns and rifles while the boys have been getting the camp into decent order again, darning and washing my blankets and garments which they sorely needed. I've sent a note in to Macheso to tell him I want Yokani again and to see if we can't come to some arrangement about our supplies of maize flour. I also sent a note into Imarenga Boma to tell the man there, who I hear is an Indian, that I have returned and to hurry up with my licence. I shall be in a bit of a hole if he tells me I cannot shoot until it arrives or that no more licences are being given in this part! But I'm not anticipating that and anyway these things might be arranged.

January 11th, 1929

This morning I found a nest of Shelley's francolin just as I was leaving camp on a look for game. There were six eggs in it and the nest seemed very obvious, very little attempt being made at concealment. The bird was not in evidence at the place, so having marked it down I went on to see what game was about. At about 11 a.m. we returned camp-wards having seen absolutely nothing, nor was there much spoor about which was disappointing after the long rest the country round here has had. On my way we revisited the francolin's nest but this time though I was looking straight at the spot where it was, near the tree we had marked, I could not see it. Another of Nature's camouflage effects, the hen bird was sitting on the nest simply blotted it from view and it was not until I was within a foot of her that I could make her out. I believe I could then have caught her in my hand so close did she sit for a 'shooing' noise did not dislodge her nor did a bit of stick which I threw and which landed right on top of her.

At about midday I went out again by myself taking a rifle with me instead of a shot-gun which I more usually take on these occasions. This time I went south and found buffalo spoor on an elephant path that runs east and west about a mile away. This I followed up for a bit and found it was pretty fresh having been left that morning. Cursing myself for not having come that way before, I considered what was to be done — go back to camp for boys or follow up myself, but finally came to the conclusion that as time was getting on my best chance of seeing them was to shape for a dambo which they might have been making for, lying a mile or so east. This I did, going through a foul country to walk in, thick grasses and low growing bushes through which one had to plough one's way, continually being tripped up by the old dead and dry stems of last year and getting scratched painfully by the thorns which every shrub in Africa seems to bear. I was greatly helped by the elephant tracks that led through it. A large herd of jumbo had paid this country a visit during my absence, we saw plenty of week-old spoor this morning and the tracks I found were only a couple of days old. All of which is annoying but speaks better luck for the future. When I arrived at the dambo I found more elephant spoor about, but a little further on came on that of the buffalo herd again much to my delight — my prognostication of their behaviour was not at fault. This I proceeded to follow and soon came on the place where they had lain down a short time before, but now they had moved on and shortly afterwards left the dambo and their tracks led round the base of a hill through the bush. I was not any too confident of my capability of getting up to them, tracking has to be a pretty speedy operation especially with buffalo on the move but I forged ahead as fast as I could until I came on some dung which to my great delight I found warm to the touch. Until then I had not had much hope really of seeing the herd but now I began to think otherwise and that if my luck held I was going to collect a buffalo single-handed. I went on for another mile or two carefully and then went astray on some stony ground in a slight depression between two ridges. While I was casting round to pick up the tracks again I heard a trampling sound in the bush ahead and lo and behold there was my herd of buffalo doubling in their tracks and coming over the ridge ahead. I was plain to view standing out in the open and the leading bulls saw me as soon as I saw them. They were some 50 yards off only and luckily stopped as soon as they saw me, giving me time to put in a shot at the chest of the largest bull. He dropped to my shot and the whole herd wheeled round and galloped off like thunder out of sight over the ridge. I hared up that slope as fast as I could, passed the bull I had shot who was lying stone dead and on down the hill on the other side. But fast as I could go, I could not get another glimpse of the herd and the noise of their trampling gradually grew fainter as they left me behind. So back I came to admire the fellow I had got and found he was a pretty fair size in buffaloes with a span of horn larger than anything I have yet shot I reckon, though I have not yet measured him up carefully.

I'll say I was pleased with myself; he was my buffalo from beginning to end with no tracker's aid to discount, so I returned to camp rejoicing.

January 15th, 1929

Yesterday was spent bringing in the buffalo, my three boys and two piccanins managed it in three journeys, four altogether with the load they brought yesterday. Two boys can just manage one hind leg of a large buffalo, while the foreleg is a good single load. Today the boys have been cutting up and smoking the meat while I went off with a shot-gun to look for a particular crake which I've noticed from time to time in marshy places. I was successful in getting it and collected also a bittern which I had not noticed before in these parts. I can't quite work him out but think he is *Ardetta payesii*. (Turned out to be *Ardetta minuta*, the European little bittern and not *Ardetta payesii*, the resident form.) The crake was *Crex egregia*, the South African variety of our own familiar corncrake. He is a much darker bird in colour and should not be mixed up with the latter species which one also comes across occasionally here at this time of the year. I am running short of shot-gun cartridges which is a serious matter. I have written to W in Nyasaland asking him to send me some, but if they don't arrive by the end of the month I shall send a boy to Blantyre to get them. Life would lose a lot of its charm if I had not the wherewithal to collect birds.

Macheso came in this evening with an answer to my letter to Furancungo Boma. The fellow tells me I may shoot game but no elephants, as he writes it, until my licence comes from Tete. Funny thing how one is always on the wrong side of the law when after jumbo. One is either poaching or shooting elephants under weight or doing something for which one might be called over the coals.If I do meet jumbo before the arrival of my licence — shall I leave him alone after waiting for him all this time? We will not anticipate but somehow I think he would be in the bag and a silence preserved until such time as it was lawful to produce the ivory.

No women have as yet come to camp to barter for meat which is rather troubling me — man cannot live on meat alone. He wants his maize flour to keep him happy. The reason I think is that the villagers are nearing the end of their yearly supply and the new crop is not yet bearing. Still I think they will come when they hear there is buffalo meat in camp. I tried to come to some understanding with Macheso to keep me in continual supply but he said he couldn't do it himself as he hadn't enough flour to last out the year. This is obviously not true as they are still making moa — native beer — in the villages and as this is made from maize it is not done when there is a food shortage. I don't know quite what his trouble is but think he just considers he can get more out of me by carrying on in the old fashion. Moa, itself, by the way, is not a bad drink once one has got the taste of it as I'm ashamed to say I have. It's just maize flour watered and fermented; but a real poisonous drink is the spirit they distil from it. Master José Fernandez gave me some at his place the other day. It is like a very bad and evil-smelling gin combined with rotten eggs to taste but not so potent as one would expect though I daresay he had watered down our tots a bit. He told me he sometimes made some, distilling it through an old rifle barrel, but was insistent in assuring me that it was very rare for him to drink it and that he was no drunkard!

January 17th, 1929

I read a story in Blackwood's once by 'Fundi', called 'The Man-eating Elephant', it was a good tale but I don't suppose it was ever intended to be taken for truth. The elephant is no carnivore though a really nasty one might on an occasion so disintegrate a human as to appear as if he had been chewing him up. But today I really thought I had found some grounds for belief in Fundi's tale of elephants who forsake a herbacious diet for one of flesh and blood. I came on the spoor of a herd of jumbo which I judged to be some 36 hours old and after following for a minute or two only came on the place where they had been standing and there in the centre of the trampled space, lying in the midst of a pool of dried blood, was the chewed up tail of a hartebeest. This was sufficiently startling but a little further on we came on the remains of the freshly killed hartebeest itself, lying right on the elephants' tracks and the grass trampled down all round. I looked at my hunter in amazement, to see that he was almost ashen in countenance. Such a thing was 'medicine' of the very worse description and he begged me to come away before the hartebeest's fate overtook us also. However we proceeded to investigate — I had no thought of following up the herd who were too far in the lead for me — but search as hard and carefully as we could we were able to find no trace of other spoor than that of the elephants. There was a solid carpet of flattened grass all round the place and nothing shows up on that sort of substance. Finally we began slowly retracing our steps towards the place were we had found the tail, but that was no go and it was not until we had quartered the vicinity in every direction that my hunter at last found on a bare piece of ground what we were in search of — fresh lion spoor — and so the mystery was solved and a good tale spoiled. I need hardly add that my hunter was then careful to declare that he knew it had been a lion all the time.

January 18th, 1929

The bag today consists of a quail (*Excalfactoria adansoni*) and the cape grass owl (*Tyto capensis*), both of which I am glad to get as they are not common birds. I found the owl devouring a rat in the middle of a marshy bit of ground and was attracted to him by his loud snores of alarm which he uttered at my approach. I wish I had had one of these birds in my shack last night when tragedy would not have befallen my egg collection. A brute of a rat came and browsed on my eggs, destroying about half a dozen warblers' eggs and five out of six francolins' eggs I took the other day. Thank goodness he didn't do worse damage, if he had attacked my other box I should have been miserable for weeks. Frazer has just rushed in to me in alarm to say that he has been bitten by a tetse fly. Clever of him to have just realized at the end of four months that there were such things about camp. I suppose that means he will be sick for a day or two.

Must seriously try to get some game tomorrow — the buffalo is now too high for my liking. Mushrooms are a great standby at such times and I eat enormous quanities of them but they aren't a readily digestible form of food. I feel I owe a large debt of gratitude to my interior economy for the way in which it plays up to all sorts of varied diet!

January 20th, 1929

Shot a wart hog and a reedbuck today but a deuce of a long way from camp. Yesterday was a blank day though I went for a long walk round the country nearer at hand, I saw nothing at all except a little stembuck who got my wind just as I was drawing a bead on him. A hyena came right into camp the night before last and stole some dried buffalo meat out of a hut where it had been smoking. I tried to fix a trap for him but had no success. I shall try for him again some night as this sort of thing is a bit too much when meat is scarce. The difficulty is, I find, to fix a sufficiently easy running string on the hair trigger of a rifle, some sort of rat trap gate might work things better. I wish someone would bring out an unfailing remedy for the healing of septic scratches. I find them very hard to treat. I have one starting on my knee now, which though still very small may grow into any size of ulcer by the time it has done its worst. Iodine and pot-permang. don't seem to have any effect. I try opening them up a bit with a razor blade but think my half-baked attempts at phlebotomy probably do more harm than good.

Tomorrow is, I think, the Sabbath, so we will treat it as such and have a rest. No boy has arrived yet from Senor Chipazi with my rice and flour, I expect he is having a burst with that foul gin he gave me a taste of. Extraordinary establishment that was. He himself is a man of some 60 summers, I should say, much blacker of countenance than the ordinary native of these parts, so it is hard to know how much actual Portuguese blood there is in him. I didn't see any of his children, but of his grand-children there was one nearly white beneath the dirt in which he was always encased. His womenfolk were innumerable — all natives of course — amongst them his mother, whom he pointed out to me one day, saying she was 86 years old. I must say she didn't look it. She seemed to be working just as hard as any of the others, pounding up maize cobs in the mortars. Her wool was a bit whitish and her skin and breasts — she was just as naked as any of them — perhaps a bit more wrinkled and shrunk but not remarkably so. I asked if she remembered Livingstone and was told that she did remember him on his journey through in '75. That would have been about five years before his death, so may well have been true. I have never seen natives working so hard as did that establishment of women. Their pestles and mortars were never at rest pounding up either maize, or more generally, the cobs. Chipazi keeps a herd of swine whose food is the bran that is obtained from the pounded maize cobs and very good food it is. Fed to swine the world over, where maize is grown and pigs are kept. In Biblical wording they are of course 'the husks that the swine did eat' of the prodigal son, trying to make a good tale out of an ordinary state of affairs. It can't have been much of a famine that! Chipazi's library of English reading material was amazing. I asked him one afternoon when I had nothing to do if he had any English books he could lend me to read and he produced an English dictionary and a copy of Gilbert White's *Natural History of Selborne*. The latter was a small tome labelled Vol. II of an edition that must have been brought out in many parts. It contained his monograph on the swallows which is always both interesting and amusing to read. He was greatly in love with the theory that swallows hibernated in winter and didn't leave England for warmer climes at all; even advocating the idea that they plunged under water and there remained until the following spring. I wonder how such a book got into Chipazi's hands — I need hardly say that he was quite uninterested in natural history himself and hardly knew the names of the common birds when I asked him about them.

January 21st, 1929

Another confounded touch of malaria came on about 10 a.m. this morning. I think I've got it under, though, with large doses of quinine and aspirin as I'm now, 5 p.m., feeling fairly fit again. It means I must put myself on a course of quinine, though, but I can't be too lavish with it, the medicine is too valuable to be used as a prophylactic when there is only one bottle to last three months.

The boys tell me that a hyena finished off the reedbuck I shot yesterday which is annoying; still I got the greater part of it so things are not so bad. What with hyenas and vultures one has to be pretty quick about getting one's meat in. The vultures were already at the wart hog when the boys went to bring it in yesterday evening. I think I must take a course in butchering the next time I'm in civilization, I never seem to get the proper cuts from any animal. It's all one to the boys of course; the whole is 'nyama' to be treated indifferently or cut up any old way in long strips for smoking. The liver and kidneys of course I can always find and I generally have cold boiled tongue when I have shot game, but where in the name of fortune does the sweetbread lie? I have always understood that the sweetbread was the pancreatic gland lying along the loins at the bottom of the stomach but though I've often made determined attempts I've never been able to find it.

January 23rd, 1929

Sent a letter today to Chipazi with a couple of boys to bring me stores which I'm much in need of. I've been trying to extemporize shot-gun cartridges most of the day. I first considered the possibility of exchanging caps of 9 mm Mauser cartridges of which I have plenty, but found it quite impossible without the necessary tools. So I then set to work turning the Mauser ammunition into shot cartridges. I extracted the bullet, rammed a wad down on about two thirds of the cordite and cut up the bullets into small slugs. I then went out to try my fortune with five cartridges so made up with varying sizes of shot or rather slugs but found they didn't fly straight to deal with a small bird, so I then set about trying to mould small shot. I got an old tin and bored a hole in it the size of a no. 8 shot and then melted lead over a hot fire until it was soft enough to pass drop by drop through the hole and into another tin of cold water underneath. I found this process took a long time and is not altogether satisfactory in result, but I'm hoping the shot will be round enough to fly straight. I shall try it out tomorrow when I have made more.

January 25th, 1929

Saw *Melittophagus bullockoides* on the Lingove today, a bee-eater that I have not seen before in the flesh. A beautiful green-backed bird with a bright red throat. I spent one of my last precious cartridges trying to obtain it but missed. I must make up my mind now only to try for birds whom I cannot recognize on the wing.

Shortly after I arrived back in camp, four loads came from Chipazi with my stores of flour, rice, beans and a couple of bunches of bananas — what luxuries to have all at the same time. I am still making shot at odd intervals and do not intend to try it out until I have enough for five or six cartridges when we shall be able to test it thoroughly and see if its going to be worth the trouble to make it or not.

January 26th, 1929

Shot another reedbuck today but though we covered it well with branches and grass and the boys were back to bring it in within a couple of hours, the vultures had already disposed of most of it. There was not a solitary one to be seen in the sky when I left to go back to camp after shooting it and I thought we could safely leave it but the cunning brutes must have been watching us the whole time from somewhere miles overhead and have dropped down as soon as they saw us safely out of the way. It's a serious business. I can ill afford to lose meat regularly like this; the vultures seem to have increased enormously during the time I was away from here, before, I used rarely to bother to cover up game I had shot and I cannot recall ever having lost any, but now I see we can't leave an animal alone for half an hour without their coming for it.

January 30th, 1929

Went off early this morning for a very long tramp in the direction where I got my only eland bull when I was here previously. I thought we might come across more signs of game in that neighbourhood as I rarely pay it a visit, but saw even less sign of stuff than I do here at the Bandi. I registered a great success, though, in shooting the black coucal (*Centropus nigrorufus*) which is a very rare bird and one that I've only once seen previously and then missed badly with both barrels. This time I spotted it flying towards us whilst we were walking in line up a marshy dambo on the look-out for marsh-loving birds. It came up to about 100 yards of us and then dived down into the thick stuff on spotting us. We went forward to the place and succeeded in flushing it after a minute or two of anxiety on my part, but that was nothing to the harrowing time that followed my dropping it. I rushed to the place calling to the boys to hurry up, but though I thought I had kept my eyes glued to the spot where it fell there was not a feather to be seen, search as hard as we knew. We searched for over an hour before finding it and only got it then because I set the boys to work cutting the grass all round with their knives. Extraordinary how a bird of pretty large size could remain undiscovered like that even though the grass was thick there. I was just about to give it up altogether thinking I had perhaps only wounded it and need hardly say I was greatly delighted when at last one of the boys produced it out of a clump of grass which we must have searched before ten times over.

After that we went on to another dambo which I have never visited before — I thought I was making for home but must have been going badly askew for from there we could see one of our land marks — the hill with the boulders on top — quite close at hand and in quite the wrong direction! Here I shot another reedbuck. I took a running chance at about 150 yards and bowled him over which was rather a pleasing effort. I wish, though, the bigger game were as easily found — reedbuck, of course, as their name implies live on the dambos and streams where there are thick grasses and reeds the whole year round and can generally be found; but other game keeps to the high bush when there is feeding for them and can only be found on the dambos during the dry weather. Nowadays it is sheer luck to bump into a herd, in fact since arriving back here for the second time, beyond the herd of buffalo, I have only seen one herd of sable and a solitary hartebeest.

February 1st, 1929

Once again out of action with another of these foul veldt sores as there are called, they are difficult and painful things to treat and I don't yet seem to have struck the right way of dealing with them. I open them up with a razor blade and then jam in hot permanganate poultices which seems to be the only thing to do. If you leave them alone they take about a week to burst of their own accord and there is then a much larger wound to heal.

February 8th, 1929

It's taken a week to get these beastly things on the road to recovery. One knee was swollen up rather painfully and enforced complete inaction.

Today was my first time out of camp when I went for a short walk in the morning but failed to find game. There is little to do when one is laid up in camp. I study my bird books which always give entertainment and at times read John Locke to try and derive benefit therefrom but find that my poor mind is continually wandering from the theme in hand and I make out according to him that when that is the case one is on the road to the nearest lunatic asylum. Bacon is more helpful and tells one to study the mathematicians to remedy this evil of thought wandering, but that would call for a very serious interest on a man's part to remedy the evil and improve his understanding. To prevent thought wandering one must either, I feel, be interested in the subject one is reading or else have some ulterior motive of benefits to be obtained that will drive one to concentrate.

February 10th, 1929

I shot another cuckoo yesterday which is new to me — *Clemator jacobinus* — he is really a very common bird and I see has a large range, taking in Southern Asia as far as Assam and Burma, but it is only recently that the species has been in evidence round here. I am again short of boys — two of the three who came with me from Matenji I allowed to depart at the end of their month's work, they were not satisfied with their pay of 6/- a month and said they wanted 8/- which I cannot afford. There is little work here for boys — I have quite given up hopes of elephant, so that they spent most of their time sitting in their huts singing songs.

February 11th, 1929

Extraordinary how things work out — I had just finished writing yesterday that I had quite given up hope of jumbo and was lying down reading. I heard Frazer sending off the piccanins to get some firewood but paid little attention. It was whilst I was browsing on Bacon's essay, *Of Adversity* 'Certainly if miracles be the command over nature they appear most in adversity' that I heard them returning in a great state of excitement and chattering to Frazer in the kitchen at the back of my hut.

'What Ho!' thought I 'Nyama'. They had probably seen a lot of harte-beest, or even with luck, buffalo which it would behove me to go and investigate. But on my calling to them and asking what the trouble was, they came up with three or four green and trampled leaves in their hands saying that they had found last night's elephant spoor on the hill side close by. I will confess I was not deeply thrilled by their news. The day was getting on — about 1.30 p.m. I suppose and my former experience of jumbo in these parts had taught me what they consider to be a short day's walk. Still calling for my dilapidated walking attire (my socks now consist of the leg part only, which I draw over the sole of my foot and my veldtschoen have soles of new buffalo hide wired or tied to the uppers in ungainly fashion) and loading up the 8 mm with solid, I went off with 'Mafio' the eldest piccanin, a boy of about 10 years old. He is rather a likeable character, very shy of me originally, and always fighting with the other piccanins in the most frantic of tempers. I often take him out with me of an afternoon with a shot-gun and think he brings me luck! I could not help thinking as we went off to find spoor how times had changed and what an insufficient little party we were to deal with a herd of the mightiest of creatures. Time was when I went hunting with a heavy rifle, a gun-bearer to carry a spare, four good and experienced trackers and two askaris well armed in case of accident! now, just a ten year old boy and myself with a light rifle slung over my shoulder. But I now have, if I may say so without any boastfulness — two things at my command worth all of such an army, experience and confidence, without which to have proceeded in such a style on the tracks of an elephant would have been mere folly.

We picked up the spoor of the herd about ten minutes out of camp and Mafio surrendered the lead to me as we set off along the tracks. There was little difficulty in following, the elephants had left a broad trail behind them over the freshly trampled grass and it was obviously, as he had diagnosed, spoor of the night before. We soon left the comparatively open bush which lies round my camp and our way led through that foul country, which I have often previously described, to the south. This country is worse now to walk in than ever it was. Last year's dead undergrowth has not yet rotted completely and this year's tall grass, bushes, wiry pliant creepers and thorns are well up. Still, our rate of progress was pretty good and we had little difficulty in following down the broad lane that the elephants had driven through it all. I was not at all confident of getting up to them at the end of an hour's hard going; the dung, though it then showed less sign of being broken up and buried by those scavenger beetles, was still pretty well dried up on top, and it had been a cloudy day. More hopeful signs were that the tracks no longer led straight to the front in one broad lane, but twisted about in all directions of the compass, often re-crossing each other and the herd was not going 'en masse', but had split up into more individual tracks. At about 3 p.m. we came down a hill side on to a large marshy dambo overgrown with tall elephant grass 12 to 15 feet in height and at one point here I was all but giving things up and going back to camp. We had emerged on to an open salt lick after about half an hour's ploughing through this vile swamp and ahead of us I could see our way led through it again. But, persisting, we plunged into it once more and zigzagged about again in the water and mire. It is curious how complete a gate is closed on one set of tracks in such a country when fresher ones cross it, one comes suddenly on a wall of half trampled reed and grass stems that present a barrier to one's progress and they have to be pushed and pulled aside before one can get back on the main road, so to speak, lying beyond them. We finally pulled out of the swamp on to slightly higher ground on the left which was comparatively open and the tracks led on, skirting the edge by about 20 yards. Thankful for such mercies we forged ahead, making better time. It was very shortly afterwards that I heard a — something from somewhere ahead — nothing I could define, just something vague that might have been a small branch, up rooted with recent rain, falling to the ground; that might have been the wind in the reed stems, or yet again — the rumble of a feeding elephant.

I stopped, but could hear nothing more and turning saw that my small companion was not a bit interested. I could not yet believe that we were close up or that the sound I had heard was really — what it might have been. I had recently been testing the dung which was obviously much fresher, but there was no vestige of warmth to it — still, with a herd circling about and re-crossing its tracks as this one had been doing — ? I went on more cautiously and then came right on them, before I knew where I was.

One animal was feeding in the open bush about thirty yards away to the left and ahead of me. He was a large size in elephants and his tusks — just shootable. The rest of the herd were right on the edge of the swamp mostly hidden by a bamboo thicket which grew right down to the edge of the tall grass. Here was a conundrum to be worked out. I knew from the tracks that there certainly could not have been more than two shootable elephants in the herd — more probably one only, of any real size. The elephant on my left was certainly one of the largest — would there, or would there not, be a larger one hidden by the bamboos and the tall grasses of the swamp in the centre of the rest of the herd? I could see two of these from time to time and they were lamentably small, but how to get a sight of the remaining six or eight ahead? It would have been folly to have turned down hill to my right and come in on the herd from the swamp, I could have seen nothing and probably have only alarmed them — madness to have continued ahead between the elephant on my left and the rest of the herd. He would have got my wind long before I was sufficiently ahead to see any of the herd leaders. There were obviously only two things to be done, either shoot this elephant on the left who was a gift from the gods standing as he was, out in the open, or else wait for him to get ahead again and rejoin the herd in the swamp when I could get forward myself after they had passed the bamboo thicket and see of what the rest of the herd consisted. I weighed these two alternatives for some minutes, while I watched our friend on the left and saw him pushing a tree over by leaning on it with his shoulder. What were the pros and cons of either step. I was offered a 'snap' at a smallish elephant — was it worth while exchanging that for a chance of getting a shot at a very problematical larger? If I had already slain the odd jumbo in these parts I would probably have waited, but as it was, I came to the conclusion that a bird in the hand was worth a larger in a bamboo thicket. The wind, too, was a bit choppy and might give away my presence at any minute, so I made up my mind and came forward to deal with my elephant. He had been rather uneasy in his mind for the last minute or two, swaying round first in one direction and then another and was gradually approaching the herd. I came right forward and had my rifle up once or twice for a chance at the side of the head and could have dropped him probably at any moment, but I wanted an absolutely still one shot affair to leave me quite free to deal with another should I get the chance.

Finally I think he caught a glimpse of me for he swung round and stood stock still facing me about 15 yards off and gave me the chance I was waiting for and I dropped him with the frontal shot to the brain.

There is little more to be told. The herd made off at my shot crossing the swamp and swinging round in the bush at the further side. As they crossed over I saw one other shootable elephant in the herd and he was certainly a bit bigger than the fellow I had downed but I think on the whole I was wise to have taken the one I did with such an excellent opportunity. I rushed off myself after them in hopes that I might come up with the big fellow but could not get forward quickly enough owing to the fact that there were two smallish bulls who would not run away but stood about aimlessly in the middle of the swamp quite un-alarmed, as if they did not know what the report of a rifle was. I suppose the poor brutes were not used to salvoes of fire from bigger batteries; either that or else they were constituting a very efficient rear guard to the retreat of the remainder, if one can assign an elephant with sense great enough to think of such a thing.

So I left them alone and came back with Mafio — (who had been my shadow the whole time, except when I was actually shooting the elephant) — to the beast I had killed, where I congratulated him on his great stoutness of heart. This was the first elephant he had ever seen and he had acted the whole time perfectly naturally and with a coolness that would have put to shame many a hunter that it has been my fortune to deal with.

We started off campwards soon afterwards, and a weary enough walk it was. It is one thing to walk down elephant tracks in the direction the herd is taking and quite another to retrace their steps backwards. The grass and trampled bushes all lie the wrong way and so impede one's progress greatly and one is continually jabbing one's bare shins and knees on dried grass stems and thorny snags.

About half way home we came on the tracks of the retreating herd and as they were making in our direction I, with relief, but unwisely as it happened, turned along them. For although they helped us a good bit on our way we finally had to leave them where they swung round again in the wrong direction and we then had to plough our way unaided by any path. I will draw a veil over the proceedings of the last hour, for my bad language did little to help blast our way ahead — suffice it that we did eventually arrive in camp just as night fell and our troubles were soon forgotten in tea, a hot bath and in contemplation of our success.

But now the next question is — what of a licence? I can get no answer to my letters to Tete, so don't know if they are sending me my new licence or not. I shall keep very quiet about this affair, we will lose the meat and the commodities we could buy with the sale of it, but whatever happens, the bloke in charge at Furancungo must not hear and if I sent for boys to come and bring in the meat the news that I had shot an elephant would be round the country in no time. It's really lucky that I am out of boys at the moment — Frazer will hold his tongue all right, and I only hope the piccanins will have the gumption to do likewise but — 'Ye gods and little elephants' why is it that one is always a bit shy of the law? Still, it adds to the excitement of life.

Today I have sent off Frazer with the two children to bring in some meat and am keeping camp alone. Things are delightfully restful and peaceful. A band of 'Pui' monkeys have just paid me a visit and made faces at me from the trees over my water pool, while the little emerald spotted doves (*Chalcospelia afra*) come down for pickings on the bare ground by my verandah. There are three of them together just now as I write, creeping about within five yards of me. I don't know why the boys are so late in getting back and fear they must be attempting to cut out a tusk which I did not want them to do, as they have no experience in that art they would only make a mess of things, whereas by waiting three or four days we shall be able to draw them both easily enough.

February 12th, 1929

I saw a new kingfisher today (*Halcyon Cyanoleucus*) who has not been in evidence round here before, though I may have seen him and taken him for *Halcyon Orientalis*, which is fairly common. There is not much difference to be seen between the two birds with the naked eye, unless one catches the greenish sheen which appears over the whole surface of the back of *Halcyon Cyanoleucus* in certain lights. Studying a bird at rest under binoculars one's guide is this bird's black lower mandible and red upper, as opposed to the completely red bill of the other. This is the seventh kingfisher I have noticed for this part of the world which is profusion compared to our single British species, though by no means the full tale of the African.

Febuary 13th, 1929

Walked down to the Bandi this morning but saw nothing I wanted. I am alone here with Frazer as we have sent the two piccanins into Macheso's to buy flour, with many injunctions to ensure silence. My fear is that the native may recognize the taste of the meat and brow beat these poor children into an admission. But I don't think that is likely. If a native's powers of taste are as poor as his powers of scent — except objectively — and touch, then we have no fear at all.

At about 4 p.m. this afternoon after a cup of tea I went out for a stroll round camp and lo and behold came right on fresh elephant spoor within 500 yards of camp. I rushed back, seized a rifle and began following up. The spoor was absolutely fresh, only an hour or two old at the most and some dung I came across an hour later was warm to the touch when I kicked it over. Another hour or two of sunlight would probably have seen me up with them, but the time at my disposal was too short for the jumbo weren't feeding but jogging along ahead at a fair rate of progress and though I put on speed I couldn't get up with them. As it was I found myself badly benighted and had a poorish time finding camp in the dark.

Febuary 14th, 1929

Left camp early and got back on the trail of yesterday's elephants — and then the fun began. I believe they were actually the same two brutes that gave us such a long chase on November 19th and 20th, their tracks were similar, one large bull and a cow and their walking powers any way left nothing between them for I did not stop, nor had they stopped to feed, in the course of eight hours hard going that I now plugged after them. I gave them up in the end on a dambo away to the north east of camp. They had started off due south — and began making tracks for home weary and disgusted but although I was further from camp than I had ever been before in that direction, I thought I knew my way all right and was not expecting another seven hours on my legs — for it was not until 9 or 10 o'clock at night that I eventually got back. Yes! I was lost all right. I was probably not more than three or four hours from home when I gave up the elephant, but all my landmarks were gone or took on a new aspect in that new bit of country that made them hardly recognizable. I have often been mildly lost before, both alone and with natives, but this has been my worst streak as I was lost alone and further afield than I generally wander. There is not much to be told of that weary walk. Once I climbed a round green hill, hoping I would find my bearings from its top but though I did get a line to go on, I nearly exhausted myself in the progress. The hill was bare of all trees and I thought I would have a clear and unobstructed view of the whole district, but I found when I was half way up that, as is so often the case where there is no timber, the undergrowth which looks so flat and smooth is nearly six feet high matted vegetation and every yard has to be fought for and won in one's progress.

It was a nightmare of a place and getting down the other side was worse as I had a longer stretch before I again reached the welcome wood lands. Here I made off in a general westerly direction for the ridge of hills which I thought I had recognized, reaching them about 4.30 p.m. but I was still in absolutely strange country and had found no guide to help me on my way so I had to force myself up another hill for a last attempt to find out where I was and weary as I was it took some effort to make up my mind to that climb after my former experience. This hill was not so bad; it was well timbered and so had no undergrowth to speak of but the steepness of the ascent nearly defeated my weary legs. From the top I could see my hill with the boulders on top lying far away in the east, but search as I would I could not make out my own little hill close to camp. It was here that I made up my mind to a night in the bush; I was nearly played out and hadn't the foggiest idea where I had got to, while the sun was already low in the west and left me only an hour or two's daylight.

I will admit that I here had visions of being properly bushed but pulling myself together, decided that things were not really so bad. There was one of my landmarks plain to view, all I had to do was to make for it and though I had no hope of reaching it that day I could get some distance on the way; I must make up my mind to rather an uncomfortable night, but then next day, after a night's rest, I would surely be able to find out how the land lay by circling round that hill. So off I started once again, it was a mercy that it was the rainy season for I was able to find water in most of the little dambos I crossed, and I was able to refresh myself. Marsh water is not the purest of filtered drinks, but it is at any rate water and what I was badly needing, for the day had been burning hot. Had it been the dry season I think I might have been exhausted long before. Just as it was getting dark I stumbled out on to an elephant path running north and south, which I thought I recognized so I made along it to the south. It was an anxious time, I couldn't be certain of that path in my own mind; at times I thought I recognized things on it at others I was doubtful; but I was borne up by the fact that I came on nothing that I **certainly** did **not** recognize and so I pushed along it until the worst happened for I came on a small thicket of jungle lying to the right of the path that I thought was absolutely strange and I made up my mind that this could not be the path I had first thought it to be. Then I decided to give up trying for that day and made my way down to some low lying ground where I buried my head in a stinking pool and lapped down gallons of that filthy water, but it was dark and it tasted to me like nectar. Then I retraced my steps and lay down on the higher ground by the elephant path from where I had decided to try my last attempt to find camp, for although I was convinced shouting would be of no use, I still had my rifle to fire off in the hope that it would be heard in camp. It would have been no use trying it before, during daylight the boys could only have thought I was firing at game, but now when it was quite dark there was a chance they would hear it in the still of the night and realize what the trouble was.

So presently I fired off a round; it is one thing to fire a shot at game when one's thoughts are merely for the effect of the shot and one doesn't notice the loudness of the report, quite another thing to fire as a signal in the hope of an answer. The strain of listening is almost painful and one's hopes sink lower and lower as second after second passes with no answer.

No good — I took off my shoes and began to compose myself as comfortably as I could for the night cursing myself for my lack of fore-thought in not even having brought a box of matches with me to make a fire, the night was getting cold, which did not improve matters, but at the same time did not prevent the unwelcome attentions of mosquitos who now began to find me out. One last try, I thought, and I again fired off the rifle, the echo of whose report seemed loud enough to wake the dead in the surrounding stillness; but not loud enough apparently, to elicit any response. I must be miles away from camp, much further than I had supposed — and then I heard it — just a faint echo of a shout in the distance, which I could scarcely believe was true and at first put it down to a betrayal of my own senses. But there it was again, louder this time, three detached notes which could leave me no longer in doubt. Once again I fired and this time had my response more quickly, I jumped up, thrust my feet back again into my shoes and made off as hard as I could in its direction. After I had been going again for two minutes I tried once again — when one has so nearly given up hope one wants **proof** and more proof to keep one's spirits up and show one that the whole thing is not a figment of one's own imagination. This time my answer was much nearer and louder and my own shouts were plainly answered.

And so, gradually I made my way to camp, shouting every few minutes to get my line and stumbling on through the darkness. Once or twice I thought I was lost again when my shouts elicited no response, but it was merely, I suppose, when I was on lower ground and my voice did not carry so far.

What delight it was to see the lights of my own camp fire and to meet Frazer who came out to meet me with a flaming grass torch and my camp bed that night seemed to me the most desirable place in the world as I crawled into it after a hot bath and a meal washed down with tea containing a generous tot of whisky.

I don't know what lessons I have learnt from the affair — I know I shall go out alone again and I know that I will not always remember to take matches with me, which seem to me to be the morals of the story — so that unless I can hope that my bump of locality has been thereby improved, the thing will have done me no good at all, which is distressing of it. I am writing this from the safe distance of the 15th, when I look on it quite dispassionately, but there were times yesterday when I would have said that I had learnt those two lessons well enough if only they could have helped me on my road to camp!

February 16th, 1929

Went today with Frazer to draw the tusks. We got the top one out easily enough though even that needed our combined efforts to pull it out. The lower one quite defeated us. We had foolishly not brought an axe as I thought that today, the sixth since shooting it, there would be no difficulty and all that would be required of us would be a few gentle tugs, but not so; F will have to go back again tomorrow or the next day to complete the work. An elephant's carcass at this stage is always rather a pitiable sight — just a solid mass of squirming maggots, but it is a great attraction for charoses butterflies. I saw some beauties round it today of two or three kinds, which would have done a collector's eyes good to have seen. I think I must really start on that game sometime and specialize on this beautiful African genus of charoses only. I suppose one would do more important and useful work in taking up something else, but the charoses alone thrill me with their wonderful colours. Curious how such a beautiful creature is so attracted by such filthy things as rotting flesh and hide and dung, especially leopard dung, which he seems to like more than anything else. Back in camp I've been cleaning and measuring up the tusk we managed to extract and I make out he should weigh some 25 lb., which is better than I expected. Whilst I was at the carcass I made a mental resumé of the whole affair and reconoitered the ground ahead. On the whole I think I should have been wiser to have waited, for the whole herd would have shortly emerged on to a more open bit of ground when I might have had a chance at the big fellow I saw and perhaps have been able to get this fellow also. But it is easy enough to be wise after the event and on the other hand they might just as easily have got my wind and left me with nothing. Anyway post-mortems in this game, as in Bridge, are invidious affairs and do little good. I did not know at the time whether there was a bigger fellow or not and — but 'nuff said, it's time we were picking up our cards for a new hand. I wonder when and where that will be played out.

February 17th, 1929

I was twice hustled out of bed last night by a safari of ants who came and invaded my bed, rendering it untenable. They were not the true 'siaper', the biting driver ants who make short work of anything they meet unable to look after itself in the bush, but something a bit smaller and not quite so vicious; nevertheless they could bite painfully enough when they found a succulent portion of me to browse on and sleep was unthinkable until I had twice shaken out and searched all sheets and blankets and got rid of the last of them. Today I woke up to drizzling rain and a foul sort of morning altogether, but it gives a good excuse for the spending of a lazy day in camp.

February 19th, 1929

Yesterday, having seen nothing in a short walk round camp, I was reduced to blowing up a wretched turtle dove with my rifle as I did not appreciate the thought of another meatless day. Bacon says that beans are a kind of meat; they are — I wonder how he knew — but they get a bit monotonous if it is all the meat one has for days on end. Curious though, in the last two things I have slain with that rifle, and a sad come down from a five ton elephant to a four or five ounce dove. Mafio went with the other picannin to draw the lower tusk and arrived back with it in the afternoon. This was the left tusk and proves, as is usually the case a bit lighter in weight than the right which is the grand tusk as a rule and as it is usually called. It is a curious fact that the grand tusk is nearly always the heavier of the two, one would expect the reverse to be the case, as it gets its name from the fact that the elephant uses it more, just as we use our right hand more than we do our left, and it is generally more blunt and rounded at the tip, but the harder work that it is given only tends to add to its strength and weight unless, of course, he had broken or damaged it in some way.

In the evening I shot a bird which I can't identify and don't even begin to know what it is unless it can possibly be an immature oriole, but I don't think this is likely as there were no signs of immaturity in the plumage and I haven't found true orioles mating here yet. It is not often I am beat to put a bird in its right family but this fellow defeats me entirely even to get as far as that on the road to identification — the lack of vol. 1 Sclater and Stark which contains the earlier families of *passeres* to one of which this bird belongs, is annoying to say the least.

February 21st, 1929

I worked out the bird in the end, it proved to be a female cuckoo shrike (*Campephaga nigra*) which I might have realized before from the stiffened spiny feathers of the rump. Yesterday I went for a very long walk away to the east and right the otherside of Mbanji Hill as the natives call my boulder hill. The little streams that start on the dambos nearer at hand all join together about there and form a considerable sized river. I walked down this river for some miles but saw little sign of game. Funnily enough, just as I was turning round to come back I saw a pair of these same cuckoo shrikes, the male and female birds together and could clearly identify them. The male is a black bird with brilliant metallic green and purple reflections while the female is more olive and grey above, yellow about the wing quills and counts, while the under side is white barred with black and washed with golden yellow.

I crossed the river to come back on the other side in order to vary my walk somewhat and once again, before long, found myself badly astray.

One would have thought a walk down one bank of a stream and up the other would have been pretty well foolproof; but I must have lost touch with my stream and continued up one of those that joins it from the north for I found myself before long on one of the dambos lying north-east of my camp. I have not got all these properly marked on the rough sketch I have drawn of my surroundings here. There are many of them and it is puzzling to know just how they lie. I have often read and heard it remarked how wonderful it was how a native finds his way in the bush. People say that they have a homing instinct and that they recognize trees, which is absurd in thickish bush. I don't think there is any secret to it. A native has been used to walking in the bush since he was a child and knows the country round his village like a book; when he is further afield all he has to go on are the higher hills in the neighbourhood and I have often heard discussions of my hunters of the right line to take from the angle or appearance of some particular hill. He then, admittedly, knows how to keep that right line as he is used to walking in the bush and will not walk round in circles as a white man may do when he gets lost. Beyond this he will recognize dambos, native tracks and elephant paths as he comes on them but not trees unless it is some particularly noticeable one standing by itself in a dambo or else a thicket of msita or heavy bush. Practice at the game and a knowledge of one's surroundings are I am convinced the only two helps to finding one's way in the bush, and of these, long years of the former is the best. When I arrived back here for the second time and went out with any one of my three boys from Matenji, I often had to ask them in which direction camp lay when we had been circling about a few miles away and they would point to any direction of the compass but the right one. Once, with the biggest fool of the three, I changed direction suddenly when we were within 300 yards of camp and then turned and asked him where camp was. He, of course, pointed straight down the line I was taking at the time, in just the opposire direction to camp. All of which shows that when a native is in completely strange surroundings he is just as liable to get lost as anyone. I write all this as some apology for my frequent lapses, for it is annoying to find oneself still apt to go astray after four months in the district and gives me many much longer walks than I had bargained for. Yesterday I did not get back until about 5 o'clock, approaching camp from the north and getting my line from Camp Hill. Things that make such a tramp worth while to my strange mentality are the sights of these cuckoo shrikes which I mentioned before; a bustard of a new variety to me that got up at my feet on my way home and a type of quail (*Excalfactoria adansoni*) a rare bird here which I disturbed in the long grass of a dambo I was crossing and its behaviour bore out the notes that I have previously written on the habits of this species. These are little things that would mean nothing at all to most people, but they will probably lie in my memory for many a year. One of the most vivid memories I have of my leave home three years ago is the sight of a redstart on the road in front of me as I was driving along in my car, a thing that I had probably seen many times before and not noticed particularly, but this time, after an absence of a year or two from home, my memory photographed it and it's there for good. These bird photographs are innumerable, they swarm on me as I write, but I think I might pick from them — my first sight of the beautiful Narina trogon in a glade amongst the primeval forest of Cholo Mountain in Nyasaland. This is a little corner which Coleridge suits well with many of his lines in *Kubla Khan* — my version:

> 'There were Forests ancient on the hills
> Enfolding sunny spots of memory
> — A savage place as holy and enchanted
> As e'er beneath a waning moon was haunted
> By woman waiting for her demon lover.'

And Kipling also:

> 'Do you know the steamy stillness of the orchid scented glade
> When the blazoned bird winged butterflies flit through?'

And here if one sits very still, one can sometimes see the Narina on the edge of the black gloom of the surrounding forest, a glory of metalic green, shot with all the colours of the rainbow, above, while his breast is crimson red, the colour that sometimes blazes from the setting sun. And his name — but there we decend in bathos from the raptures of the poets to things more mundane. '*Narina*' pretty enough as a name if we delve no further into its origin, but given to the bird by Le Vaillant, the French ornithologist of a hundred years ago, after a black Hotentot beauty for whom, as Sclater so nicely puts it, he 'professed great admiration'. I need say no more.

February 24th, 1929

Have been taking it easy for the last day or two — malaria, not to put too fine a point upon it, but am pretty fit again this morning.

Kanganqupa, one of my old boys turned up about a week ago and came back to work. I agreed, but told him he must first make a journey to Mpati Store to renew our supply of salt and sugar, he at first demurred, saying — the same old weather lie — that it was impossible to cross the rivers, in the end however, agreed and he got back yesterday, having made much better time than he did on the first occasion he went there, with a supply of salt and sugar that ought to last our time out here. I don't mind doing without most things in the grocery line, but these two, especially salt, I find are really necessary to health. I am gradually running out of most of my luxuries and have to extemporize. I drink maize coffee instead of tea in order to eke out my supply of the latter beverage as long as possible, and find it really very good as long as the grain is freshly roasted and the coffee well made from it, without dregs. The lack of good tobacco is more serious to me. I smoked my last cigarette a couple of days ago and now all I have is a few hands of tobacco leaves kindly given me by the Bivars, but it is poor stuff very much off flavour and very dark and strong to the taste. Still I cut it up and roll cigarettes with bits of 'Bromo' which satifies one's craving for a smoke but doesn't really give one much pleasure.

February 27th, 1929

Wasn't able to shake off this last go of fever so easily as I thought. I've had to keep mostly to my bed, until this morning. My picannins came in with news of fresh spoor yesterday morning, but although I tried to get after it I found I was not equal to it and doubt whether I should have been able to have held a rifle straight even if I had succeeded in getting up with the brutes. Just like them to come close to camp when one is out of action. This fever has been just typical malaria. It descended suddenly on me on the 23rd I think — just as I was preparing to go out with a picannin and a rifle and for the next three days it came on regularly every afternoon, leaving me in the early hours of the morning.

Next day

Frazer tells me today is the 27th and not the 28th, as I had thought it to be. I have taken his count on the strength of the calendar that he produced to show me how he has been keeping the date ever since we left Matenji. Today, the real 27th, I went for a stroll down the nearest elephant path, it turned out to be that on which the elephants had been going when the picannin brought me news of fresh spoor whilst I was sick and unable to go after them. I saw today that it was a herd of 10 or 12, very probably the same brutes I came across before and it is good to see that shooting one hasn't harried them out of the country. I was lucky enough to find a couple of duiker feeding just off the path, whom I spotted first in the game of 'I spy' that one plays on bush hunting, and so was able to bag. The number of rounds one expends in shooting an animal seems to me to vary inversely to its size. I am ashamed to say how many times I tried to put a bullet through the head of the second of these whom I had wounded in the first instance, but it was yet able to run a few yards and wouldn't keep still. 'I spy' is really the wrong name for the game because one side will insist on playing 'I scent' and 'I hear' too, in a manner which is hardly fair to the other whose only counter is 'I think'.

March 2nd, 1929

My only success this last day or two has been in shooting a rare form of kestral (*Falco dickinsoni*). It was yesterday evening actually, after a tramp in the morning in company with my youngest picannin carrying a rifle about as tall as he is, I again went out with the shot-gun at about 3 in the afternoon. The attraction of carrying the shot-gun at the moment is the chance of putting up a bustard which, on the evidence of a single individual seen one day about 10 days ago, I am hoping it is migrating into or through the country. Needless to say I have not again seen any sign of him nor did I meet with any better success yesterday evening when I walked up the hill south into the tall grass country that lies up there. On the edge of this, however, I was attracted by a great gathering of birds and approaching nearer I found that they mostly consisted of the European bee-eater (*Merops apiaster*) and the European hobby (*Falco subbuteo*) and that they were hawking for some large species of fly, of which a great hatch was in progress just there. Amongst them I noticed, from time to time, another small hawk that I could not identify of whom there may have been two or three individuals present in that large company. Luckily, a little later one of these came and settled on the bare branches of a dead tree some twenty yards from me and I was able to shoot what turned out to be this kestrel. I hadn't the faintest idea what it was when I went to pick it up beyond that it was a hawk of some kind, but as I came home, summing up the possibilities I put it in *Tinnunculas* for certain, whilst I would have backed *dictinsai* as the winner amongst the species of the genus.

March 3rd, 1929

Madewa, another of my old boys turned up today wanting to be taken back to work again. I must say, I thought twice about it but seeing that he has come so far and was also an original volunteer, I've decided to take him on again but have explained to him that at the first sign of laziness and song-singing in his hut as his day's work, I shall put him out; and that his one job of importance for which I pay him is to find me fresh elephant spoor. To all this he expressed his agreement and then produced a small bag of grass seed heads as a present for me. This is most acceptable; being short of cotton wool I have lately taken to stuffing my birds with these silky seed heads as a substitute and find it answers pretty well; Madewa remembered this and that the particular kind of grass was 'over' here for the year, so finding some at his village, brought it along like a sensible lad.

March 4th – 6th, 1929

Uninteresting time spent looking for game which has become very scarce.

March 8th, 1929

Rained hard today and most of yesterday as well. The Bandi came down in flood swamping out my vegetable garden and spoiling a patch of tomatoes that were flowering. I am hoping to get some edible result from this garden in a few weeks, it has not provided anything yet but things are now mostly flowering and the cob forming on the maize. If I had only started putting in vegetables last November I should now be living in luxury and be more or less self-supporting; as it is I again have to send boys to Chipazi to renew my supplies and as I'm getting short of cash will have to do without wheat flour at 1/- a kilo, which is too much for me! I don't mind doing without that, what I am really looking forward to are bananas and sweet potatoes which I'm hoping he will have by this time. Trouble is though, with this rain, whether the boys will be able to get across the Lingove for a day or two and I'm nearly at an end of all my supplies.

March 9th, 1929

My boys went off today to Chipazi, they will have to go a pretty round about way as they took the road to Macheso's to begin with, in order to cross the Lingove as there is a big tree felled in the river there which helps them over. I am hoping that the supplies they bring will last me out my time here. Indeed they will have to — I have budgeted for up to the end of April and can afford no extras during that time. If the road is not ready and I am delayed much after the beginning of May, I shall be in a bit of a hole. Of course if I shoot more elephants I shall have to reconsider things. A walk to Tete would then be advisable in order to get my licence. I quite see they are not going to send it to me — letters are not answered and they will not trouble to do anything for me except under a personal interview. Such a walk is not worth while for a smallish pair of tusks which I intend to get out of the country on the quiet if I can, but if I had two more of fairly decent size it would be different.

March 10th, 1929

Going out alone today I first saw a hartebeest at the top of the hill between my camp and 'hartebeest dambo' but he was too quick for me. I should of course have 'upped' my rifle at him as soon as I saw him defined, but not being able to see his head, which was hidden by the branches of a tree under which he was standing, I thought he had not yet spotted me, so I stepped off the path to rest my rifle on a tree — there was to be no mistake about the shot. But the brute had me cold, he was watching me all the time and as soon as I moved went off in that beastly canter they have, laughing at me. My luck was in however as skirting the edge of the dambo I disturbed a couple of reedbuck having a siesta in the middle of the dambo. They kindly stood to my 'Hoch' and I downed the buck. I need hardly say that I had learnt my lesson and did not look for a nest this time. The head is of average length, going 12 inches or so, but the horn is very thick and has a girth of 6 inches at the crown which I think is worth recording. Covering up the buck I made tracks for home, leaving a trail of branches behind me to guide the boys as I had no desire to return there myself. This worked successfully enough. Frazer and the two picannins have just got back with the meat and tell me they picked up my 'road' at the beginning of the dambo and had no difficulty in following it.

March 11th, 1929

There arrived in camp about 11 o'clock this morning an oldish native and a 12 year old picannin who said they had been lost and wandering round the countryside for the last five days without anything to eat. They said that had left their village on the Namanzi River, sometime, to go to

Muchena to look for work and were shaping for Msatwe, but not knowing the district and not finding any paths to help them, they had entirely lost their way. By sheer luck, apparently, they hit our path at the Lingove where the tree is felled across the river and followed it up to my camp. The old man was in a pitiable condition, as thin as a rake, with hollow cheeks and sunken eyes but it didn't seem to have worried the picannin much who lost no time in getting outside a huge potful of maize porridge and meat. One of their first questions when they had more or less recovered was who had shot the elephant close by? By some queer chance they had stumbled on the remains of the animal I got last month. This is rather unfortunate — Frazer expressed his complete ignorance of the whole matter, like a good lad, but I think on the whole it will be wiser to tell them we know all about it and ask them to refrain from chin-wagging, which they should do if only from a sense of gratitude in having their lives saved, probably, from my presence here. Going out in the evening with the shot-gun, I came on a pair of hartebeest lying down in some scrubby country up the hill to the south. Funnily enough after my complaint a day or two ago about the 'I scent' game that animals play, in this case the tables were turned in my favour, for it was I who first scented the hartebeest. This may sound a pretty tall story but I can only declare that it is perfectly true. Since running out of manufactured cigarettes at the end of last month I have practically given up smoking altogether, it is only on very rare occasions, about once every two ot three days that I feel I want one of my flavoured 'Bromos'. The result of this has been my sense of smell has improved to such an extent that I would never have deemed possible. In my tramps through the bush I am often now attracted off my path by interesting smells which would before have passed unnoticed. It adds a new interest to life, which I delight in like a deaf man recovered from his malady and able to hear again. Flowering trees and shrubs now mean more to me while one can now well understand a spaniel's delight and excitement on finding a 'gamey' smell in a field of roots.

Following up the gamey smells that come to me in the bush I often find spoor that I might otherwise have missed or more generally the forms in the grass where the animals have been lying down, but this time to my great delight it was the animals themselves. I was about 75 yards off, I suppose, when I first winded them, It was a still evening and the air seemed clear and fresh after the recent rain, while a very slight breeze was blowing in my direction and I followed up the scent for over 40 yards before I could see the head of one of the animals low down in the grass. He was shaking his head about in his efforts to drive away the flies and midges that were annoying him and to carry on and utterly confound my remarks on the 'I spy' game of bush hunting, I did not, as a matter of fact, see him until I had first actually heard the flapping of his ears as he vigorously shook his head about. The light was failing and it was only finally that I made him out not more than 30 or 40 yards away, but not having a rifle with me I could not deal with him at that range and they heard me and bounded off when I tried a closer approach. To the scoffer or anyone who doubts my story I can only say — go to the nearest cow shed and find out what cattle smell like, then follow them up from the byre to their pasture and see if their scent is not certainly in one's nostrils. Then, on meeting any man who has done a little hunting in Africa ask him if buffalo have not the same scent and whether it is not possible to smell them and smell them strongly as one follows up their spoor and then perhaps it will not be so hard to believe that other game leaves the same sort of scent behind and can be smelled just as easily by anyone who has this sense fairly well developed. In confirmation I shall add this — I met a man last year who in the course of 'hunting' conversation declared to me his ability to scent game and it was I who scoffed thinking it quite impossible,and that he was just going one better after a few pretty tall stories on both our parts for we had both seen much hunting. I shall have to make humble apology to that man the next time I meet him. He was a non-smoker. I should like to think that I too could now give up smoking for good but I know that a return to civilization means falling back into the old evil habit — it is one of these repressed instincts of childhood which our present day child welfare enthusiasts talk about.

March 12th, 1929

My two boys arrived back from Chipazi's today with some bananas, rice and a few beans. He tells me he is short of the last and has not given me as much as I ordered, nor did he send the sweet potatoes which is annoying, as I know he has some. The amount I eat these days is perfectly prodigious. I have four large meals a day and yet seem always hungry. I suppose some vitamin is missing in my diet, either that or else I have got ankylostomiasis, I hope it's not the latter, but when I come to think of it I certainly have not been feeling energetic for some time now and appreciate a lazy day in camp in a way I never used to — horrid thought, I hope there is nothing to it.

Saw two more hartebeest this morning but once again could not get a shot. The brutes are all too wary by half in this country and the chances are about ten to one in their favour at this time of year. But then in the dry weather the poor brutes get a rotten time of it for the odds are then massed against them by at least the same amount so it's only fair they should have some respite. Our prodigals are still in camp and it seems are establishing themselves here for good. I had the old man up this morning and asked him what he was going to do next and he could only think of staying on here to work for me. I told him I had no work for him and that he had better go back to his village, but short of ordering him to clear out, I don't think he'll go. He's found a 'good enough ole' and is going to stick to it. I suppose I shall have to give him 5/- for a month's work but every shilling of my expenditure has got to be thought twice about just now. Poor devil — there is some sort of sense of gratitude in him anyway which makes him want to stay on with me and to find such a thing as that in a Bantu is so rare that it should be encouraged when one comes across it. I asked him about the elephant he had found dead — he said it was somewhere near here but couldn't point out the direction, he also informed me that it had only been dead a few days and that they had eaten some of it! I then thought it might be some other animal than mine but he described the place he had found it so clearly that I am convinced it is not so and that they had been eating month old rotting hide. I then told him not to talk about it in the villages as I did not want the Boma to hear as they would think I had killed it and there would then be a case which I would have to attend and I didn't want the trouble of a journey into the Boma. This he quite understood and promised not to talk — and so the affair ends by my having to take him on at 5/- a month — a small enough wage, but what he is going to do for it I don't quite know.

March 14th, 1929

I believe that darned fellow Madewa is an absolute Jonah. Looking back, not only since he came back for work 10 days ago, but also when we were here before, I cannot remember shooting anything large or interesting when he was with me. I do remember one hartebeest, but that was the half grown beast that I mistook for a big one and then wasted so much time trying to find when it was already lying dead; but I think that is the largest buck I have shot in his company. Since he came back this month, the only time I have seen bigger game has been when he was away at Chipazi — seeing hartebeest each day I went out alone. Now on his return all that we've seen in the last two days has been one wretched little stembuck which I got this morning away out up the Lingove. If this goes on I shall have to give him a job about camp and take another boy in his place. I came home today by way of the second hill that I climbed the day I got lost and saw just how the land lay in that quarter. I can quite understand how I missed my way. 'Camp Hill' is from there quite hidden by a range of other hills. If I had turned south over this little range instead of doubling back east that day, I should soon have been in camp or even had I carried on I would soon have came to the Lingove and would probably have found my bearings quicker.

March 16th, 1929

It has rained incessantly since the morning I got the stembuck. On our way home that day we were caught and had a good drenching from a heavy shower, but one doesn't mind that, what one does object to is the solid drizzling rain that has been going on ever since, night and day, which seems to work its way into everything. We are out of maize flour, also, which does not add to the happiness. As usual, these fools of Bantus left it until the last minute before thinking of sending the two picannins into Macheso's to renew our supply. They went only on the 13th on which day I happened to ask how supplies were, to receive the reply that they had only enough for that day. I hustled the picannins out of camp as fast as I could and told them to come back early next day. This is the 16th and they haven't yet arrived. Madewa went off yesterday to get them and what they need is about 12 apiece on the place made to receive it. But I have little room for sympathy for the bigger boys, it was their own fault in the first place for not sending them out earlier and for one of the big boys not going with the picannins. This sort of thing has happened before and it's their pigeon entirely. A little dose of starvation will make them remember better next time perhaps. But all the same it's annoying for me also.

I've just got back from slaying three hartebeest somewhere in a part of the country I've never been to before and it will just be a matter of sheer luck if I ever re-find them. I tried to make a straight line back to camp but soon found I had lost all idea of my position once again and if it hadn't luckily cleared up just then enabling me to get a glimpse of Mbanji, I would still be wandering about; for the drizzling rain and mist has once again closed on us bringing visibility down to a negligible quantity. I must really stop going out without a boy — it's simply not worth it — besides the fact that I'm dashed sure I couldn't last out five days like our prodigals in this sort of weather, it doesn't do any good to shoot stuff that one can't find one's way back to. Back in camp I've had a warm bath and retired to bed until some such time as I felt warmer and drier. One gets so wet on such rainy days that one's skin is everywhere soft and tender and a mere rubbing with a towel does not suffice to make one feel dry, one wants a real good baking besides. The skin is very easily chafed also and gives one such pain that I would not have believed from merely a chafing pair of shorts. For an hour or two I was yelling and cursing the wretched Frazer, who hadn't done any great harm, like a raving lunatic.

Madewa came back from Macheso's about 4 p.m. with a little of the much needed flour. He told me that the Lingove was coming down in great spate and had carried away our tree, so that it was impossible for the picannins to cross. He had only managed to get over himself by swimming and was carried along by the current until he luckily struck the right bank. My earlier diatribe on the picannins was premature, but all the same, they are still to blame for not coming back on the 14th when the river was down as I saw for myself on that date. But the river must be a sight just now, that tree was a 3 foot 'mwenya' and seemed to have solved our bridge problem for good. Funny I should have found the hartebeest today when I was once again without Madewa. The boy's a Jonah without doubt and the worst I've ever come across. Still he's a stout lad and one of the most powerful and well built natives I've ever seen — there are not many who would have tackled that river crossing today.

March 17th, 1929

We found my hartebeest, there were four not three as I had supposed yesterday. Of the first herd I met I thought I had only nailed two but I remember the other animal I fired at which at the time showed no sign of being hit. We found the place easily enough by following up my own spoor which I picked up where I had left the elephant path at the hill south of the camp. I did a complete circle after meeting the first herd, my last animal was only a short distance away from the first three and I passed within a hundred yards of them again about half an hour's walk. If it had been a clear day I should have been in sight of Mbanji long before and have been home earlier. Today I came home under Kanyangele's leadership in about three quarters of an hour, after we had taken the tongues and kidneys of all the game. Madewa and he are going to sleep there tonight so as to be able to deal with it all before it goes bad, so I have given them a large waterproof sheet to make them happy. With all this meat we shall have enough to buy flour and other necessaries for at least a month and I shall not need to perform such murder again. There is enough fat too to last me the best part of a month. One animal was especially well larded, giving us as much as the other three put together. Heavy rain came on again just as Kanyangele and I were starting home, drenching us entirely; I have now, however, learned my lesson and walked home minus my shorts; a double terai hat, a dirty flannel shirt and a pair of dilapidated veldtshoen isn't just the dress for Piccadilly Circus, but its the best rig-out for wet weather in the bush, unless one can discard the shirt as well and walk about in a loin cloth. But it is too cold for that and I find that even a sopping wet shirt is better than none at all for it prevents the cold rain actually beating on your skin and bleaching out the natural oils which keep you warm.

I collected a brace of guineafowl on the way home, potting at them with the rifle on trees. Soft nose ammunition is rather rough on them, what one wants for Guineafowl is a light rook rifle, there's no doubt, then they'd give good practice and one wouldn't run the risk of disturbing worthier game. One often can't get near to them for a shot-gun and an airgun, even the BSA isn't nearly powerful enough, so the old gun has to take on an extra job. That certainly is the most beloved rifle I've ever owned. I've such confidence in it that I rarely miss with it.

I came across yet another type of bustard today making the fifth species I've seen in these parts — none of which I've as yet obtained, I also found a Bateleur eagle (*Helotarsus ecaudatus*) feeding on carrion — one of the hartebeests — in company with a solitary vulture which had found them out. Strange and unworthy behaviour on the part of an eagle, one would have thought, but I see that the Bateleur's carrion feeding propensities have often before been remarked.

March 18th, 1929

I thought this spell of rain was over this morning when it cleared up and we saw the sun until about midday. Our water pool which was right down to dry weather level ran beautifully clear after its frequent purgings. But in the afternoon it clouded over again and about 3 p.m. the heaviest rain of the year fell solidly for about an hour, bringing the Bandi down in a wall of water which made a new high water mark round about 5 yards from my kitchen. It has now settled down to steady rain again which may go on for any length of time. The two boys are still out tending to the game; they did not put in an appearance in camp today at all. I hope they will manage to deal with all the meat successfully, but this rain will make it difficult for them to dry it out before it goes bad. March is doing its yearly worst upon us in the way of rain.

March 19th, 1929

A fine, warm, sunny day for a change. I spent a most enjoyable half hour in the early morning when I got up, down by the water pool, watching a little blue kingfisher (*Alcedo semitorquata*) not the same fellow who used to haunt the pool in the dry weather, but a bird more like our own British species. He was fishing for minnows as far as I could make out and you could see him cocking an eye downwards as soon as he had spotted something to his taste and waiting for it to come up close under his perch on a bamboo tree that overhung the water, when he would dive down with a splash, spear his prey and hurry back again and sit bobbing about and flapping his wings in his efforts to swallow it. There were a lot of other interesting birds about also, and I strolled round in my pyjamas, delighting with them in the warm sunlight, a welcome change after the rain and damp of the last few daya. I counted and identified over 20 species of birds in as many minutes.

After a breakfast of guavas — the last survivals from Chipazi — fried guinea fowl, beans and toasted maize porridge. I went off with Frazer to see how the two boys were faring who were looking after the game. I did not lose my bearings this time for a wonder but came pretty straight to the spot to find Kanyangele there alone with three large loads of smoked meat ready tied up. Madewa had gone off to camp already with another load while he kept guard for there were many vultures about waiting their chance to begin their meal. I put a bullet through one of them to find out what he was exactly but have had a great puzzle trying to work him out. Of course he ought to be the ordinary 'Aasvogel' of the Boers (*Gyps kolvii*) but there are certain points about him which would make one think he was the white-backed vulture (*Pseudogyps africanus*). I don't know what to think; I can remember being puzzled by a bird in the same way in Nyasaland and can only believe that both were the ordinary vulture and that they vary tremendously in size and plumage. I have kept the head of my bird together with a foot which should be sufficient for an indentification some day, or a description if one ever has the time and inclination to write a book oneself.

March 20th, 1929

Kanyangele went today to try and sell meat at Macheso's, but couldn't cross the Lingove. He came back about 4 p.m. much to my disgust as I was hoping for green maize cobs today, which are very good for a change.

March 21st, 1929

Went today with Madewa and Kanyangele to see what could be done about the river crossing.

I found the Lingove still pretty high and absolutely no sign of our tree which may have been carried down for miles. We considered felling another big 'mwenya' which stood close to our original one but it was so long a job that I agreed to Madewa's suggestion of felling a smaller tree and pushing it over the river. It was a span of some 30 feet, I suppose, that we had to deal with and we succeeded after some heavy work in wedging one end of our tree behind the trunk of the big 'mwenya' while the other rested on a tree that had fallen into the water from the other side. This formed our bridge and we fixed up a couple of bamboos for a handrail so Kanyangele managed to get across. We told him to be quick about coming back and to come back with both picannins and a large supply of flour for this bridge would certainly not hold up to any fresh spate.

So he went off and Madewa and I stayed behind to make the bridge a bit easier to negotiate. Actually it was easy enough to swim the river, Madewa was continually going backwards and forwards while I plunged in myself and swam over with ease, just to show Kanyangele what a nuisance he was not to be able to do the same thing. Still one couldn't really expect the old man to undertake it and anyway it's necessary for the children.

As we were passing Camp Hill on the way out this morning I was attracted by a party of four or five black birds hopping about amongst the boulders at the base of the hill. I could see that they were something I had not before come across but they were so wild that it cost me much labour to shoot one. The whole party fled as I approached them hopping their way straight uphill over the huge boulders while I sweated after them. I finally managed to down one and saw as I picked it up that it was something quite out of the common. Back in camp I find that it is one of the larger warblers (*Pinarornis plumosus*) a bird that has the habits of a chat. He is only noted from two localities in Africa, so I have secured a great success in finding it here. I should like to collect another bird or two and there are points about this fellow that may make it referable to a sub-species if other specimens confirm its idiosyncracies. Madewa informs me that the bird is common at his home on the Namanzi, but the boy has an annoying habit of always trying to show off his knowledge which depreciates the value of his statements so one doesn't always know how far one can believe him.

March 22nd, 1929

A lion has been roaring his news up the hill south for the last night or two. Last night he went on for several hours on end and again this morning up until about 8 a.m. which is pretty late in the day for one of these brutes to be about. I wish I could have the luck to come across one though I don't expect to in this country; there are not many of them and one only hears them about once in ten days on the average. If I were really keen to shoot one I suppose I should sit up over a kill one night but I have had enough of that game and don't think it's worth while — I want my lion in broad daylight, perhaps one day I shall be lucky enough to get him. I'm always borne up by the thought that Selous was three years in Africa leading a hunting life before he even saw a lion. Kanyangele arrived back this afternoon with the two picannins so I've been regaling myself on green maize which is a welcome change from the smoked meat of the natives which I've been eating for the last few days. This is really not so bad as it always looks, if one pares off the outside of the strips where it has been well smoked and then fries these outside pieces with much fat. Not that one would choose it for a diet in civilization, but it adds a savour to boiled rice if mixed in very sparingly, that is otherwise lacking in repeated meals of that diet.

March 23rd, 1929

Trouble in camp today with theft of meat and lies from all concerned. Diappointing and exhausting.

March 24th, 1929

I bethought me of my camera today which had been idle for many moons. I suppose the beautifully fine morning made me think of it and I posed Mafio for his portrait, squatting on the ground between the two elephant tusks. Hope it comes out well — if ever a picannin deserved to be so photographed he does. I then went down to our bridge at the Lingove and took some photos there — one of Madewa swimming over should make a good picture but the river is not so high now as it was the day we fixed the bridge and it was difficult to know how to 'stopper' as the bridge itself was in the deep shade of the mwenya tree while there was bright sunlight outside. We then turned down stream for a mile or two cutting into our path to the south of Camp Hill and Madewa at last succeeded in breaking his luck, for we first saw a waterbuck who was too wide awake for me and then a herd of hartebeest which M spotted on the ground and of which I was able to kill one. We gralloched it there and then and found it a good fat animal. Fried liver and kidney for lunch is a pleasant change especially if there's a sweet of squashed bananas to follow.

March 25th, 1929

Madewa and the picannins had to go back this morning to fetch in the remainder of the meat as Kanyangele is away at Macheso's and the other boy who calls himself Kolenso is still hardly able to walk. They spent the rest of the day cutting it up and smoking it.

At about 11 a.m. they called my attention to some vultures who were on the tall trees down by the water pool and had probably been attracted by the sight of so much meat. I went out to have a look at them and saw they were much smaller birds than the ordinary 'aasvogel' and a closer examination through binoculars showed me they were something quite different so I loaded up the 8 mm and downed one. He turns out to be the hooded vulture (*Necrosyrtes pileatus*) and is an interesting companion to the head of the other vulture I took a week ago. I hope the head dries out satisfactorily, it's the very deuce sometimes at this time of the year to deal with skin. In the dry weather two or three days and the skins are as dry as parchment. Now one has to be continually on the look out that they don't rot on you.

Frazer had just come up to say that Kolenso and his picannin, our two prodigals, want to accompany us back to Blantyre when we go. I think he rather favours this arrangement himself but I put my foot down firmly. He's a dirty old man, even Madewa refuses to feed with him, while I found the picannin licking my plates one day, which does not prejudice me in his favour. But I know what's going to happen — the old man will depart this world, I wouldn't mind betting and his wretched youngster will have to come with us. The pair of them are a darned nuisance; I wish they would clear out and plague some of their own kind with their presence.

March 26th, 1929

This morning I was a greatly interested spectator in the final scene of the hook worm comedy which has been worrying me, when I watched a certain species of fly that we keep in these parts dropping their white worms in numbers. For the last day or two I have been inspecting this fly but hesitated to be certain of it because it seemed so extraordinary, but I spent some time this morning examining the flies and their behaviour on the droppings. The culprit is a large grey fly with a red head, general form the same as the ordinary house fly. One fly will drop several of these worms in the course of a minute or two. She can be seen smoothing over the hinder portion of her body with her two hind legs in her efforts to evaginate the worm and scurries off as soon as it is dropped to some other portion where she proceeds to repeat the performance. The worm can immediately be seen wriggling off and soon buries itself in the verdure. When there are many flies of this type 'vermpositing' — if that is the right word — at the same time it is hard to see how these worms could be overlooked. I don't know why I've never noticed them before. I count myself a fairly observant individual but I've never had such 'Hospitable' fears before, which I suppose is the reason. But its the sort of thing one would have thought that the medical men would have warned one of long ago and yet I've never heard any mention of such a thing before as far as I can remember. Anyway I'm glad enough to have found out about the matter and to know that I myself am not the host.

We have gone back again to usual March weather this morning, drizzling rain and general soppiness which makes one disinclined to stir from camp. It's been a pretty wet winter altogether, there have not been many days on which no rain has fallen, nor has it produced as yet any sort of a sign that there are elephants in the country which is uninteresting of it. This book ends with a total bag of three elephants to its credit. I was hoping to be able to record a good many more than that when I started it, I must confess. But I can quite see now that I made a great mistake in coming to this part north of the Zambezi. I should have paid another £30 for a licence to shoot south of the river where they allow you five jumbo but then one never knows; it might have been just chucking good money after bad and I'm anyway glad to have seen this part of the world and to have poached an elephant in it. They are quite a nice uniform pair of tusks and as they are not marketable — anyway in Tete — they would be a good pair to have polished up one day or have set up with a gong in the middle, if one can ever afford such trifles. But the first thing is to get them out of the country safely. No news has leaked to date and I almost am considering now whether it would be better to declare that I shot the elephant last December and so have it down on last year's licence. I don't know and I have another month at least in which to consider things and perhaps shall be able to collect another pair to go with them.

March 27th, 1929

The only excitement to record today is the collection of a brace of guinea fowl. A boy bringing in firewood in the evening brought news of a large company of them close to camp, so out I went with the rifle and brought off two most spectacular shots at them in the failing light. I apologize for thus continually harping on my success with the rifle. I must admit that I take great pride and pleasure in the neat performance, for rifle-shooting is about the only accomplishment in which I profess to have more than average skill. For these shots I opened up a new pack of ammunition, an odd fifteen rounds of Belgian manufacture. Of the four rounds I tried, two were miss-fires, which I shall keep and show to the maker from whom I got them. They and a single round of soft-nose of the same manufacture are the only miss-fires I've had on this trip, which speaks well for British cartridges. But a 50% average of miss-fires in solid ammunition is a most serious, almost criminal, negligence on the part of the manufacturers.

If these two rounds had been in the magazine and chamber at the precise moment one wanted quick shooting to deal with a charging elephant, for instance, one's quick demise could be reasonably put to the door of the Cartoucherie Belge, Liège, Belgique, to give it its full title, so that we may remember it. If these people had supplied the Liège forts in '14 there would not have been much stemming of the German advance.

March 28th, 1929

To pay me out for my boastfulness yesterday, I today missed three of the easiest shots that I could ever wish to have. One with the rifle at a hartebeest that looked at about 75 yards quite as unmissable as the proverbial haystack; the other two with the shot-gun at sitting birds which I could not identify. I didn't mind so much about the hartebeest but it's annoying to have thrown away a couple of useless shots with the gun. I think this brings down my stock of cartridges to four with no hope of getting any more on this little trip. I never had any success with my extemporised shot in 9 mm cartridges so stopped making it. I wish I could exchange 100 rounds of these for the same number of 12-bore. Next time I go on a trip I shall know how to cut down a good deal of weight in my battery and put it into shot-gun cartridges. I have three rifles with me at present that I really never use. My 8 mm and a shot-gun are really all that I want. With these I can deal with anything one can possibly want, so why cumber oneself with extra weight? If I took a third lethal weapon it would be a very small-bored collector's gun — a 410 perhaps which I've set my heart on having one of these days, to deal with warblers and small finches. A 12-bore is far too big and has too much of a spread, so I've had to leave the smaller birds quite alone on this trip.

March 30th, 1929

The episode of the wandering Kalenso and his picannin finishes this morning I hope. Frazer came to me and said that the old worm had been stealing meat and salt from the kitchen, while he himself was out for a few minutes. Rather a poor return for his two weeks feeding in my establishment, during the whole of which time he has done nothing but lie in his hut, refusing even the lightest work. So I told him to clear right out of it and he has gone, thank the Lord. I am expecting the picannin to be back though, the old man started beating him because he wanted to stay here, whereupon the young brute naturally ran off and hid in the bush. He will doubtless appear in camp when he thinks it is safe to do so and attach himself to me permanently, which I do not want.

He is back again as I write, poor little brat, and tells me he never wants to see his father again (I don't blame him) but will stay on with us and come back to Nyasaland with us. So perforce I've had to agree — he may turn out a decent youngster yet, he is only about six or eight years old so he has time enough to learn.

April 2nd, 1929

It's one thing to get rid of fever when one can get all the quinine one needs, quite another to try and shake it off when one has none. These goes are becoming a bit too frequent for my liking. There are signs now of the passing of the rains and by the end of this month I will be thinking of moving off again.

April 5th, 1929

Madewa, who had been away for a day or two at his home, came back yesterday evening saying that he had seen much spoor on the Lingove out towards Msatwe, so I today went with him for a very long walk out in that direction. We found spoor all right, two days old, of a herd that has been tramping about down that way lately. I couldn't get on to anything fresher than that and made out that this herd had gone off in the meantime S.W.

The Lingove is now so far down as to allow us to cross by wading most places, though a pretty deep, up-to-the-shoulders sort of crossing we had at a place where the river divided into two streams leaving an island in the middle. It's a most filthy sort of scrub country on the other side — no timber to speak of and the bushes and undergrowth grow thick and matted. Not so bad as the country S. of my camp, but still bad enough to walk in, except along buffalo and elephant spoor.

We didn't stay long on the other side but time enough to see that the herd was not at home that day. I shot a bee-eater though, which pleases me (*Melittophagus bullockoides*) whom I've only seen once before in a similar type of country on the banks of the Lingove.

There were two of them behaving very like a fly-catcher in the way they darted after passing insects and returned to the same perch.

Coming back over the river I found another bird of the same family, the Southern bee-eater (*Merops meridionalis*), on the look-out for its food amongst the reeds of the river bank and carrying on in much the same manner. This is the commoner bird in these parts; he is a good deal smaller and not so brilliantly coloured. As a rule he is a very silent bird, but the one I saw on this occasion entertained me greatly by his behaviour. After catching a passing insect he would fly back to his perch and carry out what I suppose was a digestive exercise in order to cast up the indigestible portion of his food.

He threw his whole head and body forwards and downwards, causing his tail to cock up in the air behind him, uttering as he did so a curious sort of snapping noise which must have been vocal but sounded as if he were gnashing his teeth — had he possessed any to gnash. He would repeat this performance two or three times consecutively after each successful sally after a fly and seemed greatly to enjoy it. Coming home again I saw the third type of bee-eater that we commonly come across in these parts, the European bird (*Merops apiaster*) who takes his food in a very different fashion, generally 'hawking' at a good height from the ground in the manner of a bird of prey. These birds must be beginning to think now of their journey north; but there are still a good number of them to be seen in the countryside.

April 6th, 1929

Followed up a honeyguide this morning who brought us up to a good swarm of bees which the boys have now gone to cut out. He was the male (*Sparrmanni*) and in his behaviour was more intelligent than I have sometimes thought the male to be, as compared with the female. After that I went to look for bustards in a particular bit of stunted tree country where I have before seen the odd bird. But today there was only one very wary bird to be found. He rose at about 50 yards, settling again within a similar distance; but he must have then run like the deuce for we saw no further sigh of him.

I wish I could circumvent at anyrate one species of these birds, but fear they have got the better of me, for with yesterday's bee-eater and a rockthrush (*Monticola angolensis*) that interested me today, my stock of cartridges is down to two No. 8's which are on the small side for bustard, unless one is really to get up at my feet while I was carrying the shot-gun.

April 9th, 1929

Yesterday evening Kanyangele came in from Macheso's where he had been buying flour with news of having seen spoor quite close to camp. It turned out, however, to be spoor of the day before of a single smallish animal that was not worth while going after.

Today I shot another vulture which is of interest being the fully adult bird of the last species I collected ten days ago (*Necrosyrtes pileatus*) and differs in many points from it.

It is just about a month since I last sent into Chipazi's so I have decided to send in Kanyangele again tomorrow to get me a load of fruit and pay my bill there. I am sending him with a load this time, anticipating a difficulty in finding carriers when I leave for Matenji again. He is taking the elephant rifle and ammunition I don't need — what ignominy to heap on the Bandi River for its failings. Those things that I can most easily spare are the very ones that I ought by rights to be most needing.

Macheso came into camp this afternoon with a letter from W in Nyasaland. The first letter from outside P.E.A. that I've had, in fact the only letter worthy of the name I've had since arriving in the country last September. The letter from W was in answer to my two to him both of which he had received. He is quite beat to think of a way of getting supplies to me here. The boys are frightened of walking in P.E.A. and say that they'll be clapped into jug if they ventured over the border, whilst everything I want is dutiable and needs a permit from the Portuguese authorities before the A.L.C. export it! So I must give up hope of receiving any supplies — not that I've had any really for the last month or two. W's letter was dated March 3rd, mine to him took over two months to arrive. Three and a half months for an answer is not so bad for a journey that could be done on foot in under a week. He gives me no news except that things in the 'baccy world show no improvement, which is a bad state of affairs, but whether the outside world still exists I know not. I suppose if there had been any really important events, wars or rumours of wars, one would have heard somehow, but I must admit that I am now quite ready to get back to civilization and pick up the threads of everyday life once again.

I've an idea though that it will be the middle of May at least before that road is passable again. I don't see how it could be got ready by the end of the month; they could not think of starting work until all signs of the heavy rains had passed and the rivers down to winter level — and that is not yet as I can see for myself from the Lingove. If I had shot-gun cartridges I should not care how long it took, but without them I must confess I shall be glad to get away again. My remaining two only tantalize me with thoughts of how I may best use them, and with fears that I'll miss something good with them; my prodigality also in the first three months of my stay here annoys me when I think of it and I regret those pigeon pies and roasted guinea fowl which at the time I ate with a clear conscience.

April 10th, 1929

I give up. Madewa, whom I had just paid for his last month's work, ran off last night because he was wanted to help with this load into Chipazi today.

It is the 10th of the month and my lucky day so went out with little Mafio to see if he would bring me luck again, and sure enough we hit spoor of a herd that had passed during the night only a short way from camp. But that was the full extent of our luck, for we did not gain a fraction on them in some 20 miles that we plugged after them. We gave it up right away down the Nehomala river, the herd still apparently going great guns ahead. As a matter of fact I don't think there was any really large animal amongst them. It's hard to tell actually of what a herd consists when animals are following each other and keeping mostly to their paths; but even on the dambos there as a rule a herd will spread out slightly to cross, I could not find the tracks of a decent sized bull. So I have at least that thought to comfort me. We saw quite a lot of game, but nothing near enough to camp to shoot.

Of course I'm lazy about this elephant hunting game. If one wants to make anything at it in this part of Africa one must be prepared to walk about very much more than I do, But I'm afraid I'm not the man for two or three days on the trail, I like to enjoy my hunting and if I can't get up to my elephant and be back in camp the same day I'm not doing that! I saw a pair of big ground hornbills (*Bucorvus cafer*) which are rather rare in this part of the world. He looks not unlike a turkey, with his naked red head and neck, and he spends most of his time sitting on the ground and saying 'Boo-woo, Boo-woo' like a mournful lost dog, if the simile may be allowed.

Mafio has just come up to say he wants to go into the village to buy green maize. Not bad for a youngster, that; seven or eight hours good hard walk in the morning and then a twelve mile tramp in the evening on top of it. I know I don't feel myself that a mere prospect of green maize would induce me to undertake a walk of that length; but walking to these people is merely a matter of putting one foot in front of the other, and is not looked upon as hard work, so long as they've no load to carry they'll go on all day and all night as well if they want to. Personally I'm happy enough to sit in my chair on the verandah and watch the birds who kindly come up to entertain me, and write at odd intervals. It is delightfully peaceful. Yesterday, with W's letter, I was rather unsettled and perhaps envying him in civilization, while Madewa's exit this morning did not exactly have a soothing effect on me, but now on the other hand 'What though the spicy breezes' — I am content and happy and more dreading the thought of a return and the necessity of looking round for a job again, when one can live this sort of life in peace on an expenditure of a pound or two a month. Still, even that pound or two has got to be earned sometime and that's not done by a pair of smallish unmarketable tusks, for which, on the contrary, I might be fined or shoved into the calaboos even.

April 11th, 1929

This is rat week! For some time past I have been plagued by swarms of rats who come into my shack every night and browse on anything that is to their taste; and the African rat is omnivorous. If he were to confine his attentions to maize and the foodstuffs one would not mind so much. But he seems to be more fond of exploring the food values of such things as book bindings and tallow candles, while there must be some particular vitamin in Lifebuoy soap to explain how it is that he finds it so irresistible. But his worst habit is that of nibbling off the rims of the buttons of all one's garments. What sustenance he derives from them it is hard to see, but unless a button is made of tin it is not proof from their attacks. I've had a roll of film spoiled by a rat nibbling through the outer cardboard case, right through the lead foil cylinder which encased it and down into the film itself. Of course if one is foolish enough to leave a bird's skin open to their attentions there will not be much of it by morning.

They bounce about on top of my mosquito net and keep me awake with thoughts of what next of my poor possessions they will destroy. So at last I have declared war and operations started some days ago when I gained a great victory by taking the tent off the top of the house and slaying six in their burrows in the thatch. The rats retaliated the same night and gained a partial success by disintegrating my measuring tape, but as I have another in reserve this is not disastrous, and since then I've had successes all along the line by trapping them. Frazer proves himself to be a great hand at this game and is made by common consent O.C. traps. He got two the first night in spring snares made by bending down a pliant withy having a noose attached to the end which was fixed in one of their runs just where it entered my shack, but the rats have lately got wise to this and he has had more success by fixing falling weight traps. A heavy flat stone, or failing that, mud plastered on a framework of bamboos is neatly fixed at an angle from the ground by bits of stick and grass-stems on the lever and fulcrum principle and to one of the stems which goes right underneath the weight, a bit of maize cob or some meat is attached, which the rat seizes and so causes the whole contraption to fall on top of him. By this means we are really making some impression on the rat hordes and are keeping them within reasonable numbers.

Mafio's overnight enthusiasm to walk into Macheso's is explained by his arrival back in camp today — dressed up to the nines in calico of colours that would put Joseph's coat to shame. They are probably the first garments the kiddy has ever had beyond a dirty bit of rag for a loin cloth, and he must have got news of their arrival from the Mfati Store when Macheso was in a day or two ago. He has been lucky in getting the outside cut of the roll of calico with the maker's trade marks and gaudy signs all over it, which is always much prized. I don't know if the Indians put a premium on this part of the cloth, but I know I should myself were I to go into business in Native Stores. There arrived with Mafio, stirred into enthusiasm for work by the sight of all his finery, three other piccanins of various sizes, amongst them Master Nyalagwa who worked for me before and ran off from Msatwe on our way into Matenji. He is rather an engaging child of nine or ten, so I've taken him on again and forgiven him his past misconduct. Piccanins now swarm in camp. I don't really need them all but they're amusing little brutes and will not mean a vast expenditure as they drop out and come to work whenever they feel like it.

April 13th, 1929

An enormous load of oranges, bananas and guavas arrived today. I didn't know the fellow had any oranges, they proved to be extraordinarily good, in fact quite the best I've ever had in Africa, except of course the Jaffa oranges we used to get in Egypt; but what he wants to send so many for I fail to see — 100 oranges all nearly at the same stage of ripeness, 100 guavas all nearly rotten, 3 bunches of bananas, luckily still quite green. Still it has made a sale for him and a bit of sleepiness won't matter to me, and gives an excuse for getting outside large quantities at a time.

I was a day out in my calculations once again, thinking yesterday the 13th, when I made an entry in this diary. In fact there has really been little to record for some days past. Fever is still hanging round me which does not make one fit for long tramps and though I've been out most days for short walks have not seen anything of interest except an odd hartebeest. It is this confounded lack of quinine that is the trouble; the old malarial bug has once again got good hold of me and will take some shifting when I can again put myself on a course.

April 24th, 1929

Rain still carrying on in an unpleasant sort of manner, while I keep indoors and brush up the odd short story I've written here and draw plans of the bungalow I want to build in a certain spot if I can get a few acres of land there. This is an amusing game and calls for more time and thought than I would have conceived possible, so is good employment so long as this wretched low fever is with me. I don't dare go out, especially in this damp weather, for each time I do so I pay for it by a bad night or two. It's an annoying business altogether, as in between times I am perfectly fit. If I could have one jolly old go and be finished with it for a respectable time I wouldn't mind; but this half feverish, half fit sort of existence is wearying and annoying when one knows that with an extra bottle of quinine at the bottom of one's kit it would never have occurred.

April 25th, 1929

There has been little to tell of these last ten days or so. I have had to take things pretty easy or else I pay for it by getting a concertina head every other afternoon, which feels as if the back of my head was going to blow out at any moment. Kanyangele came in with news of spoor one day which I chased the whole morning with him through the long grass S of camp; but it was too old, we should have got on to it the day before when we would have stood some chance of seeing Jumbo. All that we came across was a family of wart hog who made more noise in their alarm on getting our wind than even a herd of elephant did, and made me at anyrate think for a moment we were up to something worthier. Kanyangele of course knew they were just wart hog all the time which nevertheless did not prevent him from seeking the nearest tree — not that one blames a boy for that. If I hadn't always a rifle in my hand I should spend a lot of time tree-climbing myself; but it's their petty fogging little lies and excuses to justify themselves afterwards where no justification is necessary that rile one — for it is riling to be thought fool enough to believe what they say.

April 26th, 1929

My very last shot-gun cartridge — a No. 8 — bagged me a duck this evening, one of a pair which came and settled on a pool near camp. If I hadn't foolishly fired off my other barrel a morning or two ago at some other duck flighting over the river in the early hours I could have had them both; but anyway the black duck (*Anas sparsa*) is a fitting finale on this trip for the shot-gun which can now be put to bed and sent off to Matenji in company with the elephant rifle. I shall probably send a boy tomorrow or the next day to enquire about the road. The end of April, they told me it would be ready but I rather fancy that means the middle or end of May. I hope they get a move on with it though, as the other road from Tete to Blantyre will certainly be open early in May, and the sooner I'm along it now the better I'll be pleased.

April 30th, 1929

On getting back to camp today after shooting a reedbuck a boy arrived in to ask for work. I told him I was sorry but there was no work for him and that I was soon going away back to Matenji. He seemed very crest-fallen, so noticing that he had many bangles of elephant hair round his wrists I questioned him further, when it transpired that he was a hunter of some experience, knowing how to handle a rifle and with many elephants to his credit. He pleaded for a rifle and to be allowed to go and try his luck, declaring that he would shoot many elephants for me. Now I have not made any attempt previously to find such a boy, as they told me in Tete that this was not allowed under the conditions of my licence but having transgressed the law already it seems I might as well be hanged for a sheep as for a lamb, so I've given him the 9 mm and ten rounds of ammunition, and he departs rejoicing with Kanyangele and food enough for a week and more. He seems the right sort of man, and may quite likely shoot the odd Jumbo for me. Of course it is the only way to get Jumbo in these parts — go off for a week at a time and more, sleep out on the tracks and not give up a herd until one does get up to them. A native can do this — I can't — not with enjoyment at any rate; but I couldn't help envying that little party as I dished out their supplies to them before they set off. A tiny sack of maize-flour, enough to last the pair for a week, a cooking pot, a box of matches and an axe were K's 'load', while the hunter carried the rifle and a blanket. I gave him a tin of the Matenji off-flavoured tobacco, to make him happy and off they went, leaving me wishing I could go with them. It was lucky I still had the 8 mm here, I all but sent it off with the shot-gun a couple of days ago, and how those odd ten rounds of ammunition happened still to be hanging about I don't know, as the rest of the ammunition for it went off with the cartridge magazine a fortnight ago as I never dreamt I should have any need for it. All this puts a very different complexion on matters. If Kaisé succeeds in getting elephants for me and if we can keep quiet about them until such time as I can get down to Tete and renew my licence and back here again, then I should be sorely tempted to stay on for another month or two here. I shall anyway have to go and see about this licence if he nails even one of reasonable size. On the other hand, I simply must go and see my mail soon and attend to business in Nyasaland. What I may do is to dash down to Tete as soon as the road is ready, get my licence, go back to Blantyre, stay there a week seeing about various things and renewing my supplies, and then take the road for Dedza and Furancungo, as Furancungo is really nearer here than is Matenji, I could leave all my belongings here so that I would be going light and would make good time while Master Kaisé could carry on hunting while I was away, so long as he kept very 'Chup' about it. However, it all depends on what he does during the next ten days, and on what sort of luck he has. One thing is certain anyway, and that is that I beat it and renew my supply of shot-gun cartridges just as soon as I am able.

The boys did not get back with the reedbuck until after night-fall. The fools could not follow my description of where it was, though I had drawn pictures of the place and explained its position with reference to other game I had shot nearby previously, until I thought I had hammered it in. But no, they came back saying they couldn't find it, about 7 p.m., and Frazer had to have its position explained to him, whereupon he walked straight to the spot apparently — so he has a little sense after all. I had left a long and broad trail of broken branches for a quarter of a mile, leading to the spot; but they were of course searching the wrong side of the dambo.

That is the third or fourth reedbuck I have killed at or about the same place in the last few weeks. There have always been two together, a buck and a doe, and on each occasion I have slain the buck. I think she must be a very attractive young doe to lure so many bucks to her company. She is still going strong, and so I'm hoping she'll soon attract another for my benefit. Reedbuck heads in this district seem to average about 12 inches, there has been little variance in all those that I have shot — a half-inch one way or the other, perhaps, but that is all. I've a sort of idea that a really good head will go 15 inches, but cannot remember distinctly.

May 3rd, 1929

My boy came back today with an answer to my letter to Matenji, saying that the road was not yet ready — nor even begun; rather what I had feared. Abnormally heavy rains and apparently a Government who say they'll help one minute and won't the next, seem to be the trouble.

Bivar himself is away in Tete at the moment arranging about it, the Senora says he will probably get it in order himself and trust to be repaid later by his Government. I wouldn't put out much money myself under those conditions. This means, I think, that I must walk down to Tete myself. I'll hang on here until my hunter returns to see what luck he has had, and, if he has shot an elephant of any size, off I go. Even if he has had no fortune I think I may still go along to get cash, of which I'm rapidly running short. Not that I want to; there is not much pleasure in a plain 120 mile hike to Tete, nor can that miserable little town produce anything to look forward to out of its — vegetable plots. I don't suppose I shall even be able to buy an English cigarette there, and I shall spend as much money there on a bottle of beer as would keep me in fruit here for a month. Still — I'm wanting salt and sugar again, or will be very shortly, and I feel it is time I spoke English again with some one, be it only a Dago.

May 6th, 1929

No sign yet of the hunter coming back. I hope an elephant hasn't trodden on him; but we would hear soon enough if that were the case, from

Master Kanyangele who would take the best possible care to keep out of the way, if I know anything of him.

They are finding it not so easy a job as they thought, and I daresay K is holding things up, he is no stalwart and really not the man at all for slogging after elephant. I hope they won't be long now as I want to get off myself as soon as possible; but must see Kaisé first. I shall not tell the boys that we will have to walk down to Tete as the prospect would probably overawe them. If they merely think they are going for a gentle walk up to Matenji they won't mind so much. I do not intend going with a lot of loads. A boy and a couple of piccanins will have to do me, and whatever happens the loads must be light.

May 7th to July 12th, 1929

About the beginning of May, leaving Frazer in charge of my belongings, I left my grass shack on the Bandi with one boy and a brace of piccanins to do the 120 mile stretch into Tete. These were all I had in the way of carriers, and, in Makanya country dashed lucky to have them.

I am writing this here in the Barwe district after completing a successful trip, with a good lot of Chikunda natives picked up at Tete, and I've rarely had a happier trip. My boys are willing and faithful; the only one who has groused at all is a Makanya. Result: good relationship between them and me, and that I look after them and do as much for them as I can.

The Chikunda are the first decent-minded natives I have met since leaving Tanganyika, and it is such a relief. I had begun to think that it was in reality I who was at fault, and not the Amanganga, Angami, Makanya and Azumba. Then I thought perhaps it was because I'm no longer a big man and a member of a Government service that every African tribe I've met since has been unhelpful to me.

But now, thank God, I know that this is not so and that there are still tribes of the right sort. The Atonga here, though they fall far short of the Chikunda, are on the whole and with a few exceptions a generous and pleasing people. All this has done me the greatest good, and I've been more at peace with the world this last month or so than at any time during the last three years.

But to return to my journey down to Tete; that, I think, was as regrettable a show as was the rest of that unfortunate trip N of the river. What shoes I had were rapidly disintegrated on the march. I had no socks to my name and I arrived in Tete walking on poisoned and swollen feet that laid me up for a fortnight, and in fact did not get completely right for over six weeks.

I stayed in Tete with M of the Posts and Telegraph Service, who has a little shack on the north bank of the river, and was when I arrived the only Englishman in the place. He is the only permanent one there; the rest of us are birds of passage like myself.

Right well was I greeted and much did I enjoy the luxury of fresh milk and butter and an occasional cabbage or green food, though that is scarce enough in Tete. But though the rest was good, it was not altogether without its anxiety. Fortune was still dealing low-down cards to me.

I found an uproar of excitement over elephant licences and ivory, a couple of young Englishmen having just done a bunk over the frontier, fearing to meet Portuguese law over a simple matter of shooting a cow. It was almost impossible for a newcomer to get guarantees which are necessary before a licence is issued to you and the licence north of the river had been changed from free shooting to £15 for five Jumbo, like the rest of the country.

Here was I with a pair of tusks, unbeknownst to the authorities, and having to put down as much money as they were worth to be able to own them. Still it had to be done. I could see that sticking out a mile and I went to the bank to cash money on my letter of credit only to find that the damned thing was only good for six months originally and was now out of date.

So there I was stranded without a bean to my name and no funds available except in Blantyre. That took over a week to be put square — telegrams flying to Beira, Blantyre and I don't know where else. It would have been quicker to have cabled home. Blantyre, though only 120 miles off had no account with the Bank in Tete; there was Empire Day and other holidays to delay matters, and it was not until about the fourth of June that I was again in funds and each minute of it was an anxiety to me. If it had not been for M, I should have been in a real bad hole. The British Consul did nothing for me and it was M who lent me the cash for the wires.

At last, however, all was fixed up. I got my money and licences and just as I was starting off north again the Bivar's motor lorry came down and I got a lift back again on it, which was a stroke of luck. This left me only 50 miles or so to walk and I arrived back at the Bandi halfway through June.

But Dame Fortune still had her back to me and had not finished with me by a long chalk. On arrival I found that Kaishé, the boy to whom I had given the rifle in hopes he might snaffle the odd Jumbo whilst I was away, was arrested and in prison at the Boma — my rifle confiscated. The silly ass had not kept to this deserted area where it was known I was shooting, but had strayed further afield and been pinched by a police Askari.

I wrote to the Boma, disclaiming all responsibility for his actions, and was given back the rifle. Hands of horror of the Negrophilist I vision, but the boy had been well warned that if such a thing occurred he could look for no help from me and he had not only left the country I had told him to hunt, but paraded round the villages showing off his rifle. So I had no scruple in letting him take what was coming to him, which would not be more than a few shillings fine, whilst had I been impeached for arming the natives, I might expect any sentence up to two years in the calaboos, which was the fate meted out to a poor devil from South Rhodesia not so long ago, who was still in jug in Tete when I arrived there first, and that without any trial.

The next back-hander from Lady Fortune was to find that a herd of elephants had been hanging round my camp for days whilst I had been away. Frazer and the boys had seen them on two occasions and once had been driven out of camp. They had built an aerial retreat in the big trees and from there had watched them one night close by. Now of course they were off again, leaving behind one bull of large size whom we heard in the bamboos the second night after I got back. Full of hope I started off next morning on his tracks with Mafio, the small piccanin as my tracker, and we came up with him in long grass where he got our wind and gave us an exciting minute or two.

The brute was looking for us then and made those terrifying little rushes in our direction, stopping within five yards of us each time, when he appeared as an indistinct shadow through the long grass. I might have had a shot at him; but as I never had a clear view of him or his tusks, held my hand and beat a retreat to higher ground where I climbed a tree hoping for a clear view of him and his tusks.

By the time I had found a tree I could scale, the animal was making off and I saw him on the other side of the open dambo over the top of the grasses. He was still very excited, his trunk was up feeling the air so to speak, and he hadn't an ounce of ivory to his name.

So much for that. We returned campwards, my head singing like a top, and a day or two afterwards I went down with the worst go of fever that I have ever had.

Frazer had left me by then. The fellow was a poor-spirited wretch really and not suited for a life in the bush, so I paid him off and gave him his choice of clearing out.

He was not worth 15/- a month in the bush. He was continually whining for civilization and in the end I was glad to see the last of him, though I would have given much for his ministrations while I lay sick.

It was a curious bout, and I don't think can have been true malaria for I've never had a go that came in the way this did. Perhaps it was not fever at all but a heat-stroke. The symptoms were strange to me. For at least a week before I actually collapsed I used to wake in the night with a splitting headache which disappeared when I got out of bed and strolled about for a minute or two. In the morning I felt all right and quite fit for a walk in the bush. Later, these nightly headaches got worse and would wake me on two or three occasions; but it was several days before I actually felt feverish during the day.

When it did come I got it good and proper. High fever and splitting headaches which made me at one time quite delirious. I had the fear in my mind of Sleeping Sickness which probably made things worse, for I did not know the symptoms of this disease. In a comparatively lucid interval I scrawled a note to Chipazi telling him how things were, and he wrote to the Boma at Muchena for machila boys to carry me in. I had already tried the nearby Boma of Furancungo with no results as the bloke in charge, I heard afterwards, absconded just at that time with I don't know how many thousands of the native tax money, burning his office down behind him so that there should be no trace of his transactions. While no help was to be looked for from the local Makanga native without Boma orders. A sick white man was none of their business.

So for about a fortnight I lay at a pretty low ebb, and just as I was shaking off the go, a machila arrived from the Bivars, who had heard of my plight, and very kindly sent down their own machila team for me. I lost no time in packing up my loads for the last time and had the comfort of being carried into Matenji where I arrived the first week of July, still pretty weak but on my legs again.

They were very kind to me there for the couple of days I stayed with them before tackling driving the car down to Tete. I owe that family a lot for all they did for me.

Here at Matenji, I paid off what boys I had, keeping Mafio, who said he wanted to stay with me after a little pressure on my part. But the little blighter deserted me the very morning I left for Tete, leaving me to struggle with all the loads myself, and giving me a tiring journey by myself with punctures and valve trouble to sort unaided. I think I then felt my fortunes at their lowest ebb. I was alone in Africa, so to speak, and up against it.

The first day I only got as far as Muchena, which I had to visit to show my tusks and get a licence to sell them; but on the second made Tete about midday as the road on that stretch was really quite good and here I again began to consider ways and means and what was next on the programme.

My assets were a motor car and about £20, with another £20 deposited with the police to get me out of the country if I decided to return to Nyasaland where at any rate I had a house to live in any time I wanted. But the money I had was also just enough for one more trip. If I could get down to the Barwe and shoot four elephants there that remained to me on my licence, I should once more be in funds; if the trip was a failure I should not be much worse off than before. I would just be able to pay off my boys and struggle back to Nyasaland.

So I threw my glove down to a last round with Africa and Dame Fortune, and on a Friday, and the thirteenth of the month left Tete once more on my travels.

The last taunt was not deliberate, I need hardly say, a gambler does not do such things deliberately. In fact I was horrified when I realized what I had done; but by then it was too late to mend matters. What made it worse to my mind was the thought that my last trip had started both from Blantyre and from Tete on Fridays. I remembered the fact, as a hunter had said to me on the latter occasion, 'Put it off until tomorrow'. My last trip N. of the river started on a Friday and was a disastrous one!

But for me it was too late and I had not taken his advice.

PORTUGUESE EAST AFRICA
South of the Zambezi

July 13th, 1929

Left Tete by canoe down the Zambezi. Six carriers, a personal boy and a picannin. We were late getting off as I made a last unsuccessful rush round the town to try and find shot-gun cartridges. So I left the shot-gun with the British Consul together with the 9 mm rifle as there is no point in lugging round extra weight. The trip down the river was most enjoyable, though the sun was blazing hot and we of course had no sort of awning to shelter us. We saw a few hippos and crocodiles in hundreds, especially at the mouth of the Luwemya River which joins the Zambezi, I suppose about 20 miles down; but the only thing I tried a shot at was a thick flush of knob-nosed duck sitting on a sand spit. They did not allow us to approach closely so it was a matter of 'browning' and a solitary duck was collected. One other species of duck was noted (*Dendrocygna fulva*), flamingoes, ibises, a few spur-winged geese and what I made out to be the open-billed stork. Stayed the night at an Indian store at a military post just past the mouth of the Luwemya, I can't remember its name.

July 14th, 1929

Completed the journey down stream arriving at another Indian store about 11 a.m. I made a few purchases here and sent out boys to collect another two carriers of which I am in need — can't get off without them. The local chief promises two for tomorrow morning, as he says they are not to be found in the villages until evening, which of course is so. There's no point in being impatient to get away as I've heaps of time to collect my four jumbo, I hope. Went out along the banks of the Zambezi in the afternoon to sight the ·450 rifle and found a convenient crocodile lying on a sand bank about a hundred yards out, so targeted on him with both barrels much to my satisfaction. Not that I got possession of the brute — one rarely does unless one goes on pumping lead into him indefinitely. The paddle steamer went by in the evening on its journey down to Chinde and I heard rifle reports just as they passed, so I suppose the Portugoose also amuses himself by blotting an odd crocodile on his way down.

July 15th, 1929

Two boys turned up this morning so I got off in good time arriving at a small village about midday where I was given the most erroneous information. Good game and elephant country half a day away — we would get there today — no villages on ahead. Taking this to be the truth I rearranged my loads, leaving a lot of stuff behind, and went off to explore this wonderful country only to walk straight into another and larger village a couple of miles away. The chief here seemed a sensible sort of bloke and he gave me information to go on to Nyakafula's village about two days off where there is elephant and game. I asked if there were buffalo and he said plenty, so on the principle that where there are buffalo there will be elephant also at some season of the year, I decided to take his advice and sent back for the loads I had left behind. This country is full of 'masan', a little round yellow-red fruit growing on a prickly bushy tree. The fruit tastes rather like an apple and is very good when not too bitter.

The natives distil another of their rotten-egg-smelling spirits from the fermented fruit.

July 16th, 1929

Today's march to a village called Mali's. Nothing to record except the slaying of a wart hog much to the boys' delight, the first 'nyama' of the expedition. Yesterday's chief came with us as guide after a great deal of pressure on my part and reluctance on his, but departed wreathed in smiles with a ham as his 'prizie'.

July 17th, 1929

Had a glimpse of an eland bull as we left the village this morning and then, after about an hour's walk, came on fresh elephant spoor which I immediately proceeded to follow, taking blankets, food etc. and sending the remainder of the carriers on to the next village on the Nyakaluswe River with orders to await me there. We followed Jumbo — a small herd — for the rest of the morning and until about 2 p.m. when we came to some millet fields and a village which we visited to get information as to where we had got to. Here, whilst regaling myself on honeycomb, I was told by the chief that I was in the Mozambique Company's territory and had not yet reached the Barwe District of my licence. Bit of luck for me that I had not got up to those Jumbo and more that he was a sensible native who could put me straight. We had meat, millet porridge and honey — and immediately made tracks in the right direction, the chief showing me a range of hills which he said was the boundary of the two territories. A further ten miles or so brought us to the Nyakuluswe River just at dusk so we made camp and stayed the night.

July 18th, 1929

On again this morning about three or four miles to a village, or rather a single native's hut where I found the rest of my carriers so we lost no time in getting under way for Nyakafula's. I slew a pig on the way and followed a herd of buffalo whose fairly fresh spoor we hit. They gave me a merry chase up and down the steepest slopes they could find for a couple of hours when I got tired of them and came on to the village, arriving well on in the afternoon. The country round here is flat — thank the Lord — by the spoor we saw it seems to be full of game and there were a good lot of reasonably fresh elephant spoor to be seen.

July 19th, 1929

Went out this morning with a couple of boys and a native as guide who professed his confidence to show me elephant. We found no spoor worth following, but encountered a pair of leopards. They snarled their displeasure at getting our wind from a point in the long grass about a hundred yards off the path we were walking on and when I went to investigate, bounded off. The second one was a bit late in getting under way and I had a snap at him which knocked him over. I could not see him where he lay hidden by the grass and began moving forward, rifle ready, to finish him off as soon as I got a glimpse of him whereupon the confounded guide started talking. I suppose he was trying to warn me of the danger but it naturally had the effect of rousing Spots, who with one bound disappeared into the grass. I had another snap at him in mid air which missed — and that was the last we saw of him, for I'm afraid there are no heroics about me when it comes to following a wounded leopard in long grass. Not when one's livelihood depends on keeping fit for action, anyway.

July 20th, 1929

Late getting off today as that fool of a guide did not turn up betimes. He said he did not want to come as he was afraid of me. Of course I had cursed him yesterday for his behaviour with the leopard and he further showed his incapacity by taking us a ridiculously long road back to camp. I pacified him in the end, as one must have a local guide until one begins to know the country a bit, and we then went off south, first to a small water hole and then through some very heavy bush. The walk produced nothing except two nests of some type of courser, both with eggs which I took. Sent boys today to the Boma with my licences for endorsement.

July 21st, 1929

A very long tramp to the east along the foot of a range of hills where we found the leopards. We followed a herd of elephants but could make no impression on them. It was spoor of the night before but the brutes were trekking and I eventually gave up and got back dog weary late in the afternoon.

July 22nd, 1929

Another rest today as yesterday knocked me up rather. Am not yet in training for jumbo. Thinking things out I have decided to go and make camp out to the east some six or seven miles. I shall have to send for water every day but I have plenty of boys and that will be no hardship to them.

July 23rd, 1929

Started out this morning intending to carry on as I decided yesterday but came on fresh spoor of three bull elephants before I was a mile down the road from camp. It was the best spoor I have seen for many a long day and we changed plans quickly enough, sending the loads back to camp and following up with three boys. Jumbo led us through some good game country and I could have had shots at kudu, waterbuck and bushbuck but of course held my hand though we are in much need of meat. The dung was absolutely fresh and just faintly warm in the centre which meant that the brutes were jogging along slowly just ahead and a rifle shot might scare them into the next district. Spooring was the very devil; the boys weren't any too good never having had much practice at the game and this is the very worst time of year for quick work which was what we wanted to get up to them. But I was determined we should succeed and about midday sent a boy back to camp with orders to follow up after us with water, food and blankets. I think this may have shown the other boys that elephant was a more serious undertaking than they thought — all my boys are new hands at the game, picked up in Tete — and they worked harder with the result that at about 2 p.m. we at last heard the crash of a tree ahead which warned us we were up to them.

I seized the heavy rifle and went forward accompanied by Sabunete, whom I had drilled in unloading and reloading it and handing me my light rifle when I needed it. We were in pretty heavy country but so cut about by elephant tracks that one generally had a good field of view, isolated clumps of bush with their trails winding round them. I saw him — one only as the other two were feeding apart — just as I rounded one of those corners and he looked evil and malign and black. He had those half curved tusks, too, which are so disconcerting. Anyway, I made a horrid mess of it when I might have done the thing cleanly; both barrels of the heavy rifle and a magazine full of solid 8 mm were not enough to bring him down for they were all just in the wrong place and I was excited. However he couldn't go — he was stunned and all he wanted was some place where he could hide from these blows. I took over the RTP ·450 again, which I presumed was ready for me and found myself in the creature's path as he dashed for a safe retreat. "Now" I thought "I have you" and "a frontal shot for the brain" — and I pulled the trigger, one after the other, but there was only the snap of a dead cap to answer me and I turned tail and fled, waiting for Jumbo's trunk at the seat of my trousers. But a glance behind told me he had turned off and an examination showed not misfires but that that criminal Sabunete had not reloaded the rifle. Language flew both then and afterwards nor have I taken the boy with me again. But this, anyway, gave me a breathing space and I worked round and finished off Jumbo with a shot from the 8 mm. What rejoicings! the biggest elephant I have had since leaving Tanganyika by a good way — I make out there should be at least 100 lbs. of ivory on him.

But as we sat talking, there were shouts heard in the distance and up came the boys I had sent back in the morning, with water, to our great enjoyment and a letter for me from the Boma to say that I was to go in there immediately and that I was not to shoot elephant until I had done so. Once again the wrong side of the law — sending my licence for endorsement was not sufficient. The letter was written in Portuguese but I could make out most of it and the boy had been told what to tell me by the man in charge at the Boma. I didn't take it very seriously, some damn jack-in-office wanting to show off his importance — and so it turned out to be — but that's anticipating.

July 24th, 1929

The boys spent the day bringing in meat and starting to take out the tusks.

July 25th, 1929

I started out to the Boma, curse it, 50 or 60 miles away with a couple of boys — Driver, the cook and the picannin who calls himself MaryAnna. The boys tell me I will be three nights on the road — will I? — I'll show them. Walked for about nine hours in all today in three bouts, finally camping for the night when I made out the Boma to be not more than six hours off.

July 26th, 1929

Into the Boma, arriving about 1 p.m., fixed up my licences in no time, the whole thing was a farce and quite an unnecessary bit of officialdom. Started back again doing a couple of hours and making a village where I found the German, Muller, in camp. I'd met him in Tete about a month before. He's an experienced hunter who claims 200 elephants. I can believe it; I think he knows what he is talking about. We had a long talk in the evening on elephant.

July 27th, 1929

Camped tonight just past Nyakafula's village on the Nyakagombe River. This river and the Mwira join about here and the Mwira goes on down to Nyakafula's. 'River' is the wrong name for them as they are merely dry sand and the only water to be got is from deep wells. Stopping here as I found good spoor in the sand as I was coming along.

July 28th, 1929

Hunted here in the morning but failed to strike anything fresh so came on to Nyakatumba's, where after some misunderstanding I was well received by the chief and regaled with Moa — native beer. They tell me there are plenty of elephant here so I have decided to camp here for a day or two and see what's what. I have sent in to Nyakafula's for some kit so as to be a bit more comfortable.

July 29th, 1929

Got up to elephant today but the wind gave us away at the last moment and all I saw was a stern piece vanishing in the thick stuff and a gleam of tusks — no good to fire at such a target and the blighters didn't stand again though I followed them hard. Spooring is dreadfully hard — even Muller, the German, was complaining of the difficulty, so I must not be hard on my boys who are improving with practice. Shot a kudu on the way back to camp.

July 30th, 1929

Hunted the same country as yesterday but though I got a spoor we made no progress. My loads and heavy rifle have arrived from Nyakafula's, also a letter from Goucher whom I've been looking for and of whom so far I've had no news. He is near Nyakafula's and we have arranged to meet shortly.

July 31st, 1929

Again up to elephant and shot one, tusks long but thin, may go 30 lbs. A long and tiring day and in the end they got our wind and I was lucky with a snap for the heart just as he was moving off. This failed for the heart but hit him in the shoulder about six inches too far forward and I think the bone must have broken when he dashed off for he stood again twice within ten minutes. There were three animals together; a bull, a cow and a half-grown animal.

August 1st, 1929

Back to Nyakafula's.

August 2nd, 1929

To Mafundo's about 14 miles on to the north. Beastly wet and raining! No kit with me except a blanket.

August 3rd, 1929

Hunted round Mafundo's in the morning, but finding that Jumbo had not been stamping round there lately came back to N's in the afternoon.

August 4th, 1929

Rested.

August 5th, 1929

Long trek south after elephant whose spoor I found on the sand of the Mwira — quite unsuccessful in getting up to him.

August 6th, 1929

Another long trek — after a mountaineering elephant who spent all the time rushing up and down the steepest slopes of a hill I call Saddleback Hill, for obvious reasons, lying some six or seven miles west. In the evening had a visit from Goucher who has now shot four elephant and is on his way back to the Boma.

August 7th, 1929

Walked out north-west to the Dogni River, the boundary of Mozambique and the Barwe — saw yesterday's spoor, only. Shot a kudu near camp on return.

August 8th, 1929

Going west in the morning I came on a large herd of buffalo and shot two big bulls — one spanning 41 inches, the other about 36. Again yesterday's spoor only.

August 9th, 1929

Picked up spoor on the sand and followed it south past Nsusa Hill — a regrettable day as I came up with them and then wounded the bull — 'nuff said. Got back to camp 10 p.m.

August 10th, 1929

Made tracks for Gogo — a small village lying by a hill of that name past Nsusa Hill.

August 11th, 1929

Hunted west from Gogo but saw no sign of any elephant having been there for ages.

August 12th, 1929

Expected great things from this date and it paid up with my 16th elephant, a smallish animal unfortunately, which I would not really have shot in the ordinary course of events but I saw it was wounded and quite recently. My first close sight of it was from behind and a bullet wound in that quarter showed up plainly. At first I hoped it might be the animal I had a go at on the 9th but I realized this was not so when I saw that one tusk was deformed and turned right round, pointing the wrong way. It was rather an interesting day. We first inspected a water hole a few miles to the south finding yesterday's spoor there. Then, while we were climbing the bank of the watercourse we heard an elephant gurgling a few hundred yards off but when we went forward found that it was only a smallish animal. Still, I followed up for a time hoping that it would join or be joined by bigger ones. After about half an hour's trekking with no sign of any other elephant being near I gave up and turned about, intending to circle round by the east, but before we had been going five minutes heard a tremendous trumpeting from the bush ahead which went on more or less continually for about ten minutes. We went up to see what the matter was but as we were a good distance from the place where all the commotion had been, by the time we arrived Jumbo had already moved off. We found fresh spoor though of a herd and followed up. After an hour or two we came up to a solitary bull which I eventually shot though I was loth to do so at first, owing to the small size of his tusks. It was the sight of the fresh blood that made me take him and I plead to having in some way repaid the debt of my behaviour on the 9th. I think this animal was the cause of all the noise and fancy he was trying to join up with the herd on ahead, which he was still following. Poor animal he was very sick and the herd resented his presence and the smell of blood that was on him.

Coming back to camp we again came on fresh spoor which I followed for a time, but making no progress with it returned to the village where I found boys had arrived from Nyakatumba's with my second elephant tusks. Five and a quarter feet is the length of the longer tusk and if they only had been thicker in proportion would have weighed somewhat! They are beastly thin though and won't go much over 30 pounds apiece. Still I'm pleased enough with them and reckon I've made some £100 this last month.

August 13th and 14th, 1929

Two more days hunting round Gogo Hill without getting a spoor.

August 15th, 1929

Went back to Nyakafula's where the chief had made ten jars full of Moa at my bidding for my boys to dance on. It wastes a day but I want to keep these boys happy. The dance lasted until all hours but I found that the local grey beards did most of the drinking. My own boys were not much in evidence. They one and all got tight immediately and were down and out at 6 p.m. They came alive again about midnight I noticed and took further part in the proceedings.

August 16th, 1929

Made tracks for Chigombe on the way to the Boma hoping to pick up my last elephant in that quarter. I understood the distance to be much shorter than it proved to be for we struck no sort of village until about 9 or 10 p.m. except Nyahorongo, five miles out of Nyakafula. Here I was bitten by a wretched pi-dog which made a snap at my leg as I was entering the village. The confounded creature broke the skin which necessitated applications of pot permang after a scarifying operation with the razor. I had no scruple in putting a bullet through the dog though I would have contented myself with giving the blighter a hammering if I could have got to it.

August 18th, 1929

Came on today through the country I hunted for three days at the end of last month telling the carriers to go and wait for me at a certain water-hole that we knew of. My idea was to camp there if jumbo was still in the vicinity and so save the long walk each morning which I had had before when hunting this country from Nyakatumba's. However I changed my plans as I found no spoor more recent than about a week old and the water-holes dried up where the elephants had been drinking before. So on we came, back to Nyakatumba's and were lucky to find that the chief had called in the herdmen from the various out lying villages on some tax business and he promised to question them all as to Jumbo's whereabouts as they arrived. The result that I have two offers for guides tomorrow and

more, assurance that there are elephant to be found south of the Mwira.
I came in today from the north. Bought a tinful of honey this evening of
which I ate enormous quantities. I buy it at about 3/- a gallon which is
not an enormous price when one thinks of the 7 or 8 shillings that is paid
for a solitary comb of the stuff at home.

August 19th, 1929

Great luck today in finishing off this licence with quite a good elephant
who had fair tusks which should go for 30 lbs. a piece. A longish trek to
the south brought us to a small dried stream, a tributary of the Mwira. We
saw no spoor at all on the way and I thought half way through the morning
that there was nothing for us here and we should have to retrace our steps
to Gogo. But on the sand of this little stream things began to look more
interesting. Lots of old spoor and dried dung told that it was quite a
favoured spot, while a solitary bull of large size had tramped up the river
bed only a day or two before. For an hour or so we saw nothing further
than that. There was no sign of dampness to the sand and the deep holes
that elephants make in order to find water, I suppose with their trunks,
were also quite dry. On enquiring, the guide said there was water to be
found further on so we slogged ahead, the spoor of the solitary bull keeping
company with us all the way. Presently I was delighted to see clumps of
green rushes growing on the sand of the river bed , always a sure sign that
there is water not far below the surface and finally the sand grew damp
and we came to water lying in small puddles and one deep hole in
between two rocks. Here the ground showed good spoor at last and the
bright yellow of fresh dung rejoiced my eyes and fresh enough it was,
probably not more than an hour or two old, while the spoor itself bespoke
two great bulls that had taken their fill. We sat down for two minutes, had
a drink and a smoke while I envisioned the prospect of finishing my
licence with a month to spare.

Then to the day's business — and we moved ahead along the spoor. At
first it was difficult enough to follow over springy dried grass but my two
head boys, Jonack and Alfiere, are now really good trackers and it didn't
take us long to work it out. We were much helped by the enormous
appetites of those two animals and the tell-tale signs they left behind
them. Soon we left the comparatively open country where the elephants
had been feeding in the early morning and entered thick bush where
the ground was carpeted with dry leaves and here spooring was a simple
matter each footprint is plainly visible and one can follow at a good pace.

The elephants were still feeding and such was the progress we made that at the end of an hour's tracking we were close up, Jumbo not more than 15 minutes ahead and I reckoned we should see them in five. I can never get rid of that nervous excitement that attacks one when hot dung tells one is close up. I'm not sure that I want to, for therein lies one of the charms of this thrilling game; I suppose the veteran and hardened performer at the game or the cool unemotional man can go through the whole business in a calm and collected manner, but as for me even a stalk up to an ordinary hartebeest makes me say to myself 'Don't be a fool man, you've done this hundreds of times before what the — have you got to be excited about? While with elephant the signs that tell one is gradually nearer sends me into a blessed state of nervous bliss which I am all the time trying to keep under control. If I come suddenly on Jumbo while this nervousness is at its full height and there's no time to be lost, I am liable to do any sort of fool thing; but luckily there's generally plenty of time in which to sober up. So in this case, there was a long enough tramp ahead of us still, for Jumbo, who up to this time had been feeding regularly suddenly decided that he had had enough and it was time to find a good place for a doze and he started on through the bush keeping us the same 15 minutes behind him all the way. This went on for an hour or two and by the time we eventually did come up to them my only feeling was one of exasperation with these two bulls who had kept us so long in suspense and given us this quite unlooked for tramp.

We had momentarily lost the spoor and I had sat down for a rest when Jonack came up to me and said he had heard them close by. 'They had got our wind and are now off' was his remark. I was quite ready to believe it; that beastly chopping wind that always blows in the bush when the sun is high has saved many an elephant. Still I went forward and sat down where he said he had heard them intending to give them a few minutes to realize a false alarm and settle down again. But hardly had I reached the spot when a gurgle and a slight crackle of branches told us that Jonack's theory was wrong, they were still there, quite unalarmed and apparently feeding.

What Ho! thought I, this was luck indeed. And I went forward with the heavy rifle. I had rather an exciting time with them for I failed to hit the brain of the animal I fired at — heavy bush work is the very devil for a clean shot — and finally downed him at 3 yards with the 8 mm, taking the frontal shot and firing as it seemed to me straight up in the air. It was certainly touch and go. I had just fired a shot of the same rifle at him which turned him towards me and while I was reloading my sensations were: "have I time for another shot? — No — yes —" and I fired, at the same moment ducking down the nearest opening in the bush across his feet. He collapsed as I sprang aside and — "You old . . ." — I found myself reviling him — "Nearly had me that time didn't you?". In the meantime I had quite forgotten elephant No. 2 who, the boys afterwards said, had at one time been very interested in me and his tracks showed that he had indeed approached much too near for comfort, though I was unaware of it. He had now made off and we dashed after him hoping he would stand again, for although he would have been in excess of the number I was entitled to by my licence, I was quite prepared to take him and fight for him at the Boma or pay an extra small licence fee. But as things turned out we had no hope of seeing him, he was off for good and earnest and I don't suppose he halted until there was a good chunk of Africa behind him. So that was that and we came back to camp, arriving in the late afternoon to a well earned cup of tea that held more than its usual satisfactory taste. Just a month to the day since we started hunting at Nyakafula's and four elephants to our credit. Not so bad a record when one considers that three months is the full time of the licence and that most hunters need it all to complete their bag. The clerk at the Boma when I went in there shook his head over the short time I had for my four, while Muller, the German, annoyed me considerably when I told him by saying "Six weeks — plenty of time for me — yes — For you —" and a shake of the head. The man took great delight in blowing his own trumpet and talked down to me in rather a resentful manner which at first annoyed me until I realized how amusing it was to be told what good food was provided in German lines "First class, of course. Second class I do not know".

August 20th and 21st, 1929

My first thoughts after shooting the elephant on the 19th were to lose no time in getting back to Tete; but thinking things over I saw that two or three days spent here bringing in meat and collecting new supplies of flour would be worth a lot to me on my next trip, so I've spent these two days in camp writing up this narrative in bits which I had left out before, cleaning up rifles, overhauling my kit, etc. The boys are all at the elephant, engaged in chopping it up and cutting out the tusks. I don't want to delay much longer as I'm anxious to meet Goucher in Tete before he starts back here. We made a tentative plan to come out together in my car sending on the boys a couple of days ahead. We are planning to camp together for a few days on the next trip as I want to learn how to wash gold. This country is full of odd little bits of gold but one rarely meets it in paying quantities. G is a great hand at the game with a lot of previous experience though needless to say he has not yet made a fortune at it. All alluvial in this country, is free and open to the prospector, so once one knows something about the game it gives one a second string to one's bow while Jumbo hunting. Of course if one could have the luck that I've had this last month every month of the year, one would not worry about much else; but I've had great fortune and also it's a tiring game and one wants a rest from it occasionally.

Continued

I'm afraid this can hardly call itself a diary as I'm starting to write on October 9th and have to think back each day to September 9th — just a month ago — the day we left Tete and arrived at Munjana Boma — my laziness I can only blame on G whose company has been a welcome change from the usual solitary life of the hunter, for it is only now that we have split up our force for the time being that I begin to put pencil to paper — still here goes.

September 9th, 1929

Having at last got our licences fixed up — and trouble enough it was to get them for they want to close down the Barwe again — I crossed the Zambezi in the ferry pulled by a powerful motor-boat, the car once again loaded up and groaning under its weight of kit and boys. But the more you seem to put up on a two-seater Morris Cowley the more it seems to like it, for she took the steep bank up from the river like a soaring bird. Whilst in Tete I had decarbonized her and ground in the valves with the help of a young half-caste who had had a little experience in the Government Garage. Our valve grinding paste was a mixture of thick oil and emery powder, rather drastic treatment but she seemed to thrive under it. I picked up G on the other bank and after making a few last purchases we left the town about 11 a.m. My carriers had left in the early morning and I hoped would be a long way out by now, but we overtook them before we had gone ten miles, lying under a tree by the roadside — a poor enough effort for a day's march, so I left them there and told them to hurry on as fast as they could after us. We made good time to the Luwemya about 20 miles out where we had to board another ferry and be shoved and pulled across the sandy river sticking everywhere on sand-banks. The water looked very tempting after the dusty roads and I lay and wallowed in it while we waited for the boys to come over for us. The car was very refractory on reaching the other side and refused to start up until we had washed out the magneto and it was obvious even then that the points weren't functioning properly. Still we went forward merrily for another 40 miles without any mishap, but then troubles started — first a puncture and then just as we were within ten miles of the Boma a complete failure of the magneto. She occasionally showed a spark of life and at odd intervals came forward at bounds of a mile or two, then she needed more attention; but as it shortly came on to dusk I could not undertake any feats of engineering with spanners but could only throw petrol at the damned thing and wag it about until she seemed more at ease. It was dark when we arrived but the great thing was having got there at all. Tea, the old khuku and bed succeeded each other rapidly.

September 10th, 1929

Started wrestling with the magneto in the early morning and of course found I'd no magneto spanner but managed to make one from an old tyre lever, and with the help of G and the book of words got things going about 10 a.m., when we went over to the office and showed our licences. So after a long and wordy row at the Indian Store over a matter of a couple of yards of their calico which we'd had made up into hankerchiefs and for which the Indian wanted us to pay 12/- we left for Kampapa's Kraal back on the main road. Going out in the evening from there G slew a duiker which gave us fresh meat for a day or two.

September 11th, 1929

Hunted from the village, a country that had seen no elephant for many a long day, nor did I meet with anything when I went to look for a buck in the evening. The askari, or 'spy' as they call him here, arrived in the afternoon with our licences and the news that there was fresh spoor on the road about five miles back.

September 12th, 1929

Ran down the road in the car to where the spoor had been seen and then cut in through the bush and along a path lying across what should have been the brute's line to water, but had no luck. My carriers had arrived by the time we got back to camp and we planned to move off that day. A lorry belonging to Schotts, a German trader in Tete, rolled in short of petrol — just like a native driver — and I had to see him through with a promise that he would bring it straight back to me. I gave him four gallons and if he doesn't play the game I won't have anything like enough to take me back to Tete.

September 13th, 1929

By car to the Boma about 15 miles off where I garaged the car as best I might, rearranged loads and we then made tracks for Rupia's village where we'd heard there were plenty of jumbo about. The village proved to be about 18 miles away and we camped at a delightful spot by the sandy river under a large wild fig tree.

September 14th, 1929

A long trek into the country where our guide told us there would be plenty of elephant but of course found nothing that was not 'archaic'.

September 15th, 1929

Rather disgruntled, we returned to the Boma, where once again we rearranged loads, jacked up the car, two of whose wheels had been punctured in our absence whether by the sun or some evil half-caste kids, I know not, dismantled and hid the parts of the magneto, collected our handkerchiefs from the Indian store at 1/3d. — the price they wanted originally — this possibly the result of a threat of mine to tell their boss, the Indian who took me back to Tete on the last trip.

September 16th, 1929

Off betimes in the morning, arriving about 10 a.m. at Chirah, a hill, by which a small village on the Nyakatumba River takes its name. Here we were told that three big bulls had drunk the night before in the wet sand of the river bed, so taking a couple of the local boys we lost no time in getting after them. But they were too far in the lead and we had perforce to give them up and I, for one, was glad enough to see camp and get down on my valise that evening.

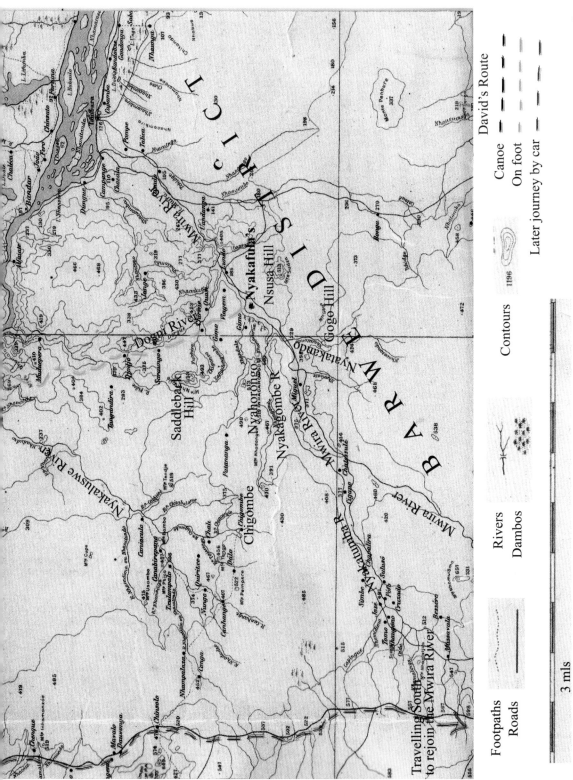

4

David's Route

Canoe

On foot

Later journey by car

Footpaths

Rivers

Roads

Dambos

Contours   1196

3 mls

(Ref.: Carta Da Colonia de Mocambique, Ministerio Das Colonias, 1936–1946)

PORTUGUESE EAST AFRICA

SOUTH OF THE ZAMBEZI RIVER

September 17th, 1929

A family party of a bull, cow and calf drank at the sand during the night and bathed in a muddy pool by the side of the river. There are no flies on Jumbo — any old water may be good enough for buffalo and other game, but Jumbo, like a sensible person, doesn't drink bath water and prefers a cool filtered drink when he can get it. Jonak and Charles came out with us, both old trackers of mine from my last trip, and much to my disgust between them managed to make a sad mess of things. They seemed quite incapable of keeping the spoor separate from that of yesterday and though we cast round many times finally always came back to the old spoor.

September 18th, 1929

Today we came up to two small bull elephants after a long trek from the water. We had one rather amusing false alarm when I saw a perfect picture of an elephant composed of a baobab tree and a long tendril of a vine and G and I advanced very much at the ready while our picture gradually dissolved itself; but it was not long afterwards that we did really get up to them only to find, as I have said, that they were too small. One of the beggars very nearly died; he became too interested in us and caused Charles and one of the other boys to retreat up trees. This wouldn't have mattered except for the fact that Charles was carrying my hat and we lost the two fearful ones completely for the next hour or two while we were chasing the bull that we had not had a fair sight of. Words were again said when next I saw them for if it had not been for half of G's double terai which he kindly lent me I might have had a go of sun that would have put me on my back for some time.

September 19th, 1929

Nothing drank at the water except our two friends of yesterday, nor was there any sign of them at the next water-hole three or four miles down stream, so we had an easy day and in the evening since the moon was full sat ourselves down on a rock in the centre of the river bed. We took a chair, one set of blankets, a couple of boys, a plate of scones and honey and our rifles. We forgot the wine which we had meant to bring to keep us happy — a demijohn of red wine was one of our loads from Tete — and that doubtless caused our bad luck for nothing came to the water that night and our vigil was fruitless.

September 20th, 1929

We left Chiwali and came on to Gombeza's Kraal where I bought some lard for ourselves and some tobacco for the boys. Later in the afternoon we came on a long and dusty dry trek past two deserted villages into Kasay's, where we arrived about dusk. We had wine and tea that evening — a drink of the gods. The tea should be very hot and strongish and should be in about 60/40% mixture.

September 21st, 1929

Found fresh spoor of a large cow and calf up by Luabeg's village, north of the river. Bulls had been there recently but there doesn't seem to be enough water about to make the spot at all attractive.

September 22nd, 1929

A long walk right out to the Nyatakando River where I shot my fourth elephant on my last trip. This lies on the south side of the Mwira — the Nyamakombe and the Mwira join just here at Kasay's — but today found nothing at all except old spoor.

September 24th, 1929

Picked up fresh spoor of a really large bull some three or four miles out from Kasay's which we proceeded to follow with Jonack, my head boy, and Dick, a local boy who has enlisted for work with me. This bull's spoor measured 27 inches to the point of the toe of the hind foot, which is a large size in elephants and we made a special effort to get up to him, telling the carriers to wait at Magasso's. But we might have known that a 'chaguambo' as the natives here call an old man, was not to be caught napping and being without our water bottles we realized at midday that it was hopeless. Chaguambo was swinging forward without thinking of feeding and was obviously making for new country, so we left him and a weary trek we had to the Mwira again. Luckily we found water and had our drink but it was a brackish and smelly beverage; still, without it we'd have been sair put to it to get back. We spent the night away from our loads at a little village on the Mwira where three old women were living. We bought some millet meal and I hit a fowl over the head as the women couldn't catch it and boiled it with a francolin I'd shot during the day and made a very good meal indeed. A cartridge bag makes a good pillow and the nights are now warm enough not to feel the need of a blanket.

September 25th, 1929

A breakfast of more porridge and fowl and Jonack and I set off down the sand of the Mwira. G. whose feet are again troubling him kept to the main Machila road while Dick went back to Magasso's to call the carriers on to Nyakafula's which we reached uneventfully about midday. Fresh spoor was to be seen along the Mwira but I didn't follow anything. The loads didn't arrive from Magasso's till evening, which grieved me.

September 26th, 1929

G and I went off together and picked up fresh spoor five minutes out of camp in the sand of the Mwira. They led us first into a thicket where I thought we had them; the dung was getting warm and I was expecting to hear them feeding any moment. But the blighters hadn't stopped there long, came out of the thick stuff and went for a walk first up the Mwira and then away through the open bush to the south. G, whose feet are still bad came home while I slogged after them as fast as I could but all to no purpose for I was left further and further behind.

September 27th, 1929

I went first under the guidance of a local boy to a water-hole lying under the hills to the north and close to camp. Here I missed a waterbuck clean at point-blank range and the herd was so scornful of me that they moved on about 200 yards only. While I was trying to get up to them again I came on fresh elephant dung which drove all thought of the buck out of my mind and I whistled up the boys and we began working it out of the network of tracks leading from the water. Jonack and Charles were both resting in camp, Charles should by rights have been with me but there had been quite a fracas with him the day before. He told me he was sick and was going back to Tete. I think his sickness was because I had slanged him for being late the day we arrived here and had set him to clean up camp along with the others. "You don't know, Bwana, how sick I am" he had told me, so, thinking he might really be having a slight go of fever I bunged him full of quinine and told him to lie down. On returning from the hunt yesterday I found him drinking beer at a village about a mile from camp which gave the show away for poor Charles. Anyway it meant that neither of my best trackers could be with me today and we spent some time puzzling out the spoor. While we were doing so a herd of eland came down to the water and I was determined to have one as we were short of meat. The boys have really had quite a hard time since the beginning of this trip and tummies full of meat are a better antidote to sickness than many bottles of quinine. Besides a shot or two doesn't really disturb Jumbo unless they are fired right on his tail. I got my eland and sending a boy back to camp to call the others to bring it in we went on again with the spoor.

We had only been going about half an hour when the boys told me they'd heard them in a thick bit of bush on the left of our path. I was behind at the time and had heard nothing; but while we were standing listening there was a tremendous crash in the bush on the right and ahead of us and I thought we were right in amongst a herd. The spoor had not yet told us anything about the jumbo we were following beyond the fact that there was one big fellow — this I knew from the size of the dung — how many of them there might be I had no idea. Here was one apparently in comparatively open bush so I went forward to have a look at him. We rounded a spur of the foothills and there was our tree down right enough, but it was one of those hollow euphorbias, fallen by itself and no sign of jumbo having been anywhere near it. This rather set me scoffing at the boys' elephants which they said they had heard on the left of the path, for we heard no more of them, though we certainly did find fresh dung round about where they said they'd been.

For the next hour or two we had a merry old time trying to work out the spoor; the boys seemed completely bewildered by it and I thought we'd have to leave them. They wanted to cast round to try and pick it up behind the thicket on our left but this I wouldn't allow as I was convinced by then that those jumbo actually were there in the thicket itself. I'd heard something myself, one time when I'd lost touch with the boys, which though I couldn't have sworn was jumbo had at any rate interested me. So back we came and plunged right into it again and before long, by the grace of God, came on really fresh dung warm to the touch. The boys then became a bit more interested and we managed to follow up with less difficulty, but it was still some time before we actually saw them.

Then Dick rushed up to me and thrust a rifle into my hands, "They're in there, Bwana" he said, pointing. This boy, Dick, comes from Nyakatumba, old Mpenso's kraal, further up the Mwira and though no hand at tracking and always quarreling with other local boys, is yet stout enough when jumbo is about.

I went forward quickly and soon, guided by Dick, got close up to them. One was well in evidence, a small bull with poor tusks, of the others there was no sign. I had seen at a point where they had crossed a sandy river that there were two only and I was sure that one of these, the good one, must be close at hand somewhere, but he made no sign of his presence and I couldn't move about to investigate for the small fellow was standing looking at us. All I could do was to stand still and trust my luck. It was after three or four minutes of perfect silence that there was a crash in a dense bit of bush on my left and a big jumbo bolted from it, much after the fashion of a fox breaking cover. An eddy of wind must have reached him from us and he lost no time in getting under way. He crashed out into a little open space and I just had time to see good looking tusks and get in a shot at his broadside before he was again lost to view. I fired my other barrel at him through a thick bush, but with what effect I do not know. One shot, anyway, must have found some vital spot, for as we followed on we heard him again, obviously in distress, and only a few yards away and I was able to work up to him and finish him off. The smaller animal had long betaken himself off so I could soon go up and see what I'd got. I knew the tusks were good but must confess I was not expecting them to be so large as I now saw them to be, for I saw at a glance that they were bigger than the 50 lber I had shot on my last trip.

After they had cut them out and brought them to camp a few days later, I measured them up to be 66 and 54 pounds and though this may not be correct I know it cannot be very far wrong. As to what effect my shots had taken to pull him up so, I could not tell as the animal fell on his right side, the side on which I had fired, but I reckon that one, at any rate, must have reached the heart.

And so back to camp where G kindly congratulated me on my success. It is hard lines on him not to be able to get about properly yet. I know I should personally be wild with envy of a man who shot a jumbo whilst I was laid up in camp.

This night we toasted our jumbo and drank to more success in a couple of bottles of the local gin — a drink by no means half bad distilled from the fruit of the 'masan'. What Masan is, exactly, I'm afraid I don't know; but I understand that it is not an indigenous fruit but was imported by the Goose from Brazil and it has spread itself all over the country. I certainly have not seen the fruit myself in any other part of Africa.

G's boys at last arrived this evening from Tete, so from now on we can be independent of each other.

September 28th – October 3rd, 1929

Spent in fruitless chases after jumbo that led to nothing. G is putting soles — a bit of eland neck skin — on to my old boots for me. He is a great hand at that game.

October 4th, 1929

Again no elephants drank so I went off up to the Mwira with Jonack, Charles and one of the Makanja boys. We found no spoor of any interest and I had just called a halt, the next water was still a long way off and I intended sitting down for ten minutes in the shade of the trees and giving things up for the day. The bush on the river bank was very thick just there, of an eminently tropical nature and the shade looked very inviting. I was five yards from the bank talking to the boys behind me when we were pulled up by a threatening growl in a deep gurgling sort of tone which made me jump for my heavy rifle.

"Elephants" said Jonack behind me but we soon pulled ourselves together — not jumbo this time but lions.

Rifle at the ready I scaled the bank and just caught a glimpse of one and had a snap at him as he was slipping off through the bush. Then J called my attention to another, giving a perfect chance about 20 feet off. I knelt down where I had him well in view underneath all the thick stuff overhead — but he was too quick and was off before I could bring the rifle to my shoulder. I followed on and repeatedly heard deep growls from the bush but could see nothing, it was far too thick. So cursing my luck, I sat down and lit a cigarette, hoping they might perhaps come back and give me another chance. Nor was I disappointed, for before I was half way through my smoke the boys drew my attention to the right and behind me — and there was a lioness some 25 yards off, standing looking at us. She must have been trying to make back to their old resting place and had suddenly caught sight of us. I gave her the ·450 at the point of the shoulder and she bunched herself together and bounded off at the shot. I went back to the river then about 20 yards along the sand and scaled the bank again, when I came immediately on a heavy blood spoor which I followed with great caution. The boys were all close behind me behaving very well and it was Charles who first spotted her. I had halted on the edge of a patch of sunlight and was peering across this into the deep black of the shade on the other side 10 yards away. I thought I'd seen something move there but was uncertain — it might just as well have been the play of the dappled shade of the leaves; then Charles pointed — and as my eyes grew more accustomed to that strange light I, too, definitely saw the dim outline of something.

I was taking no risks and put in a couple of shots and then slowly came forward. She was there all right and quite dead. My first shot would have been enough for her and she wouldn't have moved from there had I left her a few minutes. As it was I spoiled the skin rather by my fusilade at short range.

We hadn't yet finished with the lions though, for as we were pulling the lioness up to the bank, the male came back to see what had happened to his mate. I was ahead with the rifles and things while the boys were pulling the lioness out of the thick bush, when I heard a patter behind me and the three of them came running to tell me they had seen the lion coming back. So back I went but by the time I arrived there was no further sign to be seen of him and though I waited quietly there for a quarter of an hour, he did not again put in an appearance.

Well, well, there it is. It's taken me six years to get my lion but I've done it at last.

A thunderstorm and quite a heavy shower of rain came on in the evening before the boys got in with the lioness. They came in later when it had cleared up and I measured her up at eight feet.

October 5th, 1929

Sent boys to the water and they reported nothing had drunk there so we both had an easy day in camp and I took the skin off the lioness and had it pegged out.

October 6th, 1929

Again no jumbo at the water so we upped stakes and beat it for Chemba, which lies some 17 miles to the south-east I make out, rather a long march as we left it too late before getting underway. Two of G's boys went out on the way and had to be rescued with water, they got into camp at dusk.

October 7th, 1929

I went out east through a very dry country where there had obviously been a lot of elephant two or three months ago. Now there is nothing there at all as all the holes are dry. We had a long pow-wow in the evening and decided to part company. G goes off to the Pompwe River tomorrow while I go back to Nyakafula via Gogo. I heard this evening that there is a buck in this country which I can only think to be the Nyala — the rarest buck in Africa. An old native described him to me under the name of Dzau.

The bag today was three hunting dogs and one bushbuck. There were a lot of pups with the dogs which I tried to catch, but they were too old; if one could get a pair of these and cross them perhaps with an Alsatian — what a dog one should get.

October 9th, 1929

Last night we had great excitement with a leopard. We had camped in the river bed and the brute came and had a look at us in the early hours. The boys had of course let the fire out but all passed off without any untoward incident.

Today I struck out west to the Mwira and had a look at a water-hole they call Ngoma but found nothing there. The loads went straight back to Nyakafula's and had arrived long before me. I intend staying here for a few days and if nothing of interest will cut back, I think up the Mwira right up towards Nyasakarame, the Villa Gusyra district of the Province.

October 10th, 1929

Today I found spoor of a head of some five cows and calves with one fair bull in tow which I followed from 6 a.m. until 4 o'clock in the afternoon when we got up to them in some thick bush right the other side of Nsusa. I have rarely seen better cow ivory or worse bull ivory for the size of the beasts. It's time Fortune gave me something more for it is an unsatisfactory sort of business to spend the whole day tracking jumbo and then come home without a shot, especially when it's as hot as all the days are just now. I came home to camp with a gallon thirst which I assuaged in half a gallon of water, half a gallon of tea, a quart of coffee and several pints of soup — a thirst one would pay pounds for in civilization, both to acquire and to dispel.

October 11th, 1929

Shot an old sable buck this morning which I found near the water close to camp. I then walked three or four miles down the Mwira to Nyakatawa, but though I found plenty of cow spoor there were no bulls amongst them and I followed nothing. The water is running all the way on this walk and to save shoe leather I tried the experiment of going barefoot in the sand and found it very pleasant until the sun was high when the dry sand got so hot that it burnt one's feet.

October 12th, 1929

It looks as if I'm about due for another move for there was again no sign of jumbo in the vicinity this morning. I can't quite make up my mind where to go, these moves are so often a case of going further and faring worse. Here I do get spoor occasionally, anyway, but Jumbo is certainly a bit shy of this part of the country now and with reason for there have been many shot here this year.

Spent a pleasing half hour this morning on the bank of a water-hole near the river, wildly overgrown with grasses and reeds and full of birds including egrets — the biggest species; *Hydranassa alba*, I think; a grebe of some sort, the lesser moorhen, lily trotters (Sir H. Johnson's pleasing name for the jacana (*Actophilornis africanus*), pied kingfishers (*Ceryle rudis*) and a very shy bittern who effaced himself from our view in the thickest part of mitete grass he could find.

October 13th, 1929

Got news this morning of elephants being seen or heard near the road down to the Mwira late last night. The reporter said there were two only and good bulls, so I started off full of hopes this morning only to find spoor of an enormous herd of cows. There might have been an odd bull amongst them but it was impossible in the general hash up of spoor to tell exactly what there was.

I don't remember that De Luincy considered murdering or being murdered by cow elephants as a fine art — so I did not waste time on them but returned to camp demanding Toad-in-the-Hole.

'Ubi est ille reporter' needless to say 'Non est Inventure'.

'Where is this reporter? . . . *'He is out of luck'.*

Appendix 1

MY FIRST ELEPHANT

It was in Upogoro. We left camp as soon as it was light, Hassani, head tracker, Sulemani his No. 2, Ligambazi and I. Hassani was, and still is, the best tracker I have ever known, and the one man I should choose above all others to have by my side in a tight corner; but at that time I knew little or nothing of his capabilities, as it was the first time I was trying conclusions with 'My Lord the Elephant'. Sulemani I had had with me on one or two boma shoots after game, and Ligambazi also had attached himself to my party on previous occasions to carry spare rifles, ammunition and anything else that I or the trackers needed. He was keen as mustard whenever there was any chance of game, whether from pure love of the chase or not, I know not; but I rather suspect he was prompted by the more sordid motive of a succulent venison steak.

Howbeit, there we were, the four of us and a more compact and happier party I never wish to see.

The first ten minutes from camp at a village is always, to my mind, the worst part of the day; the sun has not yet risen, the native gardens seem endless, and one is drenched to the skin by the dew on the long grass which overhangs the narrow path. Today was no exception, and I was thankful when we passed the last maize shamba and were fairly out in the bush.

The sun had only just risen when Hassani, in the lead, suddenly stopped and began examining the ground on each side of the path.

"Same old thing", thought I, "elephant spoor a week old. Why can't he get on and into a better country?"

We had been hunting near that village for some days and had not struck anything new that was worth following. But no; today he seemed more interested.

Turning off to the right in the way that the grass was lying, he bent down and studied the track closely; then forward again, stooping from time to time and examining the edge of the spoor. Sulemani was following his example, and at last he found what they were looking for, a severed leaf of a low-growing shrub. This he handed to Hassani, who examined it carefully. It was still green, and had shown little or no sign of withering. Even to my untutored eye this showed that the elephant could not long have passed.

We followed on for a minute or two, and then Hassani stopped where, on a softer bit of ground, there was a clear impression of the spoor. Taking a grass stem he carefully measured the spoor, then running the stem from the fingertips up his left forearm he noted the point to which it reached. This, to an African native, is the criterion of the size of the elephant he is following. If the grass reaches only a short distance above the wrist, then he knows this is a small beast and not worth following; but if it reaches right up near the crook of his elbow, then it is a good elephant and one that *may* have large tusks. I stress the '*may*'. There are many formulae given by which the size of an elephant's tusks may be deduced from the length of his spoor, but I never found them satisfactory. Reduction of inches to pounds' weight of ivory by Rule of Three might prove even too much for a schoolboy in his wildest arithmetical throes. Suffice it that a spoor of over 20 inches is left by a very big elephant indeed, and one under 17 inches is probably not worth following, though even an estimate on these broad lines is not infallible. I have myself shot an elephant — the story is told elsewhere — whose spoor I made only 16½ inches, but whose tusks turned the scale at 58 and 61 pounds; while it is no uncommon thing to find, after following 22-inch spoor all day, that the elephant carries no ivory at all.

But I digress. In this case Hassani's grass stem nearly reached the crook of his elbow. Bending down, I too measured it by the notches cut in my stick, and made it a good 20 inches.

'How long is it since he passed?' said I, with some anxiety, breaking the silence which had been preserved ever since we had found the spoor.

"Usiku, tutafuata" ("At night. We will follow"), was his only answer, but it was quite sufficient.

I took over the light rifle from Ligambazi, made sure that it was loaded and that I had a spare clip handy, felt for my 0·450 ammunition all ready in the pouches at my right breast-pocket, while Hassani gave over the 0·450 to Sulemani and delved in his cartridge-bag for more ammunition for it.

Then we were off; slowly at first, with many halts, to make sure of our spoor whenever we came to a clear impression; then, as the novelty of measuring a large spoor wore off, the pace increased.

The elephant had been moving slowly through the night, feeding as he went, as many a broken-down tree attested. After an hour's going the droppings showed signs of becoming more recent, and on coming to a particularly large pile of dung, Hassani called a halt.

"Nitamfunga, Bwana" said he.

A literal translation of this word is, "I will close him".

Elephant hunting is bound up very closely with witchcraft among the more outlying tribes of the interior of Africa, and Hassani would not think of following elephant without the all-protecting virtues of this art. Every elephant fundi, as he is called, has his own medicine in which he puts implicit faith. A ram's horn filled with some weird concoction may serve him as an amulet or general talisman of success, while the rites that he performs at different stages of the hunt are many and various. In this case Hassani's idea was to cast a spell over the elephant so as to prevent him going far. We three underlings sat down with our backs turned while Hassani busied himself with the dung. What he did I do not know. I would never dare to encounter his displeasure by trying to see what he was doing, and we had to wait patiently until the rites were finished.

In five minutes all was over, and we were on our way again. Hassani expressing himself as satisfied that all was well.

As I passed I noticed that all the dung was piled up in a neat heap, but beyond that I know nothing of this queer proceeding. A similar procedure occurred again some fifteen minutes later, when we came on a clearly defined footmark in sandy soil. This time all the sand inside the print was scraped together and piled up in a high mound, nothing else. All done in absolute silence, and when the signal was given to go on Hassani was already a few yards away, following up the tracks as before.

Soon we came to more difficult tracking. Our elephant had joined in with a herd and kept with them for some time, then had left them and gone on again alone. This is where the inexperienced would have gone astray a hundred times; but the trackers' discerning eyes took in everything and followed the big bull right through that network of mixed spoor. It was an education to watch them.

Whenever we missed the big spoor we spread out in line, and it was never long before a low whistle from one or other of the trackers and a forward signal of a hand brought us together on the right trail again. Even Ligambazi took a hand in this, and was once or twice successful in showing us the right way. I, too, tried my best but found myself completely puzzled and finally contented myself with staying close to Hassani and endeavouring to follow the spoor as he pointed it out to me.

Later I gained more proficiency in the art of tracking as my eyes became trained by experience; but I can never hope to emulate the native born and bred in the bush who has followed game since he learned to walk.

At last the big bull left the herd and went on alone once again, and we were able to follow up at a faster pace. All this time the appearance of the droppings had been changing; they were gradually getting fresher, nor was there any sign of their being broken up by the big black-beetles, the scavengers of the bush; lately, too, the trackers had been testing them with their feet.

Soon a whisper from Sulemani, "Moto!" told me that we were in fact getting warm, and we went on with more caution. Twice Hassani climbed trees and studied the ground ahead but each time to no purpose.

It was now about 11 o'clock, and the wind, which up until then had held steadily and favourably on our faces, began to falter and chop about in all directions. This happens only too often when the sun begins to get hot. Taking some dried grass, Hassani rubbed it into powder between his hands, and from time to time let a little fall to see in which way it would go. Once, when it blew directly down the trail, he murmured gloomily: "Mphopo mbaya sana!" ("the wind is very bad").

I could only agree it could not be worse, but we could do nothing but follow on and see what happened.

A little farther on the character of the spoor changed. Instead of twisting about in all directions, it led straight to the front, and lengthened considerably, eight feet to a stride, and there were no signs of feeding. We stopped.

"Here he got our wind", said Hassani raising his voice higher than he had previously. My spirits sank to zero.

"What's to be done?", I asked him. "Must we leave him?"

"No, Bwana, but we must wait. We will wait for him for about half an hour to give him time to forget about us."

Choosing a shady spot with a tree-stump at my back, I sat down and did my best to overcome my impatience and depression. It was not the least fascinating part of elephant hunting that one minute the hunter is keyed to the highest pitch, full of hope; the next, cast down with anxiety and hopelessness of ever coming up with the mysterious beast who had left those two enormous footprints in the ground, leading on and on into the distance, and apparently never coming any nearer.

I say two, not four, because an elephant, like a cat, brings his hind feet to the same exact position as that previously occupied by the fore.

After a short drink from my water-bottle and a bite of a sandwich, I lit a cigarette and began talking to Hassani.

"Shall we come up with him?", said I.

"I don't know, Bwana, I think so; I have funga'd him well, and he must soon stop and rest for the heat of the day."

"Is he a very big elephant?"

"Mkubwa kweli kweli; look at the size of his feet; see how big the dung is; his tusks will be like the trunks of trees."

And so, little by little, he raised my hopes, until when the half-hour was over and we were back on the trail, I was once again as confident and optimistic as ever.

The wise counsel of the half-hour's wait was soon proved, for it was not long before the length of the stride lessened, until once again the elephant was moving slowly along, feeding as he went. If we had followed straight on, in all probability he would not have stopped for hours, and we should have lost all chances of coming up with him.

Suddenly away on our left front a sound of cracking timber and the noise of a tree coming down with a crash. I lit a cigarette, not through nonchalance, but to test the wind. This, to my mind, is easily the best way of getting a true indication, and though many trackers have looked at me with some anxiety when I have done so, I have never found that game of any sort have got its wind. In fact, Hassani, best of all trackers, and wisest, always now looks to me to do so when we have sighted game.

What wind there was was blowing across our front, and the safest way of approach was to make a short detour to the right.

After a hundred yards of careful going, with many halts to look and listen, a low rumbling, gurgling noise came from somewhere on our left and just ahead of us. I took off my hat the better to locate the spot — a heavy terai weakens one's sense of hearing. In nine cases out of ten the belly-rumblings of elephant, for such this sound was some queer process of digestion, whether voluntary or involuntary has not been satisfactorily explained gives away his position to the hunter.

On again slowly with increased caution, and then — Sulemani saw him!

"Sst!" Stock-still he stood, one clenched fist extended at full arm's length. For some reason a native never points with his forefinger. I could not make out the quarry at first in the uncertain light of the forest, then I saw something move, far above where I was looking. Astonished, my gaze travelled upwards; and then I saw him standing there half-facing us, quite still except for the steady fanning movements of his gigantic ears. He was like a huge flap-eared dog cocking his ears, and at first I thought that he had seen or heard us. But in reality he was quite unaware of our presence, and he went on fanning himself slowly and methodically, dreaming, no doubt, of happy wanderings over Africa in a time long past when the white man and heavy express rifles were never encountered. Poor old beast! To kill you because you are unlucky enough to carry those two tusks of ivory coveted by man! But such thoughts did not enter my head at that time.

While I was watching the elephant, Hassani had been busying himself with a small flask made of bamboo. From this he poured a white powder into the palm of his hand, then raising it he blew three times in the elephant's direction. Afterwards I found out that this was more 'dawa' or medicine, which was to prevent him turning savage and charging us.

I exchanged rifles with Sulemani, taking the 0·450 and giving him the 0·303.

"What about the tusks, though", I whispered to Hassani; "are they big?"

This was the first elephant I had seen outside a zoo, and I had no more idea than the man in the moon whether they were twenty-pounders or hundred-pounders.

"Quite big", said he, "not very big, but quite big".

A native has not much idea of size, and none at all of weight.

"We will shoot him Bwana", he continued. I was doubtful, but also longing to be persuaded. Hassani's one fault is that he is too eager for the kill, and is apt to mislead a novice when it is a question of size of tusks.

"Still", I thought, "they obviously aren't small. Am I going to leave my first elephant after all these unsuccessful days? Never!"

Hassani, watching my face, was quick to see my decision. Straight forward we went up to twenty yards, and then, resting the heavy rifle by the side of a convenient tree, I aimed for the brain. Half-way between the eye and the ear-hole, I had been told, and there I tried to place my shots, both barrels, one after the other at the same spot. I expected to see him down then and there, but no — my aim was bad or else I was over-excited. 'Stag fever' I had in Scottish forest, I hope, successfully conquered, but 'elephant fever!' The elephant rocked where he stood, and seemed to be thrown a little on to his haunches, but he did not come down. Hastily opening the breach, I threw out the empty shells while Hassani crammed in two new cartridges. Sulemani fired a shot with my 0·303, for which, even at that moment, I found time to curse him. This was my first elephant, and I wanted him all to myself. Afterwards I found that his shot had just grazed the top of his shoulder, so I need not have grudged it to him.

Meanwhile the elephant swung round presenting his broadside and started moving off. I had a snapshot for the heart with my next barrel, which seemed to have no more effect on him than a pea-shooter, and then in despair I rushed forward, where I again had a full view of him. He was three-quarters on, making off as fast as he knew how, and in five seconds would have been lost to view. I threw up the rifle for a last shot, and aimed right at his ear-hole. The effect was instantaneous; down he came at my shot — down in a heap and never moved again. I had found the right place at last.

So he died, that mountain of flesh, who but for me might have roamed the forest for many decades to come. And even with this my first elephant a feeling of remorse for my action, which I was to know so well thereafter, stole over me. So it was with mixed feelings that I went up to take stock of my prize.

Not so, however, with the others. As the elephant came down they burst into song — the song of Victory — clustered round me, and one after the other seized my hand in token of congratulation.

As we went forward Sulemani emptied the magazine of the 0·303 into the back of the elephant's head, nearly slaying Ligambazi in the process. How he escaped I don't know! He had rushed forward half-wild with excitement, and Sulemani's shot must have missed him by a hair's breadth. He was called back while Sulemani finished his very necessary precautionary measures. An elephant has been known, occasionally, to make off after being down and apparently killed. But our elephant never stirred again, and after giving him a minute or two to make certain, we went up to him — I to measure the tusks and the boys to perform their magic rites.

The formula for gauging the weight of ivory from the tusk measurements is fairly accurate on a uniform tusk that is not abnormally long or short or malformed in any way. The exposed length in inches, measured on the outside curve, multiplied by the circumference in inches at the half-way point, and divided by ten, gives the weight in pounds correct, generally, to a pound or two. I have measured up a good many tusks in this way, and have found the formula astonishingly accurate. I made out these tusks to be 32 and 33 pounds each, and I found a week or two later that this was the correct weight. So Hassani's expression "quite big" was justified, as they were just over the shootable weight.

Hassani and the other boys were now in the midst of their orgies. First the tail was cut off and presented to me. This, I was rejoiced to see, had many fine white hairs in it, as opposed to the customary black, and if I had cared to dispose of it, it would have been worth quite a sum of money. I have been offered as much as ten shillings apiece for long white elephant hairs by a Zanzibari Indian.

Then the end of the trunk was cut off, and together with the end of a third appendage was placed in a deep hole which they cut just at the back of one of the eyes. Into this Hassani thrust his 'Kisimba' or 'Little Lion', as he named his talisman of a ram's horn, which I described earlier, and left it there for a few minutes to gain strength and higher powers of protection and good luck.

For the next hour or two I was well content to rest and talk things over with Hassani and the others. We went over the whole hunt again from start to finish. I learnt a little of their queer beliefs and their medicine, and heard many stories of past adventures and narrow escapes from elephant, buffalo and lion. The African is a great storyteller and his reminiscences lose little in the telling. Later I took the usual photographs and also tried to measure up the height of the elephant. But found it a very difficult business, as it was impossible to straighten up the foreleg, and I could come to no satisfactory conclusion as to his height at the shoulder.

As the sun was getting lower we set off on our journey back to camp. Two hours' hard going brought us within earshot of the village, and there Hassani struck up the song of the Successful Hunter, the other two joining in. As soon as we were heard, every man, woman and child of the village turned out to welcome us. The men singing and clapping their hands, the women 'lillilooing'. The latter is a nerve-racking accomplishment — a quavering scream made by wagging the tongue about inside the mouth, and from time to time intensifying the effect by beating lips with the hand. Others were even rolling on the ground in transport of hysterical delight. So it was a triumphant little procession that finally reached the green tents of my camp.

I hurriedly escaped to my tent, where my boy was waiting for me, beaming with smiles. He presented me with a long drink as I sank into my chair, and, while he took off my boots, demanded the news in detail of the whole adventure. A hot bath, dinner, and bed was my programme, but there was no chance of sleep, weary as I was. The village held an 'ngoma' or dance until the early hours of the morning and the night was filled with the noise of their singing and beating of drums.

The next day we revisited the elephant as I was anxious to see the tusks being cut out. Two men had been sent off in the early morning, experts in the business, under the charge of Sulemani but when Hassani and I arrived later on we found that little or no headway had been made at all and the carcass was in possession of some twenty or thirty natives of all ages and both sexes, who were having a royal time. The elephant had been disembowelled and his enormous entrails were strewn over the ground. Men were climbing round inside his cavernous interior with knives in their hands hunting for the most delicate portions of meat. It was a revolting orgy. As I appeared one man squeezed his way through the throng round the entrance to the belly smeared all over with blood and clutching a large chunk of meat in his hands. Spying me he rushed up and danced a few paces of his ngoma in front of me. Then, depositing his prey at the base of the tree, with a wild leap he was back pushing his way inside the carcass once more.

I quelled the disturbance as far as I was able and extricating the two men for cutting the tusks out, set them to work with heavy axes and knives. The end of a tusk lies deep in the skull, right up behind the eye, at least one-third of its length being embedded in the skull. It is a long and tedious business cutting them out as great care has to be taken not to chip the ivory, which would impair its value. Every village has its own 'fundis', experts in the art. The two men who had offered their services knew their job and set to with a will; but it was a good two hours before they had hacked their way through the mass of bone and gristle surrounding the upper tusk. I did not wait to see the lower tusk extracted. To get at this the whole neck must be cut through and the head turned over, and I had had quite enough of this revolting shambles by the time the first was out.

When the first tusk was out I was standing by, watching the two fundis who were just about to pull out the long nerve from the inside of the tusk. They did not seem in any great hurry to begin and one of them, calling out to Hassani, drew his attention to my presence. Hassani came up in a great state and dragging me away told me that this was very bad medicine and I must not look on any account. I tried to pooh-pooh the idea but to no purpose.

"No", said he, "Bwana must not look. The meat inside the tusk is very bad for the eyes".

"But", said I, "the fundis must look when they draw it out. Why shouldn't I?"

"Oh, but they are fundis" was his answer. "It is their work, they can see and not come to harm. If Bwana or I or other men look we will all go blind."

So I deferred to his wishes, and sitting down we all hid our eyes in our hands until the nerve was out and taken away to be hidden in the long grass close at hand.

I was preparing to make my way back to camp when Sulemani came up to me and begged me before I went to shoot one of the vultures which were crowding the neighbouring trees, ready to start their feast whenever it was deserted by the humans.

"What for?" I asked him. "Surely he was not going to eat one of those foul-eating creatures when there was no lack of elephant meat?"

"No", but he wanted it for dawa. More medicine, thought I. What on earth can be the meaning of it this time? I pressed him to tell me what he wanted it for, and found out finally that from certain portions of its anatomy, chiefly the bones and entrails, he would evolve a concoction which would be a very potent charm and safeguard when he was hunting elephant.

I had my light rifle with me so I complied with his wishes. Seeing a vulture showing up clearly on a tree about fifty yards away I took careful aim and managed to topple him over. Sulemani, pleased as Punch, rushed off to retrieve him.

Back at camp I was content to rest for the remainder of that day — to think and dream of the future. I had passed my initiate in the art of elephant hunting. Novitiate, I had nearly written but that I was to realize, and realize only too well, does not end with the shooting of one's first elephant. Every hunter learns, and goes on learning, the whole of his life. With his first, his tenth, even his hundredth elephant, he will find out something new about that mysterious and mighty animal which roams the forests of Africa.

Late in the afternoon my tusks came in, and I was pleased to find on examining them that they were undamaged and well and carefully cut out.

And so, sitting in my chair, I watched the sun go down in a blaze of glory. Stars gradually began to twinkle in the soft velvet sky; somewhere in the bush behind me I could hear a company of guinea-fowl screaming forth their strident note as they disposed themselves to roost; away in the distance, so faint that it was no more than a pin-prick of sound, a lion roared the requiem of the day that had passed. The moon rose and cast its silvery gleam on the mysterious African night.

Mkatakhuni

Appendix 2

FATUMA AND MKATAKHUNI

We were changing camp and had a long march in front of us. Elephant seemed to have deserted the country and the only thing to do was to try and follow them. Hence a long, tiring and uninteresting trek had to be made. I was in the lead, closely followed by my three companions, Hassani, Sulemani and Ligambazi, while the rest of my safari, some ten or twelve porters and my personal boys, were already some miles behind. The sun was getting hot and I was beginning to tire of my own thoughts and company.

"Why is it", I said to Hassani, "that you call the big rifle 'Fatuma'?".

Hassani, some ten paces in the rear, hurried forward.

"Bwana?"

I repeated my question, adding, "And yet you have no name for the little rifle".

"But we have a name", he replied. "The little rifle is called 'Mkatakhuni'."

"Oh", thought I. "Mkatakhuni, the Woodcutter."

"Yes; because his voice is like the noise of a man cutting firewood with an axe."

This was interesting. The big rifle just an old fat woman, and the little rifle the worker.

"True enough", I said, "Fatuma has an easy time, she is carried all day and only has to work when we find elephant, whereas Mkatakhuni is always in my hand, ready to work for the pot. Which do you like best?"

"Oh! Fatuma. Does she not say 'Boom', and at her voice the elephant falls! But Mkatakhuni — he will only kill small meat."

All game from buffalo to the tiny dikdik are classed by the African under the one heading, 'Nyama' — meat; and as such he thinks of it, from the time he sees the spoor until it reaches its final destination — the cooking pot.

Now I had not yet shot an elephant with a light rifle, having always trusted to the heavy one; but it had long been a desire of mine to do so, and Hassani's unflattering remarks about Mkatakhuni, my dearly loved, annoyed me. His logic in nomenclature was not good by African standards, as the African woman in reality does most of the work of provider, to a large extent tilling the land for the maize, harvesting the crop and pounding the grain; but, conceding that point, I was all the more determined to show him that Mkatakhuni, besides doing all the work, could also, if called upon, down an elephant.

"Which way?" We had come to a fork, an intersection of the myriad trails, native paths, elephant trails; they all looked much the same to the inexperienced eye.

"Left", said Hassani without an instant's hesitation; and as he passed he drew a line in the sand with his foot across the opening of the other path and snapping off a leafy twig from a shrub threw it down a few paces along the one we were on. A primitive, but effective, manner of showing our followers the correct way.

"Now I", I said, continuing the argument, "like Mkatakhuni best. He is light to carry, quick to use, and he speaks five times to Fatuma's twice, and does he not give us all our meat? Some day I will show you that he, too, can kill elephant."

But Hassani was not to be persuaded. Even my argument about 'Nyama' did not carry weight with him.

"No", said he, "Fatuma says '*Boom*', but Mkatakhuni can only say 'Tcakk'."

And so we went on our way, I pondering over the bad logic of the naming of the rifles — even the difference in their loquacity was not right — Hassani and the others chattering in the rear.

At about eleven o'clock we came to a small village, the first human habitations we had seen, and I stopped for a rest. We had started long before it was light, and I reckoned that we had put a good twenty miles behind us. The Jumbe (village headman) came up to welcome us, producing a deck-chair. A buck-skin took the place of the civilized canvas cloth; but nevertheless it was a passing imitation and I sat down contentedly.

There were one or two coconut palms standing hard by and glancing up I saw with great pleasure that there were plenty of nuts. At my request the Jumbe sent a boy up. He climbed with great alacrity and threw down three or four of the larger nuts. Ligambazi seized on one with avidity. Husking coconuts can be done in many ways but Ligambazi's was a novel one to me. Cutting the fibre all round one end he seized the nut in both hands then drew off great strips of fibre with his teeth. It was curious to watch his strong teeth ripping off the tough fibre like bark from a tree. Bending his head sideways he would take hold of a loose end like a dog gnawing at a bone, then, jerking his neck back and drawing away with his arms, off would come a huge strip; back again, he seized another strip and the procedure was repeated.

I laughed, and organized a race with one of the village men who was husking another nut in a more orthodox way. He had knocked a short stick into the ground, sharpened its point, and was now beating the coconut on it and tearing off the fibre thus loosened.

It was a close finish, but Ligambazi's strong teeth won the day; he soon had the fibre off and the nut disclosed, when, knocking off the top with a few taps of his knife, he proffered it to me brimming full with the most luscious and cool drink.

I wasted no time in draining it and the other one too; then the boys immediately fell to, broke open the nuts and ate up every scrap of the coconut inside.

Greatly refreshed, I lit a cigarette and engaged the Jumbe in conversation. My first question was the natural one: "What news of elephant?"

"Last night there was one in the maize shambas. For two days he has been feeding near here."

"Is he big?"

"Big in very truth; his tusks stick out like this." He showed me. Stretching out one arm to full extent he placed his other hand on his chest just under his chin. This is always how a native tells you the size of an elephant. With his right arm stretched to the full extent there are four positions where he may place his left hand. At the crook of the right elbow means small elephant, one not worth following; at his right shoulder, possibly a shootable animal; underneath the chin, a fair-sized tusk; and at his left shoulder, a larger one. A fifth position is when both arms are fully extended, but that would be a monster to be dreamed of. A native's power of exaggeration are proverbial, but on the whole he is fairly reliable when describing the size of tusks on these lines.

"H'm", thought I, "this may be interesting".

"Did you see him yourself?"

"Yes, with my eyes I saw him."

"Not merely his spoor on the ground?"

"No. I saw the elephant with my eyes."

It is always well to make sure on this point. Elephant spoor is readily confounded with the animal itself, and a native's story-telling powers will do the rest, so the week-old spoor of a single elephant is quite sufficient by itself to produce a tale of monster-tusked elephants who raided a shamba only the night before in thousands.

Still, there was one good point about this 'habari' (news), there was no talk of impossible numbers of elephant, and the Jumbe looked a reliable sort of man.

"What do you think?", I asked Hassani.

"I will go and see, Bwana", he replied; and, quite untired after his twenty-mile march, he went off under the guidance of one of the village boys to inspect the spoor.

In the meantime I sat and rested under the curious gaze of the villagers gathered in a ring all round me. I chose a place for my tent, when it and the carriers should arrive, and the Jumbe immediately told a few men to clear the grass, while others brought bags of mealy flour for the porters and the inevitable kukuus and eggs for myself. The women, too, brought in big earthenware pots of water, each with a large leaf floating on the top to prevent the water splashing out as they walked.

"When did a Bwana last visit your village?", I asked the Jumbe.

"Three years ago", he replied, "the Bwana Shauri came; since then no Bwana has been here".

"Did he shoot elephant?"

"No; but he shot much meat."

"What sort of meat is accustomed to walk here?"

"Many kinds of meat. Mbunju, mbarapi, ndogoro" (eland, sable, waterbuck). "Eeh! Very much game! When the Bwana Shauri came we all had our bellies full."

This was very good news; we were badly in need of fresh meat, so, even if the elephant turned out to be mythical, I made my mind up to camp a few days there and see how things shaped.

"What about buffalo?"

"Two days ago a herd of buffalo drank at the river and a man looking for honey in the bush saw them. If Bwana will stay here he will kill many with his gun."

Just then a distant shout brought our discussions to an end, and round the bend of the road appeared the head of my safari. They rapidly drew nearer to the strains of one of their weird, interminable songs, the tail being brought up by the Mnyampara, or headman. He was an ex-King's African Rifles man and, much to his joy, carried an old rifle as a mark of his station.

The porters, one by one, set down their loads and started untying them. Each man carries a load of about fifty pounds' weight to which he ties his own worldly posessions, a cooking-pot, his sleeping-mat, and, if there is no shortage of game and he is of an economical turn of mind, perhaps a roll of malodorous smoked meat, which gives forth an aroma that permeates everything. The Mnyampara approached me, slapping the butt of his rifle in true military fashion.

"All correct, where shall we pitch the tent?"

I pointed out the place nearby, and up went that tent in no time. No pause for rest, each man had his own job to do and it was not until the tent was pitched and a drain cut round it that they drifted off, one by one, some to the river or to find a good place for their own billet, others to barter for flour. My cook, meanwhile, had got a fire going and in five minutes had brought me a cup of tea. My personal boy was also busy trying to put together the Roorkee chair, and it was ludicrous to watch his struggles. He never could master that chair satisfactorily and it was only by dint of great brain strain that he ever got it together. A beautiful smile broke over his features as he managed at length to fit the last rod into its socket and turned his attention to the table. This was an easier matter, and he was soon at work fixing up the camp-bed and arranging my belongings inside the tent. In half an hour everything was disposed and from the aspect of things I might have been camped there for a week.

Later in the day Hassani came back; he had found elephant spoor and followed it up for an hour, straight from the maize garden. From the signs he could read that the elephant was trekking. He had not stopped to feed but had gone straight ahead through the night, apparently making for new country, and it would not be worth while following. Game spoor he had seen in plenty. Buffalo, eland, sable and kongoni, and also more elephant spoor.

"Very good, Hassani, we will stay here and camp for a few days and shoot meat."

"Yes, Bwana, that will be good. I will make an ngoma (dance) tonight, then perhaps God will give us elephant also."

That night I went to bed lulled into sleep to the strains of the weirdest chant it has ever been my fortune to listen to. About twenty or thirty boys were sitting round the fire after their evening meal. They had one drum — buck's hide tightly stretched across a hollowed tree-trunk — on which a skilled performer was beating gently while Hassani, throned on a stool, was softly intoning the fortunes of our party since the beginning of the safari. After every sentence, just five or six words chanted in a voice and a very similar tone to that a clergyman uses when inviting responses in church, he would stop and the whole chorus would respond: "Eeh, Eeh,

Eeh!" in token of assent. Then on again incessantly, never at a loss for a word. I could understand little of it, as he used his own tribal dialect, which was beyond my powers of interpretation, so I called up a boy and got him to interpret at the end of each sentence. The simile of the clergyman was not far wrong; he was praying, praying to the ghosts of his fathers to honour us with their presence and listen to his tale.

Then followed a long description of our fortunes to the present; often not absolutely truthful, and repeated assertions that we were hungry and had no meat; then finally demands that 'they' should give us an elephant — a big one with large tusks. So it went on; but long before the singers thought of finishing I was asleep and dreaming of the large elephants they were so importunately demanding.

Next morning we were up and off early in the day, and it was not long before we struck red-hot eland spoor which we followed up. We had come to a tricky bit of tracking on hard ground and the boys were eagerly engaged puzzling it out when, happening to raise my eyes, I saw a number of black forms crossing our front, looming large in the early morning mists.

"Elephant? No; what in the name of – –."

"Nyati", in a low tone from Hassani.

"Buffalo, of course; why the – – can't I recognize things as quickly as he can?" was the feeling I had.

And buffalo they were by the hundred. Never have I seen such an enormous herd. It was impossible to say correctly how many; for one thing they were never all in sight at the same time. We were in fairly open bush, but even there sight was restricted to under a hundred yards. They were quite unalarmed and were moving slowly through the bush. The wind was right so we moved forward to get in touch with them. I went up to about twenty yards of the nearest rank — they were moving solidly through the bush at a depth of about fifteen yards — and looking for a good head, watched them filing by.

There we waited, Hassani and I — the other boys were all up trees a hundred yards in the rear — for what must have been at least ten minutes, but seemed considerably more. Then, despairing of finding that record head, which every hunter feels he is going to get sometime, and seeing that the herd had nearly all passed, I picked out a good fat cow and gave her the right with the 0·450. She went down straight away, much to my satisfaction. But the effect that shot produced on the rest of the herd was not so much to my liking.

Instead of disappearing into the bush ahead, as I had expected, they immediately turned about and went back in the direction they had originally come from, and this time it was by no means the slow procession we had just witnessed. The march past in fours had ended and they were now returning in quarter column at the double. Luckily it rested with the Inspecting Officer and his A.D.C. to give the salute and not to take it! I must admit we beat a hasty retreat, but on seeing that the herd had not spread out to any appreciable extent and were still careering down their own trail, I grew bolder and approached again to down another one. This time it was one of the original leaders that came down but it took both barrels of the 0·450 to settle him, and this further outrage was too much for one of his companions in the original lead. To my horror he broke off the trail and came straight for me and there I was with an empty rifle!

Now was the time when the quick overhead lever and ejecting mechanism of the modern sporting rifle would have been worth not their weight only but that buffalo's weight also in gold to me; but mine was an old-fashioned rifle with hammers and the underside lever which is so slow in operating.

"Why hadn't I taken 'Mkatakhuni', the despised of Hassani?" In his hands it was useless; he was ever a hopeless performer with the rifle — and the two shots he now fired had no effect.

I turned and ran back, struggling with the breach mechanism in the meanwhile, hoping to gain the extra second or two I needed in that way, but it seemed years before I had thrown out the empty shells and got in new cartridges in their stead. I managed it at last, whirled round to find the bull still seven or eight yards off and a lucky shot brought his career to an end.

We watched the remainder of that herd disappear into the bush and I for one was thankful that we had seen the last of them. Those last ten seconds were a little too exciting.

We called up the boys and went to take stock of the slain. We had three good-sized buffalo down which the boys proceeded to 'chinja' — that is to say, cut their throats — in the Mohammedan fashion. It mattered not to them in the very least that they were all three dead and showed no spark of life. These boys are only Mohammedans when it suits their purpose. I remember once going on a shoot in the middle of Ramadan, the month of Mohammedan fasting, in the hours of daytime; Hassani joined me at my first camp and it was with some concern that I asked how he was going to get through a hard week's shooting without eating through the day?

"That does not matter, Bwana", he assured me, "out here we are no longer Mohammedans".

There was great excitement and talk over the cutting up of the buffalo.

Every boy had his own remarks to make to explain why this and that happened; but each wound up his say with the poignant statement: "Vita kweli, kweli" (truly a war).

War it had been; but there was one aspect of this war which I did not like and that was that I had turned tail in the face of the enemy and run. As a sop to my own vanity I felt I must explain things. I told them what had happened and wound up my remarks by saying to Hassani: "Now, if I had had Mkatakhuni in my hand instead of old Fatuma none of these things would have happened and we should not have had to run like cowards."

"Oh, but Bwana", he urged, "did I not fire twice with Mkatakhuni with no effect".

Now this was only too true and whether a 0·303 would be sufficient to stop a charging buffalo in reality I am not prepared to say, but I was not going to lose my argument with Hassani.

"Yes, but where did you hit him?", I asked.

This was received with great merriment by the other boys. We went up to the buffalo to see what Hassani's marksmanship had wrought and I must confess it was rather to my delight than otherwise that we found that one of Hassani's shots had just grazed the buffalo's shoulder and that there was no sign of the other one. But Hassani still stuck to his guns, and Mkatakhuni remained the despised.

We covered up the buffalo with branches to protect them from vultures as best we might, and sending a boy back to the village to bring others to take in the meat we started off again.

It would be tiresome to give a detailed account of our fortunes for the rest of that day. Suffice it to say that it was not until seven o'clock that night that, tired and hungry, we eventually reached camp once again after a long and, let me confess, uninteresting trek after an elephant whose spoor we struck soon after the episode with the buffalo herd. Possibly thoughts of a satiety of buffalo meat all ready and waiting in camp interfered with the keenness of the trackers; I am convinced that we changed on to a fresh spoor half way through the morning, but that is a crime to which Hassani would not plead guilty.

It was not until three o'clock in the afternoon that I eventually gave way to the boys' requests that we should give it up, and we set our faces for camp.

Unfortunately we had a bad guide who did not know the country well and led us through the most impossible country. We were a long way from camp but the short cut he took us, through long grass and swamp, made it seem much longer and before we saw the welcome camp-fires I had quite lost my temper with him, cursing him for a fool who didn't know the country round his own doorstep.

This, of course, was quite useless and only made matters worse.

In camp we found the boys had made huge grids with bamboos and were smoking all the buffalo meat which was in excess of present needs. This is a simple performance in Africa. They make a trellis-work platform with bamboos or other tree branches which may be handy, support it with forked sticks about three feet from the ground, and light a fire over the whole area underneath. On the platform the meat is laid in strips and one night's smoking is enough to preserve the meat sufficiently for the taste of the African native. Not that it is preserved in reality, but in ten days from the time of smoking it has, anyway, not decomposed which is all that he worries about.

I stayed in camp at that village for several days but was always unlucky with elephant. I got one or two heads of game; especially a sable bull, which pleased me greatly.

It was there that I noticed the difference in tactics which a herd of eland and a herd of sable show when being hunted. Eland are, on the whole, fairly easy to get up to but if they once get your wind or see you they are off and will not stop again for may be five miles — anyway, an hour's hard trek through the bush. Sable, on the contrary, if they have not been much harried never seem to go any great distance. They are very wary and hard to approach, but if they get your wind, only move off a short way, sometimes it may be only a matter of a few hundred yards when they stop again and give you another chance of getting your shot; but chances are that a hunter's first warning that he is up to the herd again is a snort from a wary old cow, and then the sound of the whole herd crashing off again through the bush. They are annoying brutes and a sound test of a hunter's stalking powers, especially if he is lucky enough to bring down the old black bull of the herd. If others do not agree with me in this let them remember that I am writing of hunting in a still little-known part of Tanganyika. Sable which have been much hunted may, indeed, go miles before they give a second chance of approach. I went out once to shoot game for villagers when late rains had brought a severe famine in the district before the new crops were ripe, and then I found that the sable, too, would not stop after they had once been alarmed. I taxed the village headman with sending out hunters to get meat, and, although at first he strongly denied it, he eventually admitted that he had done so and that lately many men had been out with their bows. It was obvious from the face of things, but who can blame them when food was so short? But it had made things very much more difficult for me.

The day I got the sable bull I determined it was time to get down to business again. Time was getting short and I badly wanted an elephant before going back to the Boma. I had a long consultation with Hassani that evening and we eventually decided to move off again next morning into a very different type of country some fifteen miles off. This was not the open bush or orchard country, as it is sometimes called, that we had been hunting in up to the present, but real thick stuff in which you could not see five yards from where you stood and impossible to move in except along an elephant or buffalo track.

Small thickets of impenetrable thorn are common in most types of country and it is there that the elephant and buffalo so much love to spend the heat of the day; but here in our new camp there was thick jungle five hundred yards from the village we had chosen as our headquarters. Not so much thorn as matted vegetation is the best description that I can give. Forest trees, thick bushes and thorn, their branches interlaced and woven into a nearly solid mass by a network of wiry lianas, the whole covering a vast tract of country.

The first morning out from our new camp we were lucky enough to come on the spoor of a good bull straight away and absolutely fresh. After measuring up the spoor of his fore-foot we followed and to begin with made good time. The elephant had been skirting the thick stuff in the early hours of the morning, and it was not until about nine o'clock that we had to follow him into it. It was then that our rate of progress began to fall off. One would think that an elephant would leave a broad, open trail in heavy jungle, but as a matter of fact this is not so; most of the branches and creepers that he pushes aside so easily in his passage spring back again when he has passed, and following him is a laborious business.

For about half an hour we pressed on, crawling in, under, and through it all, and doing our best to move as silently as possible, when we heard a crackle of branches just in front.

"That's him", whispered Hassani.

We stopped to listen — to see was impossible; then moved on slowly and with infinite care, passing through the dense masses of bush. Then there was another crackle on our right and another behind us to the left. Here we were, right in the middle of a herd, whether our elephant was with them or not it was impossible to say; we could see nothing. It was not a pleasant position — a puff of wind might at any moment give us away to one of them, and then he would stampede and cause all the others to do likewise. *No.* "A herd of elephant in thick bush is best left alone." That is a remark that is so often made when one is talking 'elephant', and is a truism that calls for no comment. But it is a different thing when one's blood is up and one knows there is a good tusker amongst them.

It was an exciting game of hide-and-seek that we now played but what and where our 'home' was I don't know. Hassani was in the lead with the small rifle, I following with the heavy one, whilst Sulemani and Ligambazi brought up the rear. It was an invidious job for them, unarmed as they were, but I did not stop to know their feelings on the subject. It was the most impossible task; we had not only to spot our elephant but also to see his tusks, and having seen his tusks, to see also a mortal spot to fire at. The effect of what that shot would be was looking too far ahead and did not trouble us.

We got sight of one easily enough. A slight clearing disclosed him, a half-grown bull, whose tusks were a negligible quantity. Now for another.

We moved off in a direction where we heard one feeding but had only gone ten yards when I nearly fell over Hassani, who had suddenly stopped and begun edging back, warning us away with his free hand. I could see nothing and was beginning to think that friend Hassani had the wind up badly.

"Where is he? I don't see him", I whispered. "I don't see – – –." I was beginning again when suddenly a black mass that I had taken to be a shadow transformed itself into the body of an elephant, standing face on to us, not five yards off. Time enough to see that his tusks were small, and we were edging back along the path as quickly as we could. But the elephant was not satisfied. He had seen something — not quite sure what — and he took two or three strides forward to investigate. I turned round as he did so, expecting to have to fire and put an end to his curiosity, which I was loath to do while there was still a chance of our big fellow. But he was not coming on; for five seconds he stood still, then whirled round and dashed off through the bush. This set all the others off and for about ten seconds there was crashing all around.

Apparently though, it was a false alarm; they had not got our wind, so did not know what the trouble was and were soon still again. I hated the idea of giving things up and determined on one last try for spotting our big bull. We stole forward once again, peering round as intently as before. Luck was with us, or so I thought at the time, when through an opening in the bush I caught sight of a pair of tusks gleaming white where the sun caught them through a gap in the dense foliage overhead. They looked enormous, and Hassani nodded his head in encouragement. This was our bull. All very well, we could see the tusks alright, what we now wanted was to see his head to fire at, and try as I would I could not clearly define in the darkness of the shadow all around. It was no use wasting time, and this might be as good an opportunity as we were ever likely to get. I made up my mind to shoot — and to shoot with the light rifle that I knew so well, and with it perhaps stand a better chance of placing the bullet correctly.

I took over 'Mkatakhuni' and told Hassani to fire at the same time as I did with 'Fatuma'. I made my estimation of the correct place, took a steady aim and pulled the trigger, and at the same time Hassani fired both barrels of the 0·450. The effect was pandemonium all round, crashing through the bush. I had only time to work the bolt of the rifle when I realized that we were in the path of one of them. It was no use trying to get out of its road, the bush was too thick, and besides, the four of us were a pretty large mark and the chances were that one of us would not be able to get clear in time. I remember waiting for that elephant's head to appear, and absurd though it may seem, in my thoughts I compared the wait to that one experiences in a cover shoot in England when a cock pheasant is just breaking clear of the last tree-tops of a ride in a wood and one waits for a clear shot before firing. This was what I then thought of, and as I got a view of his forehead, I raised my rifle like a shot-gun to my shoulder and pressed the trigger. He collapsed in a heap, as luck would have it, and never moved again.

Whew! A bit too close to be comfortable, and I must confess that as the sounds of the stampede disappeared into the distance my fingers were none too steady as I opened my case and lit a much-needed cigarette.

But what had happened? Was this elephant that had so nearly been on top of us the same one that we had fired at originally? A glance at his tusks reassured us on that point. They were small; too small, I sorrowfully noted, to be of any value.

What had happened, then, to our first one? We moved forward to settle the point, Hassani loud in his affirmations that the other was down as well. Personally I was none too sure; it was with great excitement that I moved forward to see what our 'pick-up' should be.

Hassani was right. Our first elephant was lying there also, and had in fact, fallen in his tracks. His tusks unfortunately were also small and eventually only just topped the 25lb. mark, which luckily was the minimum in the district. The effect of the brilliant patch of sunlight in which we had first seen them had deceived us; and he certainly was not our original bull as the measurement of his feet disclosed.

But, even discounting the poor results in ivory, I was beginning to feel extraordinarily pleased with myself. I had certainly downed one elephant with 'Mkatakhuni', and the other lay between Hassani and myself. We could not tell which shots had been effective as he lay with the side of the head we had fired at underneath. If I take credit to myself of a right and left, kind reader, do not be too hard on me, such episodes occur only too seldom in a lifetime to be lightly passed over!

I now had, too, an argument for 'Mkatakhuni' which even the doubting Hassani could not refute and he was, I am glad to say, no longer able to despise its merits.

I was extraordinarily lucky, I must admit, to be able to bring it home to him in this fashion; the more so as I felt when I came to measure the distance from where I had stood to the place where lay the elephant which had so nearly done for us. Three paces forward brought me to his trunk — as near a thing as I ever want.

My shot was, indeed, a lucky one. It had pierced the skull in the one place that could have been effective in that position, right in the centre of the skull at the base of the trunk and just below the level of the eyes.

And now a word of apology and another of explanation before I bring this story to a close. My apology is due to the critic for the expense he has incurred in repeat orders for tins of 'Cerebos' because a tale of charges from both elephant and buffalo within a few thousand written words and half-an-hour's reading is, I admit, a tall order. Still, I can only affirm that I have tried to put things down just as they happened, and to escape further disparaging remarks, let me hurry to my word of explanation.

It is not so much as an upholder of the merits of the small-bore rifle as compared with those of the heavier that I take leave to subscribe the name 'Mkatakhuni' to my tale, but more because the word has a greater personal application. Mine are not the tales of the big-game hunter who visits Eastern Africa for a few months' enjoyment and shoots record quantities of game on the open plains. Unluckily, or maybe luckily, this is not the portion in life of one who has been, and is likely to remain, that pitiful personality, the Hewer of Wood and Drawer of Water!

Mkatakhuni

Appendix 3

A.M.O.

A Trader Sportsman in East Africa

I first met Ali Mahommed Omar when I got back to the district Boma from a trip after elephant in the wilds. It was in Portuguese territory and one of the few remaining parts of Africa south of the Zambezi where elephants are still to be found in goodly numbers and where an unrestricted licence may sometimes be obtained. *Sometimes* — for the Portuguese have a curious habit of suddenly throwing open a district for shooting for a few months and then just as suddenly closing it again, it may be for a couple of years. For the elephant hunter it is really not such a bad plan, for elephants will crowd into a district where there has not been much shooting for a year or two; and early information that such a district is to be thrown open and a quick getaway may result in much ivory. Not that there is no shooting at all in such a district during its close time, for, although it is illegal for natives to possess a gun of any description, yet many of them clandestinely do so possess them, whereby hangs a tale — a tale, it may be said, of poaching, the full truth of which may not be written. Europeans have something to do with that tale; and even the Portuguese themselves (the distinction does not call for comment) and their higher officials are not altogether unconnected with it.

Pleasant as it may be for the hunter that such sanctuaries are continually being declared and then thrown open, it is a very different affair for the natives who dwell in them; and on my last trip in such a district when it had already been bruited abroad that this particular part would shortly be reclosed — it had been open for six months only, after two years when no white hunter had been seen — mention of the intended closure was the cause of some despondency to the receivers of this news. Depredation of crops is a crime of which the elephant is not unguilty; and though the native magnifies his losses on every possible occasion, hoping thereby to soften the heart of the official when it is time to collect the tax of the few shillings per head which is his contribution to the revenue, and to obtain some remission of what he regards as this unjust annual imposition, it cannot be said that he goes altogether scatheless, especially in a country where elephants are not taught their business and where a herd is never followed and shot at on any occasion after a raid.

My trip had been successful: I had obtained my full quota of elephants well within the allotted time and the little district Boma was my first port of call on my road back to civilisation and its flesh-pots, represented, be it said, by a straggling and squalid collection of buildings on the bank of the Zambezi, lying some 70 miles away.

Seen from a distance — (from the other side of the Zambezi, for instance) — (and the Zambezi here is about a mile broad) the town is not unpicturesque, reminding one as it does of a southern continental town, with the gaily coloured exterior of its pink, yellow and white-washed walls. But with a closer approach, the ruins — they are little better — of these buildings can be better appreciated. Rusty corrugated iron and ominous cracks, telling of the havoc made by white ants speak of bankruptcy, while the natives are so assailed that — we had better keep on the other side of the Zambezi.

From there the two tall masts of the wireless apparatus can be seen towering over everything; though built to transmit over all Africa, owing to some defect or the absence of some particular part of the power unit which, rumour has it, Great Britain denies them (for is she not the owner of the inland telegraph?) — the towers stand in silence.

One can count oneself blessed indeed — when one *receives*, that is receives payment for the ivory which one has to sell. In this bankrupt community nobody seems to have any ready money — and if one can extract from a dealer payment in cash for a hundred pounds worth of goods, it will require not a little patience and an obstinate refusal to remove oneself from his threshold. Even so it may be necessary to haunt his office at all times of the day for a week on end and, my patience having been exhausted, I have even gone so far as to call on one such dealer at his house. Having refused to listen to the declaration of his boy that Master had gone away, I was finally ushered into his presence as he lay on his bed, and the deal was at length concluded.

In this charming city tea costs 8/- the pound, whisky £1 a bottle, while should one wish to obtain a large supply of tobacco or cigarettes to take on a trip out in the bush, we apply to the Bank, of all places, to get them. No one can afford to keep a large quantity in stock. All prices are exorbitant and they vary in a comical way with the arrival or non-arrival of the river paddle-boat which forms – – –'s sole connection with the outside world, and which is always blamed about everything. During the rains, when there is too much water in the river, the boat may not be able to beat its way against the current and in the dry weather the lack of water may prevent arrival. Altogether though the Zambezi may be an international water-way it has no reason to be proud of the fact.

In the town business is dead. 'Amanya' — 'tomorrow' — is the stock remark when business is proposed. To obtain a licence to shoot elephant, for instance, will take at least a week to accomplish. Countless visits to countless Government offices must be paid, where different applications must be made out, each in its proper prescribed form and each on its own particular bit of government stamped paper which one has to purchase in reams at a great price. A form of tax, they call it, but then these applications have to be stamped again with a different form of stamp before they are finally sent up for approval, so they have you twice over.

The most outstanding aspect of each and all of these Government offices — except perhaps that in which affairs of the subjects of His Britannic Majesty are looked after — is the number of the typewriters in each — all of them brand new and of the latest and best make. Heaven knows they need them all, for their red tape seems to be of an even deeper hue than it is in British Government offices. I once watched a government official signing a document for the importation of a few dutiable articles. The document was in sextuplicate and he signed his name, not his initials only, in seven different places on each copy. What it was about I have no idea and doubt if the official himself was very much wiser. To fail to remove one's hat on entering a government office, or to put one's hand, unintentionally, on the table at which the official works (and on which certainly stands at least one of their superb looking typewriters) is looked upon as the greatest of insults. By touching the table, let alone leaning on it, it is supposed that one makes a gesture of claiming possession of that office and thereby of the country. What a crime to commit! I can scarce credit, though, that even the more coloured of the queer-looking Portuguese really suffer so badly from the inferiority complex as to think one's action denotes anything of the sort. Rather I am prone to believe that he is afraid of one's trying to sneak off with that typewriter or at anyrate touching it and spoiling its highly polished lustre.

The colour question is indeed one of some moment to people in these parts and not a little amusement can be had therefrom. When I first entered the country regulations necessitated my appearance at the local police station where my passport was examined. Now long sojourn under a burning African sun has burnt me as brown as a berry and as such the colour of my complexion is described in my passport. This was very disconcerting to the official who examined it and I was amused to see that in the form of permission to reside in the Territory which I received on leaving the office, departure was made from one of the extracts taken from the passport 'Colour of hair — brown; colour of eyes — brown'; that was all right — but 'complexion — *white*'!

But I seem to have strayed rather far from my friend Ali Mohommed Omar with whom I opened my first paragraph.

He was a short tubby little Goanese and the keeper of the store at the boma where he sold the usual array of cheap cotton goods, trade blankets, copper and brass wire, salt, flour and all the other commodities for which every Indian store successfully tempts the native to part with his shekels.

I approached the ramshackle wattle and daub building, not unwilling myself to be separated from an odd shilling if I should chance to find any tinned foods displayed there and Ali Mohommed Omar rose from a deck chair on which he had been taking his ease on the verandah as I came up.

"Yes, plenty good" said he in answer to my enquiry if he stocked any European delicacies and he followed me inside, where I purchased a tin of sugar-topped biscuits and a couple of tins of sardines.

"Verree good, all best qualitee" he informed me as we retired again from the shop. As if anything of that quality was likely to be found in that atmosphere of dirt!

He waved me into his deck chair, which I was glad enough to accept after a long, tiring morning's march, summoned a boy and ordered him to bring me a cup of tea with which I might wash down the queerly ordered repast that I had chosen for myself.

I was as yet unaware of his name and when I noticed that the henchman, who presently bore to me that sustaining beverage, displayed the word 'Amo' on his shirt front for all the world to see memories only of the first conjugation of Latin verbs assailed me. I stared at this lucky youth in some surprise and began dreamily to wonder who the object of his passion might be, that he should thus be unable to restrain his amorous declaration. Perhaps it was not just *one* that he loved and the word was rather a general statement of fact or capacity.

'Amo' . . . But the voice of Ali Mahommed Omar broke in on my thoughts and I had perforce to give up my speculations. He had taken a seat on an upturned paraffin case and in a mixture of broken English, Portuguese and the local vernacular was trying to engage my attention with questions as to how I had fared on my trip.

"Plenty marfim?", he asked and when I had explained that my ivory was as good a lot as I had hoped for, his next was the critical question beloved by every Indian.

"What pl-a-i-ce?" There was a gleam in his eye as thoughts of a good bargain stole over him and he began to inform me how incredibly low the ruling prices had now dropped. I was not greatly interested. To sell one's hard-won spoils at the first offer and right away out in the bush before one had any time to become au fait with the state of the market would only be adding one more middleman to collect his share in the profits; and Ali Mahommed Omar was no fool to be caught making an offer that would put nothing in his own pocket. He soon stopped trying to tempt me but his next essay found me lending a more willing ear.

"Where you go now?" I explained that I was on my way to $---$ where I hoped to dispose of my ivory at a satisfactory price and to obtain a licence for another shoot.

"How you go?"

Now my intention had originally been to walk; but the sight of a big road never makes me feel in the least energetic. It is one thing to walk along a narrow native path out in the bush with a rifle slung over one's shoulder and with a wary eye on the look out for game or elephant spoor or such like entrancing things that keep one from thinking how tired one is. It is quite another to trudge heavily down the centre of a broad highway, the dust of an occasional passing lorry or motor car flung up in one's face to make one feel more and more dissatisfied with one's own slow rate of progress. I had noticed an old Chevrolet lorry parked under a tree in the compound and my thoughts had been concerned covetously with the possibility of hiring it, or perhaps of obtaining a lift should it be proceeding my way. Not that I should tackle old Ali Mahommed Omar about it. The suggestion had better, if possible, come from him. Better for *my* pocket, that is to say.

"I'm going to walk" I told him and I could see that he was slightly taken aback at the suggestion.

"Maningi ndawa" he put forward. This means 'Much trouble' and was one of his stock phrases, used on every possible occasion.

"Two-three day — not far" I answered and the question, though of burning interest to me, was for the moment shelved.

We began to discourse on other topics, principally about elephants; the number I had got, the size of the ivory — we brought it all down from the boma office and weighed it on the store scales — and other matters of interest. He expressed a desire to see my rifles and when I had shown them to him and he had asked how much each had cost, he produced his own rifle for my inspection. Quite a new Mauser it proved to be; but the barrel, when I came to look down it, was in such a state of filth that I very much doubt whether it had ever been cleaned at all. I shouted to my own boy to bring some oil and a cleaning rod and thereupon, having nothing better to do, started in to give it such a cleaning as it had never known before.

A.M.O. looked on in rather a shame-faced way, grunting 'Maningi ndawa' from time to time in a manner that told me this would certainly be the last cleaning the rifle would undergo for some considerable period. For all that he was obviously gratified by my efforts and sat talking to me as I worked, telling me tales of his own prowess as a hunter, more especially of buck shot from his lorry as he went along the road by day and night.

I thus discovered that the Chevrolet was indeed his own property.

When the rifle had been properly cleaned, he said, as it were à propos of nothing — "My camiao go – – – tomorrow". (*Camiao*, it may be said in passing is the Portuguese for *lorry*. They seem to have borrowed the 'camion' of the French and altered the word to their needs; in fact 'camion' itself is sometimes used by the educated man.)

I could scarcely conceal my pleasure. The necessity of hiring it had at any rate passed.

"Oh", said I, "are you going also?"

He explained that he had to go in to buy new supplies, petrol and oil (he had a government contract for transporting grain) and new stock for his stores. "Maningi ndawa", of course, all of it. Then to my delight he put forward the suggestion that he should take me also and now that the proposal had come from him we could begin to come down to terms.

"Five pounds" said he, "you and your ivory".

This, of course, was an absurd price to my way of thinking. The lorry was going in anyway, I was not hiring it; he had himself made the suggestion that he would take me, and to take just my ivory and me was no good without the rest of my loads and a boy or two to look after everything. I pointed all this out with some heat and he conceded me the rest of my loads and a single boy without much hesitation; but over the other boy and the price I had not a little difficulty. The haggling was all perfectly amicable and was interspersed with talk on other matters.

From time to time as the long afternoon wore on strings of natives would come in with their bags of grain for sale or exchange for measures of 'limbo' and women from the neighbouring village arrived with tiny little baskets of flour for which they wanted salt in payment.

A.M.O. would then arise and help his satellite behind the counter. With each and all the same formality was repeated. The pinch of salt given as each woman proffered her basket was the signal for lamentation by the recipient, kept up until a second and more generous handful was added. The procedure never varied. If the correct amount had been given all in one fell swoop the women would have fancied themselves cheated — but *two* helpings — that was different and they went their way, satisfied.

These little interludes never lasted long and A.M.O. was soon back at my elbow.

"Palibe ndawa — five pounds" he would begin in his husky voice as a start to conversation, and my "Three pounds, Ali, all my loads and two boys" would answer it. ("Palibe ndawa" is the reverse of "Maningi ndawa" and means "No trouble".)

Then I made a bad mistake by paying off a couple of boys who wished to return to their homes in the district from which I had come. The old ruffian knew he had me, for without my full contingent I could not carry everything should I really choose to walk.

Finally we met each other half way at £4, my ivory, all my loads, myself and two boys. I fancied this was not a bad stroke of business and the question having been satisfactorily settled as the long day was drawing to a close, we proceeded to discuss arrangements of another matter that was exciting the interest of Ali Mahommed Omar.

He was, for some reason, very keen to come shooting in my company and earlier in the afternoon had once or twice suggested that we should take our rifles and go together into the bush to look for 'nyama' (meat). I was not in the least enthusiastic about the proposition myself, though he declared there was lots of game to be had. After a march of five and twenty miles or so, I was loath to stir from the comfort of his deck chair.

Time passed and I was just congratulating myself that there was no need for any further show of energy on my part, when there wandered into the store, a coloured man, a clerk employed in the boma office, armed with a rifle and with a shooting lamp bound round his head. These lamps are made in various designs. That which the clerk sported was very much like an ordinary acetylene bicycle lamp with a padded leather strap running through the back. Attached to it was the rubber tube leading to the generator worn hooked into the belt round his waist. Ali Mahommed Omar, who must have been Bahram himself in an earlier incarnation, greeted him with effusion and before I knew where I was I found myself roped into an agreement whereby we should all three take the field that evening and proceed into the bush in an earnest endeavour to slaughter an innocent buck. A.M.O. was enthusiasm itself; he scarce gave me time to finish my supper in peace before summoning me to the fray. He donned a pair of thin rubber-soled shoes of the type generally known as 'sand shoes' and produced a pair of puttees which he began to drape round his chubby little legs over the top of the pantaloons that reached down to his ankles. He crossed and re-crossed the puttees up to a point half way up his calf and then pulled down voluminous folds of pantaloon over the top of them so that they looked like very baggy Turkish plus-eights and there was no more than about three inches of puttees showing in all. Then he began loading his rifle, pressing round after round down into the depths of the magazine with a ferocity of purpose that was appalling. I retired to a safer distance while this was going on for the muzzle of the rifle was describing circles in all directions; but when the rattle of the bolt told me that there was round ready in the chamber I came forward again, cautiously, and breathed with relief to see him applying the safety catch properly. Still, I was taking no chances; and taking the rifle from him, I showed him how by keeping the trigger pressed as the bolt was pushed forward he could close the breach on a round in the chamber without compressing the striker spring. This, besides avoiding a continued tension on the spring, which will finally weaken it, allows of no possibility of danger such as is caused by a faulty, or a slipping safety catch, and by merely raising and reclosing the bolt lever the rifle is brought to full cock just as easily. A.M.O. was hugely taken by this device; I had to demonstrate it to him several times over.

"Maninga ndawa" and "Palibe ndawa" he called the two methods, 'ndawa' meaning this time 'danger'.

But I was to find that in his hands there was more danger in the new method and before long I bitterly repented ever having shown it to him. He seemed unable to grasp the fact that the trigger had to be held *while* he was pushing the bolt home — and not *afterwards* — with the result that disaster nearly overtook us before ever venturing on our expedition. A loud explosion followed his first attempt — but the muzzle was luckily pointing downwards and the bullet merely ploughed its way into the packed earth floor of the verandah and did no damage. His second attempt was more successful and thinking that he now understood, I proceeded to bind on my forehead the shooting lamp which he insisted I should wear. As the buckle was tightened at the back of my head I realized that I was in for it. I borrowed yards of cloth from the store with which I swathed my forehead in the form of puggrie, but even with this protection, it was not long before that confounded strap started to eat its way, I felt, right inside my head. I turned on the water of the generator and after giving a succession of fizzing and poppings, as is the alarming habit of all acetylene lamps, the burner finally burst into flame as a match was put to it. I placed the generator in the pocket of my shirt and we headed out into the darkness of the night.

Our master of ceremonies was the boma clerk who led the way with his rifle, I was glad to see, slung over his shoulder. I followed next with A.M.O. behind me, while the rear was brought up by a heterogeneous collection of hangers-on who had come out to see the sport, among whom I recognized my own cook and his picannin mate.

Our way led first down the main road but our guide soon took us from the security of that highway and we ventured out into the bush. And here it was "maningi ndawa" all the time; not so bad for us who were in the lead and had the lamp to light our path, but poor old A.M.O. stumbling along in the rear had a bad time of it. The night was pitch black and only a veil of impenetrable darkness met the eye outside the dazzling beam of the lamp. A.M.O. struggled along behind me, striking matches to light his way and murmuring profanities beneath his breath. The going really was bad as the ground was much cut about by little ravines and old water-courses. Here and there I would turn round to light his way but for the most part my duty was to walk slowly forward, turning my head from side to side so that the beam of the lamp swept the bush where it might be expected to pick up the gleamimg eye of some unfortunate buck, dazzled by its glare.

The noise of our passing must really have been sufficient to frighten any buck out of its wits long before we approached anywhere near the twenty or thirty yards that was within the power of the lamp to illuminate. What with our stumblings over fallen trees, cracking branches, the excited whisperings of our tail of followers and the fitful spurts of Ali Mahommed Omar's matches, we must have made the queerest and most optimistic party that ever thought it was going to shoot buck.

We did have one exciting moment when my lamp picked up the gleam of what was an indubitable eye — it was of a reddish hue and though I knew well that it belonged to a nightjar I could not resist giving Ali Mahommed Omar his thrill; I felt he deserved it after passing through so much tribulation and woe, so I whistled him up and let the light of my lamp again play on it. He was thrilled to the marrow.

"Nyama — shoot" he whispered to me and began to fiddle with the bolt of his rifle. But the nightjar chose that moment to give the show away and spreading his wings he flapped lazily off down the beam of my light, the long streamers from his wings waving his adieux behind him.

I was turning to resume my way when more sounds of a rattling bolt reminded me that Ali Mahommed Omar had been prepared to do battle with the nightjar — but before I could turn my light to see what he was about, the roar of his exploding rifle thundered out into the silence of the night and a bullet whistled past my ear. I took cover in exemplary fashion and pleaded with him to have a care, but "Palibe ndawa" was the only response and apology I could get from him; so I carefully approached from behind and helped him to put his rifle safe again. Would that I had never shewn him that accursed new method. I begged him to return to his old practice of using the safety catch but to no purpose; so considering that discretion was now the better part of valour, I made excuses that the lamp was beginning to make my head ache and surrendered it to its owner, who gallantly remained in lead, while I retired like a craven and for the rest of that evening stayed in rear of that dangerous rifle. There was nothing to laugh about really, though our followers seemed to think it a fit subject for merriment. Perhaps my remarks had been a little scathing but it was with an understanding sympathy that my cook received me out of the danger zone and I handed him my rifle to carry. Thereafter I felt I should have enough to do in looking after that of Ali Mahommed Omar, and unhampered, I thought I might be able to avert a calamity, should I see one approaching.

We proceeded on our way — easier going now through the old gardens of the village, which was lucky, for Ali Mahommed Omar's box of matches was finished and he had requisitioned mine. I was glad enough to be rid of the torture of the lamp about my brow and of the generator, which was growing hotter and hotter in my breast pocket so that I felt that an explosion was imminent and a disaster of that sort in the region of my heart, I felt, could have been nothing but fatal in result. But gladder still was I when we finally emerged again on the main road and set our faces for home.

A.M.O. was still game, I must say that for him. He had taken several headers into prickly bushes and ravines and on one occasion into an ant bear's earth from which we had pulled him — "Oriana!"; and even now it was all that I could do to persuade him that the time had passed for finding buck — in fact it was only when I finally pointed out that the lamp was beginning to fail — I believe that the clerk, with an understanding with which I had not credited him, had turned off the water — that he submitted to be led down the road.

And so back to home and bed; patches of sky on the horizon glowing pinkly spoke of distant bush fires and a nearby hillside was ablaze with long ragged ribands of light that travelled their way over its length and reflected in a reddish glare by the road beneath our feet. The air was heavy with an acrid smoke and the oppressiveness, heat and stillness were as though a thunderstorm were approaching.

Tired out by our adventures I sought only to fling myself on the blankets of my valise, where a cup of hot tea and a couple of aspirin tablets did much to comfort me and to dissolve the headache which the wearing of that detestable lamp had left and it was not long before I was asleep and dreaming dreams of a rifle that fired itself repeatedly without the aid of any human hand.

I awoke to bright sunlight and the explosions of the rifle of my dreams resolved themselves into the poppings and back firings of the old Chevrolet lorry which the driver was trying to wake into life. Strolling about in pyjamas with a matutinal cigarette, while my cook prepared breakfast, I met Ali Mahommed Omar who informed me that the lorry had to take a load of grain down to the next boma, seventy or eighty miles distant, but that on its return we would straight way proceed to our destination. A hundred and fifty miles would mean at least ten hours on those roads and I had perforce to curb my impatience throughout that day, for actually it was not until after 5 o'clock in the afternoon that at length it returned and we were able to board it. There was only about an hour of daylight left when the loads were finally tied securely in place and a queer collection they made; half a dozen large sacks of grain, a bicycle, a battered tin box or two, which contained the more beloved possessions of A.M.O.; my own ragged collection of loads, cooking pots, valise, camp kit, rifle case, ivory; apes and peacocks in the form of a couple of crates of fowls and the half-dozen black apes who were perched above everything, clinging precariously to whatever they could reach. In front, on the driver's right, sat Ali Mahommed Omar while I took my seat on the driver's left. We each had our rifle ready to our hand in case any game should be met on the way — and so we finally pulled out on the long road to – – – –.

It is with amusement that I recall that journey. The driver, an English-speaking native, was one of the worst that I have ever seen. He was so proud of being able to speak English whereas his master knew only a few words — that he tried to keep up conversation with me most of the time and could scarcely keep his eyes on the road in front of him. He seemed to think it was a good plan to declutch whenever he came to a hill and let the lorry free-wheel down it. He said he was saving petrol thereby and persisted, even when I told him that such a practice would soon mean the renovation of his clutch-plates — indeed when next I returned that way I heard that his lorry was laid up from this cause — but it pleased A.M.O.

who knew nothing whatever about cars. The reason of his anxiety to save petrol was apparent after we had gone seven miles along the road for we then had to stop and refill the little vacuum container under the bonnet for this had long ceased to function properly and was disconnected from the main tank. So it was that every seven miles we had to stop and refill it while I had to nurse a four-gallon petrol can between my knees all the way.

We were not without our excitements. Once a couple of wild hunting dogs came bounding along the road to meet us, sheering off in amazed terror as our thundering juggernaut bore down on them; and once, just after our lamps had been switched on, we ran into a small herd of kudu. This was the signal for much groping for rifles and rattling of bolts; but before either of us were ready the kudu had bounded off the road and neither of us had a shot at all — at the kudu, that is — for A.M.O. naturally once more fired off his rifle in his endeavours to recompose it to safety. I have often wondered whether he did at length succeed in mastering this little manoeuvre or whether he is still firing off his rifle at odd occasions into thin air. I hope he learned for the sake of his retainers, anyway, for before long he would certainly have managed to hit something more solid than thin air.

At about 9 o'clock at night when we had put some forty or fifty miles behind us, we found our way blocked by two other lorries drawn up in the centre of the road in front of us. They were facing in opposite directions and there was no room to pass in between. The occupants, a mixed collection of half-castes, Portuguese and natives, had descended and were engaging each other in conversation while they watched the efforts of a couple of boys to mend a punctured tyre. No effort was made to move out of our way though one car was perfectly able to do so. Move — not they, if such important people as Portuguese half-caste officials had to wait, then anyone else might wait with them. We stopped and I got out to see what the matter was, and pointed out that as they were perfectly able to deal with their trouble themselves, one car might be driven ahead to allow ours to pass. This suggestion was only greeted by a storm in Portuguese which I made no pretence of understanding and A.M.O. came up and in rather a worried manner explained that they would only be a short time and that we should wait. Seeing that the lorry was his property and that he had no desire that I should take up cudgels on his behalf, I deferred to his wishes and returned to wait until such time as the Portuguese official in charge might think fit to let us pass. But I could not resist one pull at his fat little leg.

"Fire off your rifle, Ali", I shouted so that all might hear. "They will be frightened and run off quickly."

This sally was greeted by a storm of laughter from the boys behind, and whether it was that they were afraid that my advice might be taken or that they objected to being the butt of the boys' merriment I know not, but it was not long after this that the repairs were finished and the Portuguese were pulling out on their way.

And so at length we arrived at the ferry of a little river some twenty miles from our destination, but it was too late to cross that night. The ferry men had gone; the ferry itself needed repairs before it could take another lorry over, so perforce we spent the night on the verandah of a little store near by, Ali Mahommed Omar in one corner and myself in the other. We shared a meal of another box of those same sugar-topped biscuits that I had purchased from him, and retired to bed, and of the two of us he was probably the more comfortable. He was the possessor of a camp bed, whereas I had only a couple of blankets between me and the hard bricks of the floor.

Next morning we were up in the still of the early dawn and down to the riverside. The big lorry was unloaded and successfully steered onto a punt that looked all too small to hold it, while the loads were packed into a large dug-out canoe into which we also climbed and were punted across the shallow river by boys using long bamboo poles. Not a breath of air was stirring; the water was as smooth as glass and painted in dappled pink by the red rays of a rising sun; a solitary spur-wing goose standing on a sand spit in mid-stream took wing at our approach; and a crocodile slid silently into the water as we neared the further bank. The lorry, looking huge and grotesquely out of place, perched as it were on the top of the water, for its weight allowed the punt little freeboard, followed slowly behind us. Once it stuck on a sandbank, but the boys, leaping off into the water, pushed and pulled it free and finally it was manoeuvred into place opposite the path made of hurdles laid across a mile of soft sand to the main road beyond. Two planks were run from the punt to the sand of the river bank and up these the lorry was at length steered and having reloaded all our possessions we were at last on our final lap into – – – –, that city of the dead, where we arrived without further adventures an hour later and I paid my farewell to my sporting little friend, Ali Mahommed Omar.

Appendix 4

HONEYGUIDES

In bygone days when travellers first came back from Africa with tales of a bird that would lead men in the search for bees' nests and honey it was thought, and perhaps excusably, by a European public that these were romances that found their origin only in the mind of their author. The very words "travellers' tales" are symbolic of hyperbole in its best and richest form, so it is no wonder that these tales were at first not believed. As time went on and naturalists and explorers all corroborated each other in their descriptions of the bird, the voice of the scoffer was stilled; but it was not until towards the end of the 18th century when Sparrmann first obtained examples of the species and wrote his delightful accounts of its habits that all doubts were finally expelled. *Cuculus Indicator* he called it — the bee cuckoo — but in recognition of his services to science and since the bird itself deserved more definite classification it was finally placed in a special sub-family of Picarian birds and given the name of *Indicator Sparrmanni* by scientists. Sparrmann's honeyguide is not the only member of this sub-family, *Indicator minor*, the lesser honeyguide and *Indicator variegatus*, the scaly-throated honeyguide, have since been discovered and added to it while it further contains another genus *Prodotiscus* of which *Prodotiscus regulus*, one of the rarest of African birds, is the sole species. Other honeyguides may since have been discovered or local sub-species may have been made. Africa is a vast continent and it is easy to make mistakes in matters ornithological owing to scarcity of literature on the subject.

There is one Himalayan member of the family, but I do not know that it has been noted to adhere to the characteristics of its African brethen. Since Sparrmann's [*Indicator Indicator*. Ed.] honeyguide is by far the commonest member of the family, it is the only one that will be considered in this article. The other African species have all been noted to lead the way to bees' nests, but they have none of them come definitely under the observation of the writer.

Sparrmann's honeyguide is a small bird not unlike the ordinary English sparrow but slightly larger in size. It is brown on top, greyish underneath and has a single golden spot on each shoulder. Its centre tail feathers are like the back in colour but the outer ones have increasingly more white, until the outermost are pure white. The male bird differs from the female in having the cheeks black in colour whereas in the female these are like the underside — greyish. Both male and female will summon one to the search of honey but the writer has thought to have noticed that the female is the better guide of the two and perhaps the more insistent in her solicitations, but I hesitate to state this definitely.

Walking through the bush at any time of day one's attention may be attracted by a shrill twittering sound coming from a nearby tree, which is the call of the honeyguide summoning one to the search. 'Twee-twee-twee-twee-twee' — 'Twee-twee-twee-twee-twee' on and on he goes and if one pays no attention he will follow, repeating his summons, but let us pay heed to his demands and see how and where he will lead us.

It is the dry season and we are on our way back to camp after an early visit to a distant dambo where we hoped to find game. As we have been unsuccessful, here is a chance that may save us returning without any spoils.

Any marshy part of country bare of trees might be called a dambo, but more commonly it is a narrow riband of low-lying open ground that drains the surrounding bush. During the rains it will be swampy and overgrown with tall grass while a small stream may actually be flowing down the middle. Tributary dambos joining in, each with its own little stream all help to swell what will eventually become a little river flowing down to the main water system of the neighbourhood. In the dry weather these dambos are quite dry but after forest fires have swept over the country, while the surrounding bush is burnt up and lifeless, they will be the first to be carpeted in shoots of new green grass which is the reason why they are at that season the favourite haunts of game animals.

As we reach the edge of the dambo a sudden chattering breaks out from the bush near at hand and we have no difficulty in recognizing it to be a honeyguide calling. He is obviously so pleased with himself at finding us that it is not in our heart to disappoint him. We have matches with us and one of the boys is carrying an axe which is all the paraphernalia we need for cutting out a bees' nest, so we come nearer to him and whistle a reply to his chatter. Delighted at this attention the honeyguide redoubles his efforts. He sits very still on the branch overhead and it may be difficult to spot him, but if we succeed in doing so we shall actually see his bill moving in the effort he is making and studying him under our field glasses we try to make out the golden spot on the shoulder that will indicate beyond all doubt that the bird is Sparrmann's species. Even with glasses it is difficult sometimes to see this spot, but if we can make out that the whole underside is a plain uniform grey in colour, we need have no doubt of our identification for the lesser honeyguide is yellowish, while the scaly-throated bird, as the name indicates, is streaked with black about the throat.

More often our first glimpse of the bird is when he flies off, as he will do when we come nearer, in the direction of the bees. Twenty or thirty yards away he settles in another tree and resumes his chatter while we follow his lead whistling encouragement to show that we are indeed coming. We need not be afraid of frightening him by whistling too loudly, he knows that he has nothing to fear from humans and our talking or whistling or beating two sticks together which is the method some natives employ, only serve to show him that he has our attention. As we approach him he flies off again, using an undulating flight to the next high tree on the line he wishes us to take, where he again waits for us. He always chooses the highest tree he can find and sits waiting for us on one of its higher branches. It may be out of our sight but he keeps on calling to give us our direction, nor does he show any hesitation when we come up to him, but flies off while we are still some distance away, straight over the tree tops to his next point of vantage. In more open country he descends lower and we can then see that his flight is a series of undulating bounds through the air.

We go on whistling and talking to him, though once he knows he is being followed there is not much need for us to do so.

With his third flight he increases the distance and we lose sight of him altogether, but as we stand uncertain which way to go and whistling for him to come and help us, he comes back and with renewed chatter denounces our slow rate of progress.

Thereafter his flights are always of greater length, a hundred yards and more sometimes; for long periods we may not catch a glimpse of him and only his voice guides us, summoning us from a distance, as we stand silently listening for it. We follow up at our best pace though we need really have no fear of losing him; he is far too keen to let us go astray. Once while I was following up a bird, a heavy thunderstorm came on when we were still only half way to the bees. I took shelter under a thick tree and as the rain continued for at least half an hour, I thought we had seen the last of our guide for that day. But when the rain stopped there he was again, summoning us to hurry up, so on we went with him to the honey. He had understood, and had himself taken shelter from the storm in the same tree under which we were standing.

But no such storm interferes with us this time and we keep on following, it may be for a mile or more until his flights once again grow shorter, which informs us that we are coming near to the bees. It now behoves us to keep a sharp lookout for likely looking trees, for some birds are not at all clever in showing the actual tree in which the bees have taken up their abode. A clever bird will hover for a second or two over the actual hole in the tree and then fly off at an angle and take up his position in another tree nearby, thus showing the exact spot, but others do not seem to have the sense to do this; they think their duties are at an end when they have led us to the vicinity and that it is our job to discover the bees for ourselves. They fly round in an uncertain sort of way, but if we look about carefully it will not be long before we find a hole where bees are entering, or perhaps passing bees will show us in what direction to search.

Having led us up to the bees the honeyguide's share of the work is finished and he sits quietly up in a neighbouring tree to watch our part of the business. Quite silent and still he sits as long as he sees that we are getting on with the job of cutting out the honey, but should we for some reason or other not proceed with the work, he again begins to chatter at us.

I once followed up a bird to bees, and having no axe I made tracks for camp as soon as we had found them, meaning to send a boy back later to cut out the honey. This so upset the honeyguide that he followed us most of the way home, hurling at us all the curses of the bird vocabulary. I hasten to add that a boy went straight back to the place to cut out the honey, with the strictest injunctions to leave a generous piece to satisfy the outraged feelings of the bird. The bird did not again show the way, but came up whilst the honey was being cut out, so he doubtless enjoyed the feast that was left for him. This time, having an axe with us, there is no need to risk the bird's displeasure, so we light a fire beneath the tree, piling on quantities of grass to make as much smoke as possible, while a boy proceeds to enlarge the hole with his axe. He keeps a smoking grass torch ready and from time to time blows smoke into the hole. It is a job at which a well-clothed European might look askance, nor could we blame him for reluctance to tackle it, but the native, naked though he is, except for a loin cloth, seems to have no qualms, he will certainly be stung once or twice but he won't mind that so long as there is plenty of honey. When the hole is big enough his hand and arm are plunged inside in a most fearless manner and reaching up he will soon produce a good pile of honey which he places in the basket prepared to receive it — a half circle of bark cut from round the bole of another tree. An examination of the combs shows us that in some there is a good supply of honey, but in others there are only the young grubs of the bees and it is these last that will be the honeyguide's portion. We discard them and leave them in a conspicuous place.

If we now retire and hide at a little distance away it will not be long before the honeyguide reappears. He will probably first be seen sitting on a branch high overhead, but he will gradually descend — rather hesitatingly — until he reaches a branch right above the place where we have left the combs and there he will sit eyeing them from time to time turning his head downwards to do so in a most comical manner. He is too shy to begin his meal in public and though once he flutters down for a close view of the feast, he retreats again to his branch without so much as a taste of it. He knows there are humans still somewhere around and he is distrustful of them, so gathering our spoils we make tracks for camp and leave him to enjoy his meal in peace.

Far out in the bush away from all human habitations there is no need to go looking for honeyguides for they will come right up to the camp. If we stay at the same place for a week or two birds from all the surrounding countryside get to know where to find us and not once or twice only but many times during the day they will come to summon us to the fray. Indeed their attentions become wearisome. We do not always want to go honey searching, especially during rainy weather when we shall find no honey but only combs full of young bees, and the continual chatter of the honeyguide begins to annoy us. It is hard to drive him off too, even throwing stones at him only makes him retreat a little and he settles down on a branch out of range and changes the tune of his chatter to a complaining note. He keeps a sharp look out though for any sign of activity and should anyone move about in camp, or at any noise, he at once resumes the full force of his remarks, until at last in desperation we send a boy to follow him and get rid of him. Should we ourselves leave camp in any direction he follows, entreating us to come away with him until at last he realizes that it is no good and that we are paying him no attention.

When watching birds at close quarters like this, one soon learns to tell the male bird from the female; young birds can also sometimes be recognized, and of these beware for though they like to chatter at us and are obviously delighted when we pay heed, they as yet do not seem to have acquired the necessary intelligence to lead us to honey. They just fly about aimlessly if we happen by mistake to follow. Many little characteristic actions will also be noted, amongst them a curious way they have of shaking out their feathers accompanied by a sharp beat of the wings. Our attention will probably first be drawn by the 'frufff, frufff' of the sound of it, and I can only think that they thus rid themselves of stinging bees for though their skin is certainly very tough and thick, almost like parchment to feel, it cannot be quite impervious to bee stings.

Distances to which honeyguides will take us naturally vary a great deal. When nests in close proximity to the camp have been exhausted, we may be taken a couple of miles in the search, but more usually and certainly when we find a bird out in the bush, we will not have to go so far and we shall find the nest within a mile or so. A honeyguide seems to patrol a certain area in which he may know several hives, to any of which he can lead us. On more than one occasion I have noticed a bird obviously trying to entice us to follow in a direction in which we had no wish to go, but when we did not respond, flying on ahead in the direction in which we *were* going and finally leading us to a swarm of bees right in our path.

A bird that I picked up one day out in the bush led us first to an old hive near at hand that had already been cut out and despoiled, he waited for us on a branch immediately above it and cruised round while we were examining it, finally resuming his way and calling us to follow. The hive to which he finally led us, a goodly swarm in an old termite heap, was a long distance away and it was just as though his action had been a demonstration of good faith and that he had thought that we might lose interest if he did not give us early proof that he was in earnest.

It is never much use to follow birds near a village for they generally only lead us to the native's own bee hives. These are curious affairs, four or five feet long, contrived out of a hollow strip of bark cut from round the whole bole of a tree so that when the strip is tied and pegged together again it presents the appearance of a hollow tree trunk. 'Mzinga' is the name of this cannon-like object, and indeed the Swahili when he first saw the big guns of modern ordnance made this name serve for them as well. One end of this hive is completely blocked with grass while a small aperture is left in the other for the entrance of the bees and it is then carried out into the bush and securely tied horizontally in the topmost branches of a high tree where it is a conspicuous object, and sooner or later a swarm of bees will be attracted by it. These hives are a common feature of the countryside all over eastern and south-eastern Africa in good bee country and probably throughout the continent as well, wherever there are tribes of Bantu stock, and are a welcome sign to a tired hunter who has been following elephant far out in the bush that he is at last approaching a village.

Honeyguides seem to be more active in the early morning than at any other time of day and it is then that we shall most frequently hear them, not that their activities are by any means confined to this period, we may be summoned to the search at all hours but it is not unnatural that during the heat of the day they should not be quite so anxious to lead us. As evening approaches and the sun loses its heat there is again a recrudescence of eagerness.

I have never been led up to bees by more than one bird at a time. On arriving at a nest I have noticed that there were two birds in evidence, the male and female I have made them out to be, but the second bird only put in an appreearance after we arrived at the nest or perhaps had been waiting there and had despatched his consort to fetch us. Such a habit of solitariness is providential for if two birds or a whole family started calling us at the same time it could only lead to a confusion of interest, with one bird calling us in one direction and a second in another.

It is interesting to speculate how and when these birds first began to look for man's co-operation in their search for the honeycomb and young bee grubs for which they had developed a taste. The Achewa tribe of Nyasaland have a fable on the subject which is perhaps worth repeating. "Kale, Kale kudala" they say, which means "Once upon a time long long ago", two little birds built a nest in the hole of a tree standing close by a road. The road was much frequented, so the choice of that particular tree was not a good one, but family matters had proceeded so far that they had no time to look round for a better tree in more secluded surroundings.

"If we are very quiet", said they, "and careful to see that no men are coming when we fly to the nest, all will go well." Time went on, two eggs were laid and the hen bird had just started sitting when one day a swarm of bees flew into the tree.

"Where have you come from?" asked one of the birds. "We had to leave our home", murmured the bees in reply. "Men came and cut down our tree and took away all the honey." "Well, you can't come in here", said the honeyguides, "this is our home". "There is plenty of room for us", insisted the bees, "we have flown far and are very tired". The birds considered this for some time between themselves and at last, out of pity for the bees' fate, decided to let them come in. "You must be very quiet though", they said, "and promise not to make that loud humming noise of yours." Delighted at this the bees were ready to promise anything. "We promise", they said, "we will be very careful and only come in one by one with our honey, also we will give you as much honey and comb as you and your children are able to eat".

So matters were decided and for some time all went well; the bees were very good and tried to stop humming as much as they were able, whilst the hen bird continued sitting on her eggs until she had hatched out her chicks. Then one day when the chicks were a week or two old, men passing by on the road heard the humming of the bees from the tree and looking about spied the hole. "Aha", said they, "Bees". And they lit a fire and started to cut out the nest, but when the honey was removed the men discovered the two fledglings right at the back of the hole and these also they took away.

When the birds returned to their ruined home and found their children had been taken from them, they were furious with the bees. "Why didn't you do what we told you", they said to them, "and stop all that humming? Now our children have been taken away to be killed and eaten and it's all your fault." So angry were they that when the bees left in search of a new home the birds followed them there, and from that day to this they and their descendants after them have lived on nothing but young bees and honeycomb, and whenever and wherever they find a hive of bees they summon men and lead them to it — and all out of revenge for the loss of their children, long, long ago.

So runs this rather pleasing story. One might also add to it that from that day onwards no honeyguide has undertaken the responsibility of housekeeping and raising a family. For in their nesting habits they are parasitic like the cuckoos and lay their eggs in the nests of other birds. This fact, though long held to be doubtful, has at length been proved.

The black collared barbet (*Lybius torquatis*) is generally the host selected and I have myself seen a honeyguide trying to enter the nest of one of these birds. I was attracted by an unusual volley of bird language coming from a dead tree out in the bush and approaching saw the two barbets flying round in a great state of excitement. Their nest hole could be seen high up in the deadest and rottenest branch so that it was quite impossible to climb to it. I did not at first see the honeyguide so could not understand what all the fuss was about, and it was not until the little brown form of one of the birds was seen to make a dive for the hole that I realized what was happening. Time after time the barbets chased her away, and once as she was clinging to the entrance hole itself, but I had no doubt that she finally succeeded in entering and laying her egg inside. A cuckoo is known to carry her egg in her bill to the chosen nest, but I don't know that a honeyguide had been observed to do this. Birds that have been shot by collectors when attempting to enter other birds' nests have been found to have an egg in the oviduct, nearly protruding from the vent.

A common superstition among natives about honeyguides is that they will sometimes lead the way not to bees and honey but to some noxious animal — a lion or a leopard or sometimes even a big snake. It is not stated that this is also part of their revenge for the part played by man in the fable, but I have heard it declared by some tribes of natives that the reason is that the bird is displeased because on a previous occasion men have not put by the honeyguide's portion. The true reason, is I am afraid nothing so picturesque, for it is quite understandable that where boys are continually following up these birds, a lion or leopard will sometimes be encountered on the path or it may be that a snake will be found in the tree from which they are taking the honey and a single fatality from such an incident would certainly be sufficient to spread abroad rumours that the whole affair was the bird's doing, and that he intentionally led the boy to his death. Superstition and witchcraft are still very much alive in Africa today, though the grosser infamies of the past have been greatly suppressed.

There are superstitions also as to the direction from which the birds are first heard calling. On the right-hand side of the road for good luck and on the left for bad luck. Mr. W. D. M. Bell in his book *The Wanderings of an Elephant Hunter* tells a pleasant story of how on one occasion in Uganda, he came to a country so swarming with honeyguides that they greatly interfered with his hunting. Each time he came up to Jumbo it was in company with one or more of these birds and the noise made was enough to warn the herd of his presence so that he had no success. He goes on to relate how finally at the entreaty of the boys, he went to consult the local Witch doctor as to how to get out of his quandary and how that worthy, doubtless for a suitable fee, promised that on such and such a day in a week's time (I quote from memory and apologize if my details are wrong) he would himself come and help and that they would no longer be troubled by the attentions of the birds. All fell out as the Witch doctor had ordained and from the date specified they ceased to annoy him.

Now that Witch doctor was a wise old man. He knew that such an eruption of birds was extraordinary and that they would not take long to disperse over the country, for honeyguides, like so many African birds, are certainly partially migratory in their habits, appearing with the seasons in different localities at different times.

I have often wondered that more interest is not taken in these remarkable birds. They are unique. No other country in the world can claim a bird of similar habits, but surprisingly few white people, even people who reside in Africa, are aware of his existence even, and fewer have ever taken the trouble to follow one up. Should these lines chance to catch the eye of anyone in England who contemplates a shooting trip to these parts, I would say to him — make enquiry of the gun-bearers or trackers employed and insist that whenever a bird is heard calling it shall be pointed out.

'Mrendi' is the name for it in certain parts of Tanganyika where Ki-Swahili is spoken and 'Sadzu' the common name in Chinyanja and its dialects further south; the boys will most certainly know the bird when its habits are described and if the trouble is taken on one occasion to follow a bird up to the bees, a memory will be carried back to England that will be worth as much as any other experience of the trip. The chance of witnessing one of the greatest of Nature's many marvels is surely not one that any of us can afford lightly to spurn aside.

Watercolours by J. C. Harrison
1898–1985

J. C. Harrison was a successful wildlife artist whose work was published in limited edition prints by the Tryon Gallery, Bury Street, St. James', London SW1Y 6AL.

J. C. was born in Tidworth in Wiltshire. By the age of six his drawing was already showing exceptional talent. As a young man he moved to British Columbia where he took the opportunity to study bird life. After serving in World War One he studied art at the Slade School. He made his home in Norwich and during his life travelled to both Africa and Iceland to paint birds.

In the early 1960's J. C. and his wife took me to see an exhibition of his work at the Gallery and afterwards they took me out to lunch. My first experience of a visit to an art gallery and a slap-up meal in a London restaurant. I can still remember the crêpes Suzette being flambéed at the table.

J. C. Harrison and his wife visited Malaŵi on several occasions and stayed with my parents on Kanongo Estate. The owl and the kingfisher were both painted as thank-you gifts for them. The owl, a Spotted Eagle Owl, used to live in the very top of a tall tree in the middle of the garden. Our swing hung on this tree and if you looked up into the treetop as you swung, you could see the owl looking down at you. The owls used to breed each year in the garden and the fledglings would practise take-off and landings on the roof of the house at night, a very noisy affair.

Isabel Macpherson

Woodland Kingfisher (*Halcyon senegalensis cyanoleucus*) — Watercolour by J. C. Harrison

284

Spotted Eagle Owl (*Bubo africanus africanus*) — Watercolour by J. C. Harrison

285

ON THE BUA RIVER — Watercolours by J. C. Harrison

287

Ah, my Belovéd, fill the cup that clears
TO-DAY of past Regrets and future Fears –
To-morrow? – Why, To-morrow I may be
Myself with Yesterday's
Sev'n Thousand Years.

from the Rubáiyát of Omar Khayyám

DATE.	PLACE.	GUNS.	ELEPHANT Grouse.	Water Buck Pheasants.	Kongoni Partridges.	Impalla Black Game.	Woodcock.	Snipe.	Guinea Wild Fowl.	Hares.	Rabbits.	Various.		TOTAL.
Dec 10th	Slopes of Inkerera.		1											
Dec 14th	Rupia's on Kilombero.		1											
Dec 15th	On way to Jumbe Rupia's				1	1								
Dec 16th	Injoni ko's			1	1	2			6					

REMARKS.

Weight of tusks 27, 28½. The first elephant I have seen. A choppy wind made following him difficult, several times he got our wind & moved off

A female shot for meat. 4 days ineffectual elephant hunting since 10th

This country abounds in game. The impalla has a poor head. The Kongoni average only.

At junction of Lukombero & Kilombero. Very good game country. No good heads. I shot the Kongoni & Impalla with the same shot, firing at the Kongoni I did not see the Impalla standing behind which got the bullet through the head.